MONEY PITCHER

WILLIAM C. KASHATUS

MONEY PITCHER

Chief Bender and the Tragedy of Indian Assimilation

The Pennsylvania State University Press
University Park, Pennsylvania

A KEYSTONE BOOK

A Keystone Book is so designated to distinguish
it from the typical scholarly monograph that
a university press publishes. It is a book intended
to serve the citizens of Pennsylvania by educating
them and others, in an entertaining way, about
aspects of the history, culture, society, and
environment of the state as part of the Middle
Atlantic region.

Library of Congress
Cataloging-in-Publication Data

Kashatus, William C., 1959–
    Money pitcher : Chief Bender and the tragedy
    of Indian assimilation / William C. Kashatus.
        p.   cm.
"Keystone Book"—T.p. verso.
Includes bibliographical references and index.
ISBN 0-271-02862-9 (cloth : alk. paper)
1. Bender, Charles Albert, 1883–1954.
2. Baseball players—Pennsylvania—Philadelphia—
    Biography.
3. Philadelphia Athletics (Baseball team)—Biography.
4. Indians of North America—Cultural assimilation.
5. United States—Race relations.

GV865. B36K37 2006
796.357092—dc22
2005028567

CONTENTS

for BOB WARRINGTON

ACKNOWLEDGMENTS

Money Pitcher could not have been written without the help of many individuals. At the top of the list is Robert D. Warrington of the Philadelphia Athletics Historical Society. Not only did he inspire the idea for this book, but he read earlier drafts of the manuscript, offered invaluable criticism, and gave me permission to publish rare photographs from his extensive collection. Bob cultivated my own interest in the Philadelphia Athletics many years ago when I curated an exhibition at the Chester County Historical Society entitled *Baseball's White Elephants: Connie Mack and the Philadelphia Athletics*. Since then we have collaborated on baseball conferences, radio interviews, and historical marker dedications. In the process, Bob has become a dear friend whose work on behalf of the Athletics deserves to be honored with the dedication of this book.

Special thanks are due to others who reviewed earlier drafts of the manuscript and provided constructive criticism, including John Bloom of Shippensburg University, Bruce Brownell of Abington Friends School, and Philip Deloria of the University of Michigan. Still others were helpful in discussing my ideas on Native American culture and baseball, including Barbara Landis of the Cumberland County Historical Society, Carlisle, Pennsylvania; Patricia Loew of the University of Wisconsin, Madison; Jeff Powers-Beck of East Tennessee State University; Jeff Schultz of Luzerne County Community College of Northeast Pennsylvania; and Timothy Wiles of the National Baseball Hall of Fame Museum and Library in Cooperstown, New York.

Since the Benders had no children and attempts to contact any extended family proved unsuccessful, very little information exists about Charles Bender's childhood. Information about his life after his major league career ended is also lacking because of his desire for privacy. Thus I am grateful to those who shared their memories with me, including the late Eddie Collins Jr., Eddie Joost, Lester McCrabb, Rube Oldring Jr., and Bobby Shantz. Special thanks are also due to those who assisted in the preparation of the book, especially the staffs of the Bucks County Historical Society, Cumberland County Historical Society, Free Library of Philadelphia, Historical Society of Pennsylvania, Minnesota Historical Society, Philadelphia Athletics Historical Society, and the National Baseball Hall of Fame Museum and Library, all of whom provided important access to their collections. I am grateful to Hall of Fame artist Dick Perez for giving me the permission to use his handsome painting of Charles A. Bender on the cover of this book.

I am also grateful to Robert Janosov, Nicole Saporito, and Clark Switzer, who gave me their support and friendship at a very trying time in my life. Finally, my parents, my wife, Jackie, and our sons, Tim, Peter, and Ben, deserve special thanks for continuing to indulge my twin passions for writing and baseball. They are my biggest heroes.

INTRODUCTION

On October 10, 1905, a crowd of 24,902 packed New York's Polo Grounds to watch the hometown Giants play the Philadelphia Athletics in Game Two of the World Series. Christy Mathewson, the fair-haired pitching ace of the Giants, had already shut out the A's, 3–0, the day before in Philadelphia, to give his team a one-to-nothing lead in the Fall Classic. Now it was the A's turn to even the Series.

Philadelphia manager Connie Mack sent his twenty-two-year-old right-hander Chief Bender to the mound against "Iron Man" Joe McGinnity, the Giants' number-two starter.[1] Both hurlers had at least eighteen victories to their credit and could boast of having surrendered fewer than three runs per game that season. Their mental approach was just as unyielding. Each man was a fierce competitor, refusing to give an inch to the opponent, especially when the stakes were this high. Under the circumstances, even the slightest advantage would help.

New York's sportswriters did their part to intimidate. Seizing the opportunity to belittle the A's pitcher, who was part Chippewa, the *New York American* ran an earlier parody of Henry Wadsworth Longfellow's poem "Hiawatha," predicting the "scalping of the Chief" by New York.[2] Not to be outdone, Giants manager John McGraw, a pugnacious Irishman known for his vitriolic bench jockeying, approached Bender during his warm-up tosses and snapped: "It'll be off the warpath for you today, Chief!" Refusing to honor the remark with a reply, the A's hurler simply stared back in stolid silence.[3]

Throughout the game, Bender was forced to endure a running fire of racist epithets from the bleachers. Slurs like "Back to the Reservation!" and "Giants grab heap much wampum!" were inevitably accompanied by imitation war whoops, creating a despicable scene that went far beyond the usual ragging of the opponent by the hometown crowd.[4]

Bender managed to maintain his composure, holding the powerful Giants lineup to four hits and completing a 3–0 shutout to even the Series. Afterward, when he was asked by a Philadelphia sportswriter if his Chippewa background was the reason for his remarkable poise under pressure, the A's pitcher replied: "I want to be known as a pitcher; not an Indian." Bender's remark appeared the following day in the *Philadelphia Inquirer*, accompanied by a cartoon showing him with a large feather protruding from his pillbox cap and a tomahawk attached to his belt. He was staring into the eyes of a Giants player and hypnotizing him with an Indian sign.[5]

Even in victory, Chief Bender was the subject of mock derision. His request to "be known as a pitcher" and "not an Indian" was just as tragic for a man who unwittingly became a pioneer for Native American athletes. In the process, he also became Connie Mack's so-called "money pitcher," the hurler he counted on to pitch the single most critical games during the Athletics' first championship dynasty of 1910 to 1914, and one of the greatest pitchers in the history of baseball.[6]

By the dawn of the twentieth century, the white man had come to the conclusion that the only way to save the American Indian was to extinguish his culture. During the previous two centuries, white America had tried to achieve that objective through missionary efforts, warfare, disease and starvation, the removal of Indians from their tribal land base, and by fostering a culture of dependence on the reservation. Still, the Indian persevered. Forcible assimilation was the only weapon that remained in the federal government's arsenal.

The Bureau of Indian Affairs, the federal agency responsible for assimilation, began by sending Native American youth off the reservation to government-sponsored boarding schools in places like Carlisle, Pennsylvania, Hampton, Virginia, and Lawrence, Kansas. Here, Indian children were introduced to white ways of thinking and acting, along with strict military discipline. Long hair, a symbol of manhood for young men, was shorn in a close-cropped fashion. Tribal dress was abandoned for the dark woolen uniforms similar to those worn by U.S. soldiers. Speaking in one's tribal language was strictly forbidden; both written and oral communication was to be done in the English language. Those who rebelled were chastised, or punished by the military instructors who ran the school. The system worked quite effectively. Once they entered the boarding school, many students never returned to the reservation, seeking instead to build a life in the white mainstream. Some, like Charles Albert Bender, came to regret the decision.

Bender, a standout pitcher for the Carlisle Indian Industrial School, became the great hope of Native American athletes. Just six years before his arrival at the central Pennsylvania boarding school, the federal government, fresh from its final military encounter with Indians at Wounded Knee, South Dakota, instigated an aggressive assimilation process designed to extinguish Indian culture. Baseball was an important vehicle in that process. The game was taught at all government-sponsored Indian boarding schools as a means of cultivating Anglo-American values of teamwork, sportsmanship, and individual achievement. Those who excelled at the sport could enter the white mainstream through semipro and minor league ball.

Nicknamed "Mandowescence," or "Little Spirit Animal," Bender grew up on the White Earth Indian Reservation near Brainerd, Minnesota, before going east for a boarding school education, first at Philadelphia and later at Carlisle. Along the way, he learned how to pitch so impressively that his talent captured the attention of Connie Mack, who signed him to an A's contract in 1903. Bender was a soft-spoken, highly intelligent individual whose dark complexion and coal-black hair gave him the distinctive appearance of an American Indian, though he was the product of a mixed marriage. Because of his physical appearance, he shouldered the burden of racism from the very beginning of his career.

At Philadelphia's Columbia Park, fans taunted him with war whoops and such vitriolic jeers as "Back to the Reservation!" Teammates nicknamed him "Chief," considered a racial slur by Native Americans. Bender also became a popular object of derision on the Philadelphia sports pages, where he was often caricatured in buckskin, moccasins, and feathers. Nor was he the only Indian ballplayer to suffer such indignities. More than 120 Native American major leaguers—and dozens of others who played minor league ball—were treated with mock disdain by white fans, opponents, and sometimes even teammates.[7] Public humiliation was an inescapable burden for all Indian athletes.

Because Native Americans have told their history through oral tradition, there are few written records revealing the Indian perspective. Not until 1969, with the publication of Vine Deloria Jr.'s *Custer Died for Your Sins: An Indian Manifesto*, did Native American writers succeed

in reaching a mass audience with published works on the discrimination of their peoples.[8] Dee Brown's *Bury My Heart at Wounded Knee:
An Indian History of the American West* followed in 1971, paving the
way for other revisionist histories of the Indian wars and the evolution
and nature of the reservation system.[9] Still others turned their attention to the Indian boarding school as a vehicle for Indian assimilation.
These studies examine the relationship between policy formation and
education, specifically how reformers and government officials came
to view the off-reservation boarding school as an instrument for accul-
turating Indian youth to white ways of thinking and behavior, as well
as how educational policy was translated into institutional practice
and how students responded to those efforts.[10]

More recently, historians have begun to explore the relationship
between Indian assimilation and sports, especially baseball. Harold
Seymour was the first to point out that while Indian ballplayers might
have experienced discrimination, organized baseball still accepted
them because their differences with whites were "mainly cultural,"
not "racial," as was the case with blacks, who were banned from the
professional game.[11] Seymour's argument encouraged others to look
more carefully at the issue of American Indian discrimination. Ellen J.
Staurowsky's insightful essay on Louis Sockalexis (1998), for example,
examined the cultural exploitation of the first Native American major
leaguer, who inspired Cleveland's "Indian" mascot but was never
credited for it.[12] David L. Fleitz and Brian McDonald followed, in
2002, with detailed accounts of Sockalexis's meteoric rise to fame and
equally rapid downfall. Both writers offer a tragic tale of a young
Native American who was victimized by baseball, its owners, fans and
the press. Sockalexis was the object of tremendous fascination as well
as bigotry. As a student athlete at Holy Cross College, his ability to
run, hit, and throw captured the imaginations of scouts and the national
media alike. But when he arrived in Cleveland, his exceptional talent
was surpassed only by the war whoops and jeers he received each
time he stepped onto a baseball diamond. Fleitz and McDonald mini-
mize Sockalexis's role in Indian integration, being primarily concerned
with his remarkable playing feats and struggle with alcoholism. They
also dismiss the possibility that he might have consciously used baseball as a means of self-empowerment.[13]

Jeff Powers-Beck, in his work *The American Indian Integration of Baseball* (2004), goes further than these historians by examining the mixed legacy of Native American ballplayers as well as the roots of discrimination against them. Surveying the careers of more than 120 athletes of Indian ancestry, he argues that professional baseball was "a crucible of *both* racial and cultural prejudices" against Native Americans, who were forced to shoulder the burden of racism.[14] Cartoonists made them popular objects of derision on the sports pages. Fans taunted them with war whoops and vitriolic jeers. Even teammates insulted them with nicknames like "Chief," "Nig," "Squanto," and "Kemosabe." "This was not simply a 'cultural prejudice' toward someone who lived differently," insists Powers-Beck. "It was a starkly racist prejudice toward someone who looked different." He adds that the roots of discrimination can be traced to government-sponsored boarding schools like the Carlisle Industrial School in central Pennsylvania. Carlisle used baseball "as a tool for assimilation as well as for the prestige and profit of the school," which fielded some of the finest athletic talent in the nation.[15] At the same time, Powers-Beck views Indian ballplayers like Bender as assertive individuals who used baseball as "a means of cultural resistance and a source of pride."[16] In fact, Bender pursued a major league baseball career in order to distance himself from his Indian heritage, and it was a decision that haunted him for the rest of his life.

Money Pitcher: Chief Bender and the Tragedy of Indian Assimilation explores the life and times of Charles A. Bender in the context of American Indian assimilation. In an era when baseball's reputation was forged by mean-spirited personalities like Ty Cobb and John McGraw and colorful characters like Shoeless Joe Jackson and Rube Waddell, little attention has been paid to Bender, who was one of a very small group of unusually upstanding players. What appeared to be a docile nature, however, was a personal struggle to repress the anger and frustration he felt against a white society and sport that exploited him personally and financially. Eventually Bender sought revenge by pitting the renegade Federal League against the American League Athletics for his services and by costing Mack a fourth world championship.

Chapter 1 gives a historical context for the book by examining the federal government's Indian policy and its implications for Native American children. Bender became a casualty of that policy. Sent east to Philadelphia for an education, Mandowescence was one of hundreds of Indian children who were divorced from their tribes in order to be acculturated into the white mainstream. After four years away from the reservation, Bender returned to discover that he had no future there and ran away to enroll at the Indian Industrial School at Carlisle, Pennsylvania. Chapter 2 discusses the educational and acculturation experience of Indian children at Carlisle. Between 1896 and 1902 Bender, like many of the students, embraced the military regimen of the boarding school. He also learned to play baseball, a sport at which he excelled as a pitcher. After matriculating to nearby Dickinson College, Bender competed at the intercollegiate level and, for pay, at the semiprofessional level. Offered a contract by the Philadelphia Athletics in 1902, the young hurler decided to build a life in the white man's world through professional baseball.

Chapters 3 and 4 chronicle the colorful—and controversial—origins of Connie Mack's Athletics in the brash and sooty environment of Philadelphia at the turn of the century. Bender's rise to stardom amid the racial and cultural discrimination of a white urban society is detailed in these chapters. The creation of Mack's first championship dynasty between 1910 and 1914 is the subject of Chapter 5. Bender was a mainstay on those teams and one of the few soft-spoken members of a rough-and-tumble gang of ballplayers known collectively as the "White Elephants." During these years he built his reputation as Connie Mack's "money pitcher," the hurler to be relied on in the single most important game of a series.

The name "money pitcher" assumed a different meaning during the last year of that remarkable dynasty. Caught in a battle over salary negotiations with Mack, Bender, who was never paid more than $2,500 a season by the A's, was offered three times that amount to jump to the renegade Federal League. Chapter 6 focuses on Bender's decision to "pitch for more money," a choice that corrupted the 1914 World Series and raised the question of whether the Chippewa hurler was involved in a game-fixing conspiracy or whether he simply "lay down" when he was called upon to pitch the opening game of the Fall Classic. It is a controversial event that is inextricably tied to the game's unsavory culture of gambling, roster raiding, and financial exploitation of players in the early twentieth century. But the circumstantial evidence against Bender is damning.

The Athletics, who had captured three world championships in the previous four years, were 10-to-6 favorites going into the 1914 World Series against the Boston Braves, a team whose offense and defense were significantly inferior to Philadelphia's. But the A's lost the Series in four straight games. The circumstances surrounding that blown championship suggest that some members of the team purposely refused to give their best effort, being disgruntled with Mack and his tightfisted ways. Chapter 6 explores in depth those circumstances and Bender's critical role in the tarnished World Series.

Chapter 7 chronicles the decline of the Indian hurler's major league career with the Baltimore Terrapins of the Federal League and the Philadelphia Phillies of the National League, and how he resurrected himself as a pitcher-manager for several minor league teams. At the same time, Bender's attentions turned increasingly to a more successful—and financially lucrative—life off the playing field. Trading on his name, he worked first as a haberdasher and later as the owner of a sporting goods store. He also increased his real estate holdings by purchasing several properties in Cumberland County, Pennsylvania. In short, Bender had finally learned how to become "successful" in a white society based on the accumulation of land and capital, one that had never fully accepted him because of his Native American heritage. The final years of Bender's life, and how he reconciled his differences with Mack and the Athletics, are discussed in Chapter 8.

Chapter 9 provides some final thoughts on the achievement and tragedy of Charles A. Bender in the context of American Indian assimilation. Bender's remarkable playing career, which paved the way to the majors for dozens of American Indian ballplayers, and the singular honor of being the first Native American to be inducted into the National Baseball Hall of Fame, serve to underscore the tragic legacy of his life—the abandonment of one's native culture to chase after the white man's American Dream, a dream that proved to be a personal nightmare. It is the same tragedy of Indian assimilation itself.

William C. Kashatus
Lake Silkworth, Pennsylvania
Spring 2005

1

MANDOWESCENCE,
1884–1896

In the spring of 1761, an English trader by the name of Alexander
Henry traveled from Montreal into the Chippewa (Ojibway/Anishi-
naabe) territory of Lake Huron. The wilderness was breathtaking.
Thick woodlands of birch, cedar, and pine hugged the lakeshore and
stretched across the mountains as far as the eye could see. The lake
was perfectly calm, its color a pristine blue. Henry, accompanied by a
Canadian boatman, navigated his canoe along the picturesque banks
of the Huron and landed at Michilimackinac, where he was visited
by Minavavana, the war chief of the local Chippewa tribe.

Being familiar with Anishinaabe history, the Englishman appreciated
the tribe's expertise at trapping such wild animals as beaver, moose,
and bear. He also realized that since the mid-1600s the Chippewa
had figured prominently in the French fur trade, but he hoped to
persuade them to establish an English trading post in the region.

Minavavana, a figure of commanding stature, was accompanied by
sixty warriors dressed and painted for battle. Surprisingly, Henry thought
little about his safety. The Anishinaabe rarely fought the whites, not
because they were any less warlike than the other Algonkin tribes of
the Great Lakes region—the Potawatomi, Menomini, Sac and Fox
and Cree—but because there were no extensive white settlements in
their country. While the Chippewa sometimes allied with the French

against the English, and had proved to be valiant in native warfare, Henry believed he could tempt the tribe with promises of greater material wealth than they already enjoyed.

Not a word was spoken as the Chippewa chief and his men seated themselves on the floor, filled their pipes, and began to smoke. Eventually Minavavana asked the Canadian boatman a series of questions about the purpose of the white men's visit, all the while gazing steadfastly at the English traveler. Finally, he addressed Henry:

"Englishman!" he barked in a deep, imposing voice. "It is to you that I speak, and I demand your attention." The Anishinaabe chief removed any doubt as to who was in charge of the gathering as Henry sat in respectful silence.

"You might have conquered the French, but you have not yet conquered us! We are not your slaves. These lakes, these woods and mountains were left to us by our ancestors. They are our inheritance, and we will part with them to none. Your nation supposes that we, like the white people, cannot live without bread and pork. But you ought to know, that He—the Great Spirit and Master of Life—has provided food for us in these broad lakes and upon these mountains."

It was a noble speech, designed to assess the courage and character of a potential enemy. Noting, however, that the two travelers were not armed, Minavavana presented Henry with a pipe to smoke as a token of friendship and assured him of the Chippewa desire to regard him as a "brother."[1]

To be sure, the Anishinaabe chief was determined to limit his tribe's relationship with whites to the fur trade. The Chippewa, like most Indians, were receptive to European material goods but were unwilling to surrender their traditional ways entirely and assimilate into an alien culture. Despite Minavavana's resolve, the white man imposed his culture on the Chippewa people.

Between 1768 and 1775 Native American tribes west of the Appalachian Mountains sold off their vast hunting grounds to English settlers. The upheavals of the Revolutionary War, followed by conflicts with the United States Army led to large cessions of inhabited Indian lands, especially in the Great Lakes region. At postwar treaty negotiations, Native Americans were haughtily told by U.S. commissioners that they were a "subdued people" and that their "country is claimed by conquest."[2] The first such treaty negotiated between the government and the Chippewa took place at Fort McIntosh on January 21, 1785.[3] Other treaties followed, and by 1847 the Chippewa had ceded all their possessions in Michigan and Wisconsin.[4] By 1867 the Ojibwa and Dakota Sioux of the Minnesota Territory had ceded another 24 million acres to the federal government and were crowded onto two large reservations under the control of the Department of the Interior's Bureau of Indian Affairs.[5]

Westward expansion was the catalyst for nineteenth-century Indian removal. At a time when the railroad was knitting the continent together from the Atlantic to the Pacific and the growth of industry was transforming a once rural, small-town society into a more congested urban one, the U.S. government needed to find a safety valve for its burgeoning population. Expansionists validated their movement with the rhetorical term "Manifest Destiny," coined by John L. O'Sullivan, a New York journalist. "Our manifest destiny as a nation," wrote O'Sullivan in 1845, "is to overspread and to possess the whole continent which Providence has given us for the great experiment of liberty and federated self-government entrusted to us."[6] Implicit in the expansionist movement was the ethnocentric notion that white, Anglo-Saxon Americans were a chosen people destined for greatness because of their democratic institutions, and that they had a divinely inspired obligation to extend the benefits of those institutions to the inferior peoples who inhabited their borders. Using lofty language and routinely invoking God and Nature to sanction expansion, Protestant missionaries joined with federal policymakers and reformers to proclaim the divine mission of Americans to "Christianize" and "civilize" the "weaker races" on the North American continent, especially the Native American Indian.[7] Among the reformers were Lucius Q. Lamar, U.S. secretary of the interior; Carl Schurz, commissioner of Indian affairs, and his successor, Henry Price.

During the 1870s and 1880s, Lamar, Schurz, and Price defined the federal government's Indian policy. These reformers insisted that there were three interrelated obstacles in the way of Indian assimilation. First, they argued that the reservation system served to propagate the Indian attachment to tribal institutions and placed a higher value on communal than on individual property. Under these circumstances, it was difficult for tribes to recognize federal authority, and the U.S. government would be compelled to negotiate for land with tribes instead of individuals, frustrating attempts to secure greater holdings in the west for white settlement. Related to this problem was the need to extend the U.S. legal system to Native Americans so they could become citizens of the country. The final obstacle, as the reformers saw it, was the need to educate the younger generation of Indians as a matter of both assimilation and economic necessity. Lamar, Schurz, and Price realized that the elder generation might adopt the white man's ways, but in their hearts they were still attached to tribal ways. The younger generation, however, could be assimilated into the white mainstream through a common education, making Indian youth economically self-sufficient and relieving the federal government of having to feed and clothe another generation tied to the reservation.[8]

The Dawes Severalty Act, passed by Congress in 1887, addressed these issues and established federal Indian policy for decades to come. Under the act, the president was allowed to distribute land not to tribes but to individuals legally "severed" from their tribes. Those individuals who "accepted the allotment of 160 acres and agreed to allow the government to sell un-allotted tribal lands" could "petition to become U.S. citizens." These unallotted lands could be sold to whites and the profits from those sales were to be held by the federal government for the tribe's "education and civilization."[9]

Price extolled the benefits of the Dawes Act, noting that "the allotment of land in severalty and the breaking up of tribal relations" would speed the process of assimilation by developing in the Indian "a personal sense of independence and the universal adoption of the English language."[10] While the tenets of the Dawes Act appear from a contemporary perspective to be discriminatory, if not insidious, reformers like Lamar, Schurz, and Price pushed for its passage because they were genuinely concerned about the Indians' plight. They were outraged not only by the bloody atrocities of the U.S. military's suppression of the Plains tribes, but also by the federal government's flagrant abuse of its Indian treaties. They believed that in such a hostile environment the Indians were confronted with two alternatives, as Lamar succinctly put it, "either speedy entrance into the pale of American civilization, or absolute extinction."[11] "The idea of exterminating a race," added

4

Schurz, "once the only occupant of the soil upon which so many millions of our own people have grown prosperous and happy, must be revolting to every American who is not devoid of all sentiments of justice and humanity."[12] Still, the humanitarians, no less than the most brutal advocates of extermination, played a part in diminishing an ancient culture; and they did it by redefining the behavior and values of Indian youngsters like Charles A. Bender.

Born on May 5, 1884, near Partridge Lake in Crow Wing County, Minnesota, Bender was the mixed-blood son of Albertus Bliss Bender, a German homesteader, and Mary Razor, who was of part Chippewa descent.[13] One of nine children, young Charles was given the Indian nickname "Mandowescence," which means "Little Spirit Animal."[14] A Chippewa was known by his nickname throughout his life, and it frequently contained an element of humor. It was different from the Indian birth name, which contained a spiritual significance that originated in a dream. Whether Bender received a "dream name" at his birth is not known. But his nickname suggests that his "spirited" behavior as a boy resembled that of a small animal.[15]

Because of Mary Razor's Chippewa ancestry, the family was allotted 160 acres on the White Earth Reservation near Brainerd, Minnesota, when Mandowescence was still a toddler. Located in present-day Gregory Township, Mahnomen County, the reservation was established in 1867 by the federal government in order to concentrate all of the Minnesota Chippewa on a single tract of land. But there was a growing division between the full-blooded Anishinaabeg and the metis, or those mixed-bloods who descended from marriages between fur traders and native women.[16] Metis tribal members demonstrated a strong adherence to market values such as the individual accumulation of wealth. They were cash-crop farmers and merchant-traders who lived in the western part of the reservation, which was composed of prairies dotted with hills and marsh. Metis tribal members used wage employment, anglicized surnames, and the English-language churches. As a result, they tended to serve as intermediaries between the Anishinaabe and white society. Traditional Anishinaabeg, on the other hand, were more oriented toward kinship and band. They were gatherers or subsistence farmers who resided in the eastern part of White Earth, covered in thick woodland, and were content to achieve a comfortable subsistence level. Only sporadically did they use wage employment, and they tended to use Anishinaabe surnames and participate in Anishinaabe-language churches.[17]

The Benders were considered metis tribal members at White Earth. Their land—which eventually totaled twenty-three contiguous plots of eighty acres each—was located on a section of prairie where they raised vegetables and livestock.[18] Mandowescence learned how to farm from his father, and at age seven he took a job working as a farmhand off the reservation for $1.00 a week.[19] Aside from these scattered facts, there is no documentation or oral history regarding Bender's childhood on the reservation.

It is tempting to believe that the young mixed-blood might have learned how to play baseball at White Earth. After the American Civil War baseball spread rapidly throughout Minnesota as teams were organized on a statewide basis. "Baseball is emphatically a national game," proclaimed General Henry H. Sibley, president of the Minnesota State Association of Baseball Players. "The game contributes to the health of its devotees, occupies their time, and prevents them from indulging in habits which are improper and ought to be avoided."[20] While Sibley saw baseball as an enjoyable pastime that promoted physical fitness and created competitive rivalries between such amateur teams as the North Star Club of St. Paul and the Vermillion Base Ball Club, pressure for professionalization came when many of the amateur teams began to hire ringers, talented athletes who were paid to play. In 1884 professional baseball made its debut in St. Paul with the establishment of a twelve-team Northwestern League. Although the circuit lasted just one season, minor league baseball had found a home in Minnesota.[21]

Nor was the sport uncommon among the Lake Superior Chippewa at the turn of the century. Since 1887, when the Dawes Act was passed, the Ojibway had been adapting their own traditions to white institutions and pastimes. In addition, the Chippewa familiarity with ball-and-stick sports like lacrosse and cha ha allowed them to embrace baseball with a passion.[22] Youngsters played pickup games, sometimes using lacrosse sticks as bats. Catholic missionaries, who ran day and boarding schools on some reservations, promoted baseball as a "wholesome" recreation that embodied strong Christian values of sportsmanship, individualism, and competition.[23] Adults soon began to play the game as well, not so much for its assimilationist value but because the game resonated with certain Anishinaabe traditions.

While the Chippewa honored a tribal way of life, their egalitarianism still "allowed for and even celebrated individual feats of distinction and heroism." At a time when Indian agents and white men were controlling their lives and their native lifestyle of fishing and hunting was quickly disappearing, Chippewa men had fewer opportunities to distinguish themselves. Baseball, like tribalism, was one of the few opportunities in which an Indian could assert himself as an individual while also uniting with other members of a team.[24] Indeed, baseball had the potential to become a powerful form of Indian resistance waged on the white man's playing field, as Cherokee, Potawatomi, Winnebago, Wabanaki, and Choctaw joined the Chippewa in playing the sport by the beginning of the twentieth century.[25] Thus Mandowescence, as a metis tribal member, may very well have been introduced to the sport at White Earth. What is certain is that he was among the brightest of the children on the reservation.

In 1889, shortly after the Benders relocated to White Earth, the metis made a pact with the federal government to sell reservation land to white lumber interests in return for federal subsidies. While the agreement allowed the federal government to sell reservation land to lumbermen and farmers, often at a fraction of market value, a significant portion of the profit was applied to the education of the most promising child from each Chippewa family.[26] Two years later, in 1891, Mandowescence, at age seven, was chosen by his parents to attend the Educational Home on the East Coast.[27] Considering that the few Indian youths who attended off-reservation boarding schools returned to White Earth to assume some of the most desirable jobs, such as storekeepers and postal workers, enrollment at the Educational Home was considered an honor to be coveted by those fortunate enough to be chosen.

Located at 49th and Greenway Avenue in Philadelphia, the Educational Home was a boarding school for orphaned and destitute white and Indian children. It was operated by the Episcopal Church and in 1884 merged with the Lincoln Institution, another local Episcopalian school that educated Indian children exclusively. With an average

7

enrollment of one hundred, the school taught students ranging in age from seven to twenty-two years old. Many students came from White Earth because of the intercession of the Reverend Joseph Gilfillian, the head of the reservation's Episcopal mission. Mandowescence was one of twelve White Earth children enrolled on July 15, 1891.[28]

The experience of being thrust into a white urban culture must have been painfully shocking. The train ride from White Earth to Philadelphia was traumatic for a seven-year-old who had never been more than a few miles away from the reservation. Luther Standing Bear, a Native American youngster who attended such a boarding school in the East, later wrote about the fear instilled in him by older students as the train traveled across the Great Lakes region and into Pennsylvania. "The big boys began to tell us little fellows that the white people were taking us to a place where the sun rises," he wrote. "There, they would dump us over the edge of the earth as we had been taught that the earth was flat with four corners, and when we came to the edge we would fall over. As the full moon was rising and we were traveling toward it, the big boys were singing brave songs . . . [and] we expected to be killed any minute."[29] Of course, nothing happened to the youngsters, but their relief was short-lived. No sooner did they reach their destination than the children were taunted by white onlookers. "Many of the little Indian boys and girls were afraid of white people because they acted so wild at seeing us," wrote the youngster. Whether in simple jest or mock derision, these white observers "tried to give the war whoops and mimic the Indian" in an effort to get the children "all wrought up and excited."[30] Nor did the situation improve much once the Indian children arrived at the Educational Home.

The primary objective of the off-reservation boarding school was to prevent a relapse into old tribal ways, something that could not be avoided at the reservation schools.[31] Once removed from the tribal environment, the Native American youth was totally immersed in white culture, customs, and values. Without the interference of Native American culture, the Indian child would acquire the skills necessary to join the white mainstream. He would learn to read, write, and speak the English language; accept a Christian lifestyle; develop a deep devotion to the United States and its laws; and, above all, embrace the ideal of individualism by learning a trade so he could become self-sufficient

and embrace the value of property ownership.[32] All of these assimilationist priorities were reflected in the charter of the Educational Home,
which began with the following prayer: "Be Watchful over them for
good; provide for their necessities; make them dutiful and submissive
to authority; preserve them from sickness and accidents; and turn
their youthful steps unto thy testimonies . . . so as these children grow
in years, they may grow in wisdom for the good of society and the
prosperity of true religion."[33]

Once an Indian child arrived at the school he remained there, at
least until the age of twelve, unless he was dismissed for disciplinary
reasons. There were no trips home to the reservation. During vaca-
tions, students were placed in local homes and farms to learn a trade
such as farming, shoemaking, carpentry, and tailoring. This so-called
"outing system" prepared Native American youth for self-sufficiency
in adulthood.[34] Great efforts were made to ensure that once a student
completed his education, he would not return to the Indian lifestyle but
would take his place in white mainstream society. In fact, the school's
board of managers, in its 1894 annual report, proudly noted that of the
180 students who received their schooling at the Educational Home,
to that date "not more than four have gone back to the old life."[35]

Mandowescence was thirteen years old when he returned to White
Earth. Much had changed during his six years in Philadelphia. While
the Dawes Act had done little to integrate the traditional Anishinaabe
into white society, it had promoted an alliance between metis tribal
members and the federal government. Encouraged by self-styled "Indian
reformers," the metis wrested control from the Anishinaabeg of valuable reservation land for lumbering interests and left them with inferior
farmland, inadequate tools, and little training for agricultural self-
sufficiency.[36] To facilitate the white takeover of White Earth's resources,
the metis were permitted to sell reservation land without any restric-
tions. The Anishinaabeg were forced into surrendering their land and
then made dependent on government subsidies for their livelihood.
White Earth had become little more than a white lumber camp. Anishinaabe tribesmen were now struggling with idleness, intemperance,
and environmental degradation.[37]

Whether Albertus Bender participated along with other metis in
selling off White Earth's resources is not known. If he did, his family

9

certainly didn't profit by his actions. Mandowescence had difficulty readjusting to his own family, who lived in a cluttered one-room log cabin with an earthen floor and lean-to kitchen. It was also overcrowded, for his mother had given birth to an eighth child while he was away. The living arrangements were the complete opposite of the well-ordered lifestyle he had known at the Educational Home.

With few prospects for employment, there wasn't much of a future. "At the end of two months," Bender recalled years later, "I decided to run away from home and go to Carlisle Indian Training School, where I arrived the first week of September, 1896."[38]

Mandowescence had made a fateful decision.

2

CARLISLE,
1896–1902

Mandowescence was not as innocent as the other Indian youths who arrived at Carlisle, Pennsylvania, on September 5, 1896. Many were Chippewa boys and girls who had never been off the reservation and were desperately lonesome for their native Minnesota. Some of the older boys began chanting like warriors when the group stepped off their eastbound train. Organized by twos they marched like soldiers along Hanover Street, attracting the stares of the white townspeople, some of whom would eventually apprentice them to their businesses in the summer months.

Carlisle, located in south central Pennsylvania, was a small farming town of some 7,000 residents. Since the opening of the United States Indian Industrial School in 1879, the townspeople had grown to accept, even appreciate, the presence of Native American youth. The town's churches and charitable organizations donated funds and supplies to the school. Local businessmen hired Indian students at minimum wage so they could learn the white man's ways. Most of the inhabitants seemed to applaud the special efforts of the school to assimilate Native American children into white society. While there may have been no overt resentment of the Indian presence by 1896, there did exist a patronizing, if not haughty, attitude that the white man's way was the "only way" for these children to lead their lives. Indeed, there was a popular belief that the community of Carlisle itself was a virtuous partner in this progressive experiment to civilize and Christianize these small heathens.

As the band of Indian émigrés crossed the trolley tracks and began the final leg of their journey down the narrow lane to the Indian Industrial School, the war whoops became louder and more piercing, as if the young braves were going off to do battle with the white man, if only in their imaginations. But their chanting only served to make the girls cry. Some became so terrified that they tried to break ranks in a futile attempt to return to the train. Mandowescence, however, paid no attention to the spectacle that was unfolding before his eyes. He had already experienced a similar scene five years earlier when he first left the reservation to attend the Educational Home in Philadelphia. Besides, he had to be strong for his younger brother, John, who accompanied him. John was also enrolled at the Indian Industrial School and it was his first time away from the reservation. At the same time, Mandowescence's calm exterior belied the irrepressible anxiety he felt inside over the uncertainty of attending this new school.

The children passed the guardhouse that fronted the redbrick gates and entered the Industrial School at the southern end of the campus. As they crossed a footbridge passing over a small stream, the youngsters were awestruck by the immaculate grounds before them and their orderly design. At the center of the plush green campus stood a small white bandstand, built a few years earlier by student band members, who would also provide musical entertainment from its wooden deck during spring and autumn afternoons. The bandstand was like the hub of a wagon wheel, with buildings surrounding it in every direction. To the northeast stood the girls' dormitory and gymnasium, another structure built by the hands of student labor. A grand two-story Georgian structure clothed in white clapboard was situated to the east. Fronted by eight ionic columns and a hip-roofed pediment, the structure was the home of the school superintendent, Captain Richard Henry Pratt, and gave the appearance of a southern plantation house. More modest teachers' quarters were located directly across the campus, and just beyond, the boys' dormitories, one for the older students and another for the younger boys. Predictably, the disciplinary quarters was sandwiched between these two dormitories.

Fig. 1   Carlisle was a small, growing town of about 7,000 people at the turn of the century. Located in Pennsylvania's Cumberland Valley, the town could boast of an early transportation network, with trains connecting the western part of the country to major cities in the East. (Cumberland County Historical Society, Carlisle, Pennsylvania)

The school building was located to the south. It contained classrooms for both vocational and academic training, a chapel, and an auditorium. But the pride and joy of the campus was the athletic field, located at the far northeastern corner. Carefully tended by the students, the field resembled a thick green carpet. Here, on spring and autumn afternoons, Carlisle teams would compete in football and baseball against some of the top collegiate teams in the nation. A small wooden grandstand was built on the western periphery of the field, where fellow students gathered to cheer on their athletically gifted schoolmates. It was on this athletic field that Mandowescence would develop the talent to become a professional baseball player.[1]

Pennsylvania, the place that Charles A. Bender would call home for the rest of his life, had quite a different Indian history from his native state of Minnesota. Long before English colonizer William Penn and the Quakers arrived in 1682, Pennsylvania was the domain of the Lenni Lenape ("Original People"), who lived in small bands along the tributaries of the Delaware River to the Delaware Bay and eastward to the Atlantic Ocean. Called the "Delawares" by white settlers, the Lenape numbered about 5,000 and survived by planting corn and beans and fishing during the spring and summer months. During the winter the small bands divided into family groups and relocated further inland to hunt deer.[2]

Dutch and Swedish traders, who arrived in the 1640s, developed an antagonistic relationship with the Lenape, which was worsened by the irresponsibility of those who gave them guns and alcohol. While Penn also took advantage of the barter economy, he was determined to establish a friendly association with the Indians. Indeed, the Quakers, members of the Religious Society of Friends, and the Lenape shared common beliefs in participatory government, consensus decision making, and a mystical religious tradition, all of which allowed the two groups to forge a lasting friendship. Because Penn sought to create a "Holy Experiment" in Pennsylvania—a colony dedicated to religious toleration and pacifism—he refused to raise a militia for the defense against Indian attacks. He also recognized the Indians' right to the land, making sure to purchase the Lenape title to any territory he wished to settle.[3] Penn's peaceful relations with the Indians was truly exceptional at a time when Puritan colonizers to the north and Anglican settlers to the south warred with Native American inhabitants. Penn, like many of the early Friends, believed that the Lenape could be assimilated into their society and attempted to convert their Indian neighbors to the Quaker faith because of a mutual belief in a mystical divine presence within each person.[4]

Word of the Quaker proprietor's friendship with the Indians spread to other dislocated tribes who found sanctuary in Pennsylvania, including the Shawnee, Nanticokes, Conoys, and Tuscaroras. This unique friendship was eventually reinforced by a "Covenant Chain," an interlocking alliance between these tribes and the seat of Pennsylvania government at Philadelphia. Relations remained peaceful as long as Quaker principles were followed. But after Penn's death, in 1718, the Indians grew wary of the white man.

With the increase of German and Scotch-Irish immigrants, pacifist sentiment declined, along with the benevolent treatment of the Native Americans. Driven from Europe by hunger and war, neither group of settlers shared the Quaker ideal of racial harmony; both were concerned only about farming and the acquisition of land. Different cultural interpretations of property ownership only worsened tensions. The Lenape believed that land was a gift from Kishelemukong, the Creator, held in common by all those who shared it. Europeans, by contrast, considered land "private property" to be bought and sold and made the Lenape frequent victims of land fraud. During the early eighteenth century, the Lenape learned to manipulate European land laws to further their tribe's own interests. Still, white settlers continued to encroach on their territory, sometimes encouraged by land agents of Penn's own sons, Thomas and John, who assumed the proprietorship of the colony after their father's death.

When the Penns saw squatters from New York settling in the Lehigh Valley and along the upper reaches of the Delaware, they conspired to cheat the Indians out of existing land claims in order to increase their own income through land sales and the collection of rents. The resulting "Walking Purchase" of 1737 covered sixty miles of choice land from Bucks County into the Pocono Mountains.[5] It also claimed virtually all the remaining Lenape lands in eastern Pennsylvania. Demoralized and distressed, many Lenape relocated to the Susquehanna Valley or moved further west to Ohio, where they established their own towns or lived among the Shawnee, Miamis, and Wyandots.

When the French-Indian War broke out in 1754, Lenape warriors abandoned the Covenant Chain and sided with the French against the British and their Iroquois allies because of the Pennsylvania government's failure to protect their land. Realizing that Indian survival required independence from all European powers as well as unity among themselves, the leaders of the scattered Lenape settlements formed a Delaware nation in the Ohio Valley. On May 8, 1765, the Ohio and Pennsylvania Delaware Indians signed a formal peace treaty with the British victors. Under the terms of the treaty, the Delaware were forced to accept any general frontier boundary demanded by the

English and their Iroquois allies. Three years later, when the Iroquois sold the Susquehanna Valley to the English, the Delaware were left without a Pennsylvania homeland.[6] Not until 1879, with the founding of the Carlisle Indian Industrial School, would Pennsylvania again play a critical role in the assimilation of Native Americans. This time, however, it wasn't the Quakers who were spearheading those efforts, it was the federal government and the United States Army.

Carlisle was one of twenty-five off-reservation boarding schools established by the federal government at the turn of the century. Founded in 1879 by Captain Richard Henry Pratt, the Indian Industrial School was designed to introduce Indian students to white ways of thinking and acting. Students were given a vocational education and ranged from ten to twenty-five years of age.[7] While the institution enjoyed the academic reputation of a college among Native Americans, it was in reality more of a secondary boarding school. Carlisle's survival depended largely upon the efforts and perseverance of its founder, who, for his twenty-five-year tenure at the school, was the single most important figure in Indian education.

Born on December 6, 1840, at Rushford, New York, Pratt was the eldest of three sons of Mary and Richard Pratt Sr. Six years later the family relocated to Logansport, Indiana, where they settled along the banks of the Wabash River. In 1849 Richard Sr., restless and wanting to seek his fortune in the California gold rush, headed west. While there he was robbed and murdered by a fellow prospector. At the age of thirteen, young Richard became the head of the household and left school to support his mother and two younger brothers. For the next eight years he tried his hand at printing, tin-smithing, and rail splitting, but proved to be just as restless as his father until, at age twenty-one, he enlisted in the U.S. Army.

Serving with distinction on the battlefields of Kentucky, Tennessee, and Georgia during the Civil War, Pratt was promoted to first lieutenant of the cavalry. After the war he returned to Indiana and opened a hardware store. Bored and failing in business, he applied for a commission in the regular army and was promoted to second lieutenant. In the spring of 1867 Pratt was assigned to Fort Gibson in Indian territory. There he was given command of a newly formed African American unit called the "Buffalo Soldiers," composed of recently freed slaves

Fig. 2   Captain Richard
Henry Pratt, Indian reformer
and founder of the Carlisle
Indian Industrial School.
(Cumberland County
Historical Society, Carlisle,
Pennsylvania)

and Indian scouts who had served in the Civil War. It was during
these eight years that he became sympathetic to the injustices that
both blacks and Indians had to face as second-class citizens.[8] "Talking
with the Indians," he wrote years later, "I learned that most had received
English education in home schools conducted by their tribal government. Their intelligence, civilization and common sense was a revelation
because I had concluded that as an Army officer I was there to deal
with atrocious aborigines."[9]

Pratt also witnessed the federal government's aggressive campaign
to relocate the Plains Indians to reservations, especially the Kiowa,
Comanche, Cheyenne, and Arapaho, who refused to surrender their
hunting grounds to be herded onto those government parcels. In the
summer of 1875 General Philip Sheridan, under orders from President
Ulysses S. Grant, pursued the raiders, imprisoned them, and sent them
east to stand trial for their hostilities. In April 1876 seventy-two of the
Indian prisoners were sent to Castillo de San Marco, an old Spanish
fort at St. Augustine, Florida, later known as Fort Marion. There Pratt
began to acculturate Indians to a disciplined military lifestyle, though

not without compassion for them. Shackles were removed. Indian dress was replaced by government-issued military uniforms. Daily drills and gymnastics were introduced. Soldier guards were eventually dismissed and the prisoners given rifles to police themselves. Industries were established to encourage greater contact with the townspeople, whether it was teaching archery for a fee, offering fishing excursions to tourists, or creating crafts to sell. By creating these opportunities for interaction, Pratt promoted a better understanding between whites and Native Americans. After they had spent three years in exile, the War Department released the prisoners to the Bureau of Indian Affairs, which gave them the choice to return to the west to live on a reservation or to continue their education in the east.[10]

When Pratt applied to several schools seeking admission for those former prisoners who wanted to continue their education, however, his efforts were rejected. "Their case was pre-judged," he complained to the Indian Bureau, "because they were prisoners of war with reputations for atrocities."[11] Pratt, who was beginning to flatter himself that he was a reformer, had found a purpose for his life and pursued the goal of Indian education with the zeal of a campfire preacher. Appealing to Samuel Chapman Armstrong, the founder of Hampton Normal Agricultural Institute in Virginia, he secured the admission of seventeen former prisoners in April 1878. Hampton, originally a school for blacks, was now a biracial institution. Its program was carefully monitored by the federal government, which was beginning to realize that their Indian policy of relocation, segregation, and annihilation wasn't working. When Hampton proved that acculturation could be successful, Pratt persuaded Secretary of the Interior Carl Schurz to recruit more Indians for the school.[12] Eventually President Rutherford B. Hayes agreed that Hampton's program of acculturation was "destined to become an important factor in the advancement of civilization among Indians."[13] But Pratt still was not satisfied.

He believed that Native Americans needed more exposure and interaction with the white race than Hampton, with its predominantly black enrollment, could provide. His educational philosophy was paternalistic and simple: "Immerse the Indians in our civilization and when we get them there, hold them under until they are thoroughly soaked in the white man's ways."[14] Therefore, he began to lobby key officials in the War Department to realize his vision of a school exclusively for Indians at an abandoned cavalry barracks at Carlisle, Pennsylvania. Once a training ground for Indian fighting tactics, Carlisle's geographic proximity to Washington, D.C., would allow the federal government to monitor its progress. Securing the approval of General William Tecumseh Sherman, in August 1879 Pratt was named superintendent of the United States Indian Industrial School at Carlisle and traveled to the Indian territory to recruit students among the Sioux, just three years after that tribe defeated Custer's forces at the Battle of Little Bighorn.[15]

While it may seem ironic that the children of the Sioux were selected to attend the school when more malleable minds could have been recruited among the Kiowas, Comanches, and Cheyenne—tribes with which Pratt was more familiar—the choice reflected his personal philosophy. "If we take pains with those who give us the most trouble," Pratt reasoned, "their children would be hostages for the good behavior of their people."[16] In other words, the ultimate success of Indian education depended on the acculturation of the white man's fiercest enemies into the white mainstream. To this end, Pratt convinced Sioux leaders that acculturation was inevitable and that if their children were to survive in white society they would have to enjoy "the same education as the white man" and "be able to take care of themselves and their property without the help of an interpreter or Indian agent."[17] With such high expectations and little margin for failure, Carlisle was run like a military training camp.

When children arrived, their long hair, a symbol of manhood for young braves, was shorn. Tribal dress was abandoned for dark woolen uniforms similar to those worn by U.S. soldiers, or, in the case of girls, stiff Euro-American dresses. The students were assigned a trade such as tailoring, carpentry, or stenography. Speaking in one's tribal language was strictly forbidden; both written and oral communication was to be done in the English language.[18] All of these actions were taken to create uniformity among children from several different tribes. Individuality was actively discouraged in order to discipline and acculturate students to white customs and behavior. In the process, the student's identity as a Native American was also diminished. "When my hair was cut short, it hurt my feelings to such an extent that tears

Figs. 3 and 4 "Before" and "after" photographs showing the same Carlisle students, first on their initial arrival, with their long hair and tribal dress, and then a few years later, after they had been transformed into docile students. (Cumberland County Historical Society, Carlisle, Pennsylvania)

came into my eyes," admitted Luther Standing Bear, the son of a Sioux chief and among the first students to arrive at Carlisle in 1879. "All I was thinking about was the hair that the barber had taken away from me. I felt that I was no more Indian, but an imitation of a white man."[19]

Pratt shrewdly commissioned a series of "before" and "after" portraits showing the same students, first on their initial arrival at Carlisle with their long hair, tribal dress, and wild-eyed appearance, and then a few years later, after they had been transformed into docile pupils. The portraits served as an important public relations tool to prove that the school was making remarkable progress in training these young "savages."[20] After seeing the photographs, one Indian reformer remarked enthusiastically, "The years of contact with ideas and with civilized men and Christian women so transform them that their faces shine with a wholly new light, for they have indeed 'communed with God.' They came children; they return young men and young women; yet they look younger in the face than when they came to us. The prematurely aged look of hopeless heathenism has given way to that dew of eternal youth which makes the difference between the savage and the man who lives in the thoughts of an eternal future."[21]

The portraits seemed to offer positive proof that Pratt had accomplished his goal of "killing the Indian to save the man." At the same time, the look of "eternal youth" that was celebrated by the reformers may just as easily be interpreted as a state of cultural shock, the dazed look of children who have had their personal identity stolen from them. Not only were they groomed to look like Euro-Americans, they were taught to think like them.

Carlisle's curriculum trained each student according to his or her own abilities and included instruction in English, chemistry, history, geography, mathematics, and biology. Since the government's allotment system consigned Indians to an agricultural life, farming skills were also taught at the school. In addition, the students were taught a trade so they could become constructive members of the economy after their graduation from Carlisle. Boys were assigned to such trades as tin-smithing, carpentry, shoemaking, tailoring, wagon making, blacksmithing, and steam fitting. As little machinery as possible was used to teach these trades so that each student could learn his trade by becoming skillful with his hands. Girls were instructed in the domestic arts

21

Fig. 5   Carlisle's students were taught a balanced curriculum consisting of math, English, history, geography, and writing. This photo of ninth graders was taken in 1901. (Cumberland County Historical Society, Carlisle, Pennsylvania)

of cooking, dressmaking, and childcare. It was a practical curriculum that met the needs of the individual student as well as of the school. Carlisle relied on student labor to become self-sufficient because of inadequate funding by the federal government. Produce cultivated on the school's three working farms was sold locally or sent west to other Indian schools. Students also made their own uniforms, furniture, and even some of the buildings on campus.[22]

The most critical part of the curriculum, however, was the outing program, through which students would spend summers working on the farms or in the homes of families throughout Pennsylvania and New Jersey. Each student was paid for his services and the money was deposited in an interest-bearing bank account by the school to be handed over to the student upon his graduation. An outing agent visited students to report on their progress. According to Pratt, the system was an "unconditional success," as "barriers and prejudices between whites and Indians were removed" and the students "received training that no school can give."[23] In fact, many students were made to feel like servants by their host families, being given little time away from their chores and receiving low wages.[24]

The outing system, like the rest of the curriculum and the military lifestyle observed at Carlisle, was an integral part of Pratt's plan to eradicate Indian culture among his young charges. "It is the nature of our red brother that is better dead than alive," he wrote in a phrase that was hauntingly similar to the often-quoted remark of U.S. Indian fighters that "the only good Indian is a dead one." Carlisle's mission, according to Pratt, was to "kill the Indian as we build up the better man" and give him "something nobler and higher in the ambitions and aspirations of his more favored white brother."[25] For, as genuine as his intentions might have been, Pratt's philosophy was an ethnocentric one. His strict rules and rigid routines were deeply offensive to Indian culture, which placed great value on personal and tribal freedom. Those who rebelled were chastised or punished by the military instructors who ran the school. In the process, the integrity of the Indian lifestyle and culture was broken down among those who were most responsible for carrying on the old way of life. To be sure, Carlisle's system worked quite effectively. Once entered into the boarding school, many students never returned to the reservation, seeking instead to build a life in the white mainstream. If Charles Bender was stifled by the strict discipline and regimented lifestyle of Carlisle, there is certainly no record of it. In fact, he appears to have been the kind of student the school intended to graduate.

Bender attended Carlisle from September 5, 1896, to May 14, 1902. Because of his Chippewa ancestry, he belonged to one of the largest tribal groups enrolled at the school.[26] But soon even that tribal identity was lost. Carlisle's students were recruited from many different tribes and the school was careful to separate students from the same tribe. The purpose was to eliminate any connection to the Indian's past in order to cultivate the white man's culture, language, and behavior. Bender, a scrawny five-foot three-inch youngster, weighed just one hundred pounds when he arrived at age thirteen, but he grew to a formidable six foot two inches and weighed 185 pounds by the time of his departure.[27] His younger brother, John, was the only other member of his immediate family to attend Carlisle, though a younger sister, Elizabeth, would later teach at the school.[28]

There are no existing records of how Bender performed as a student or what course of study he took. However, he did learn the watch and jewelry business during an apprenticeship with Conlyn's Store in Carlisle, a trade he put to use as off-season employment during his years as a professional baseball player.[29] In addition, Bender was, according to one account, soft-spoken but highly intelligent, "passive and inexpressive, but very tall and handsome."[30] Bender's "passiveness" *might* have been acquired through the strict routines of Carlisle, but it appears to have been a part of his natural disposition. His summers were spent working on farms in rural southeastern Pennsylvania and New Jersey. According to his school records, Bender was assigned to the following families:[31]

Patron's Name	Address	Dates
Joseph E. Beck	Penn's Manor, Pa.	March 31–April 24, 1897
Eleazer Thomas Doan	Buckmanville, Pa.	Sept. 11, 1897–Sept. 16, 1898
S. Bennett Dudbridge	Jamison, Pa.	September 21–November 1, 1898
Elvin Allen	Edgewood, Pa.	May 20–September 15, 1899
Gerald McScudden	Lawrenceville, N.J.	June 21–September 1, 1900
David L. Hertzler	Williams' Mills, Pa.	June 24–July 29, 1901

With the exception of Gerald McScudden, the heads of these families were Quaker farmers from Bucks County, Pennsylvania. They ranged in age from the early forties to early fifties, had been married on average for twenty-two years, had one or two children who were away at school, and had a history of employing Carlisle students on their farms.[32] Apparently their Quaker faith and lifestyle held a strong appeal for Bender. Years later he would speak most fondly of those "good Quaker folks" and credit them with the "best training" he received during his time at the Indian school.[33] But it was on the athletic field that Bender distinguished himself.

Carlisle competed against the nation's top collegiate teams. The school's football program particularly enjoyed great success and constantly sought to expand its pool of talented players, thanks to Glenn

Fig. 6 Glenn "Pop" Warner, Carlisle's athletic director and highly successful football coach. (Cumberland County Historical Society, Carlisle, Pennsylvania)

"Pop" Warner. Warner, who played for Cornell, would go on to a distinguished career as a football coach at the University of Pittsburgh, Stanford, and Temple University.[34] But in 1901 he was just beginning his career and coached baseball and track as well as football.

Baseball was an important vehicle in the assimilation process at all government-sponsored Indian boarding schools. Reformers viewed the game as a means of cultivating Anglo-American values of teamwork, sportsmanship, and individual achievement. Those who excelled at the sport could enter the white mainstream through semipro and minor league ball.[35] For the Indian students, baseball "re-figured the warrior tradition" and "created a context for the celebration of intertribal cooperation and identity."[36] The marriage between assimilationist goals and intertribal cooperation made the sport wildly popular among the students at Carlisle.[37]

Students played baseball on an intramural basis, organizing teams by vocational shops. They also competed at the collegiate level against some of the most highly rated programs in the nation, including Penn, Army, and Yale. Not surprisingly, Carlisle produced an impressive number of major leaguers during the early twentieth century, among them Jim Thorpe and Louis Leroy, both of whom played for the New York

Fig. 7   An early Carlisle baseball team. (Cumberland County Historical Society, Carlisle, Pennsylvania)

Giants, Mike Balenti and George H. Johnson, who played for the Cincinnati Reds, and, of course, Bender, who signed with the Philadelphia Athletics in 1902.[38]

At Carlisle, Bender, initially a right fielder, captured Warner's attention as a relief pitcher. During the 1901 campaign he relieved Carlisle's top pitcher, Louis Leroy, in an April 12 game against Albright College. "Given an opportunity to show what he could do," Carlisle's *Daily Herald* reported, "Bender, a new and inexperienced pitcher," was "a little wild at first but kept the visitors' hits well scattered" to record an 8–3 victory.[39] Impressed by the performance, Warner started the right-hander against Lebanon Valley on May 1. Bender "pitched the game in a very credible manner, striking out eight men" en route to a 13–8 victory.[40] The Chippewa hurler's speed and poise on the mound earned the respect of his teammates, who elected him captain of the team the following season.[41]

With the graduations of Louis Leroy and Arthur Pratt, Carlisle's two top pitchers, Bender became the ace of the team. But the team was not as strong as the previous year's and Bender became a hard-luck loser. In one hotly contested game against neighboring Dickinson College, he "seemed to strike out the [opponent] at will and allowed but two scattered hits," but lost, 2–1.[42] Shortly after, Bender was suspended for "for treachery to the baseball team."[43] While the specific details of this incident have been lost to time, Bender's suspension made him conspicuously absent from the Carlisle box scores for April and May and the team finished the season with an extremely disappointing 4–15 record.[44]

Carlisle's baseball teams were overshadowed by the school's football and track programs in subsequent years. After the 1902 season Warner resigned as baseball coach in order to focus on the football program. Many of the student athletes later complained that he was "selfish, abolishing branches of athletics that he was not capable of coaching like baseball" and, worse, that he "used the football team for the purpose of gambling."[45] To be sure, Warner was first and foremost a football coach. While charges that he used the football program for gambling interests were never proved, there is reason to believe that he was concerned about his football players competing on semiprofessional baseball teams for pay in the summer months. Such a practice was widely condemned by college presidents and athletic directors across the nation on the basis that student athletes were "commercializing themselves" in violation of the spirit of amateur athletics. Determined to avoid a scandal that would damage his football program, Warner abolished the baseball program in January 1910.[46]

After graduation, Bender attended Dickinson College, perhaps as a way to stay connected to Carlisle, which had become the closest thing to a home for him. He also learned that he had the talent to earn some money playing baseball. His brother, John, who had been expelled from the Industrial School for unknown reasons two years earlier, was already playing for semiprofessional teams in nearby Harrisburg and may have convinced his older brother that the pay was fairly good.[47] Recruited by the local Dillsburg team during the summer of 1901, Bender agreed to pitch for five dollars a game. In his very first contest he struck out twenty-one batters and hit a grand-slam home run—yet still somehow managed to lose, 9–5![48] The Dillsburg manager, who had agreed to pay Bender $5 for his services, reneged on the deal, paying him just $3.50. The manager explained that "expenses were

too high and the collection too low" to give the young hurler any
more and promised to pay Bender the $1.80 difference "the next time
I see you." Forty years later Bender received the money in a bag full
of pennies and dimes along with the following note: "In going over
our records we have discovered an outstanding account due you from
the Summer of 1901. We are enclosing the money reserved for you,
which amounts to $1.80. We are not enclosing any interest as we felt
we were overcharged."[49]

The following summer Bender signed on with the semipro Harrisburg club for the more substantial sum of $100 a month. Realizing
that he couldn't use his real name if he hoped to preserve his amateur
status and compete athletically at Dickinson, he assumed the moniker
"Charles Albert."[50] His big break came in a 3–1 exhibition game victory he pitched against the Chicago Cubs. Jesse Frisinger, a scout for
the Philadelphia Athletics, was in the stands and immediately signed
the young right-hander to a $1,800 contract.[51] The following spring
Bender began his professional baseball career in Philadelphia.

Charles A. Bender's experience at the Carlisle Industrial School
taught him to emphasize those talents and abilities that white society
valued and *not* his Indian heritage. Mandowescence, the Chippewa
mixed-blood who entered the school six years earlier, had grown accus-
tomed to the white man's ways and had come to prefer them to those
of his native culture. In that sense, Bender was a role model for the
kind of student Carlisle hoped to cultivate. At the same time, Carlisle
was engaged in a horrific act of cultural devastation. Operating on the
ethnocentric principle of "kill the Indian to save the man," Superintendent Richard Pratt and his faculty actively destroyed Indian culture
by seeking to expunge it collectively and individually from the children. Theirs was among the most deplorable episodes in the long and
tragic history of white-Indian relations. To Bender's credit, or perhaps
disillusionment, he would survive the psychological abuse to prosper
in the white man's society. His ticket to success would be his ability
to pitch.

3

PHILADELPHIA, 1903–1905

Philadelphia greeted the twentieth century with a surge of cheer and confidence. The city's population of nearly 1.3 million was a rich mix of immigrants, natives, and transplants. Bluebloods, whose ancestors founded the city, inhabited the quaint Victorian neighborhoods of the downtown and the picturesque mansions of Fairmount Park. At the other end of the spectrum were the foreign born and poor blacks, who crowded into the shabbiest sections of the central and southern wards along the Delaware River. South Philadelphia was a mix of ethnic ghettos offering its residents the security of familiar languages and customs. Italians from Sicily settled "Little Italy" below Catharine Street. German Jews clustered at the corners of Marshall and Poplar streets, while the "shanty Irish" and Poles lived in vermin-infested dwellings just beyond. Blacks were relegated to the back-alley shacks of the river wards.

Philadelphia was hardly a "City of Brotherly Love," though. The roots of intolerance ran deep, especially for new immigrants who competed for jobs and territory not only with each other but also with native-born workers who resented them bitterly. Industrial employers often paid foreign labor lower wages than the natives. Anglo-Saxon homeowners looking for domestic help specified in their newspaper advertisements that only "white Protestants" need apply. Even among the different ethnic groups there was a purposeful effort at segregation. Children learned at an early age that you only "played with your own kind." As the early years of the century unfolded, these unskilled immigrants relocated to the north and east of the downtown, finding employment in the small industrial villages that surrounded the city. Frankford and Olney became home to the Germans. The Irish lived and worked in the factories of North Philadelphia, while the mills of Manayunk attracted the Poles. Strawberry Mansion was an enclave for eastern European Jews, whose ambition and financial acumen enabled them to transform the area into a prosperous marketplace.

Industry was the city's backbone as well as its future. Philadelphia's crowded row-house neighborhoods moved to the clang of the forge and the hum of factory machinery. Philadelphians made Baldwin locomotives, Stetson hats, Schmidt's Beer, Breyer's ice cream, Quaker lace, and countless other products for a prosperous nation.[1] Anything could be purchased in the City of Brotherly Love, even the vote.

City politics was dominated by the powerful Republican machine of Boies Penrose and Bill Vare, both of whom perfected the art of "backroom" deals, "election fixing," and the "spoils system." Penrose was the penultimate party boss. Disdainful of the Quaker merchant aristocracy from which he descended, Penrose had run for mayor in 1895 but lost the primary thanks to a well-publicized photo of him coming out of a downtown brothel. Instead, he ran for the U.S. Senate and won, a feat he accomplished repeatedly between 1904 and 1922. Penrose was independently wealthy and sought no personal graft. But his appetite for power spurred him to serve the industrial tycoons of the city faithfully by dispensing contracts, patronage, and campaign funds.

Vare came from a different background. Raised on a pig farm, he was one of three highly ambitious brothers who shamelessly sought political power. Their introduction to politics came when the City of Philadelphia paid them to collect garbage, which they fed to the pigs. As they became more affluent, they used their money to buy influence and political office. Bill Vare won a seat in the U.S. House of Representatives with the help of his brothers, who fixed the election by having the dead cast their ballots for him. His power base consisted of the ethnic slum wards of the downtown, shipyards, docks, and factories of South Philadelphia. The former pig farmer possessed a unique

Fig. 8 Cornelius McGillicuddy, better known as "Connie Mack," was awarded the Philadelphia Athletics of the new American League in 1901. (Robert D. Warrington)

understanding of ward leadership and how to use it to his own advantage. Controlling each ward through patronage, false voter registration, and purchasing votes, Vare strengthened his authority by wielding a hefty war chest that he increased through lucrative contracts won by his own construction company.[2]

So complete was the Republican hegemony in Philadelphia that even the chairman of the city's Democratic Party, as well as the rest of City Council, yielded to the wishes of the machine. Reform movements ebbed and flowed, but none could cleanse the city for long. No wonder Lincoln Steffens, the muckraker, dismissed Philadelphia in 1903 as the "worst governed city in the country."[3]

Into this optimistic, brash, and sooty society stepped Cornelius McGillicuddy, who would make Philadelphia the baseball capital of America within the decade. Better known as "Connie Mack," the tall, scrawny Irishman looked more like an undertaker than the baseball genius he would soon become. Dressed in a black three-piece suit complete with necktie, detachable collar, and derby, Mack was a baseball entrepreneur who embodied the colorful nature of the game. Born December 23, 1862, at East Brookfield, Massachusetts, he was the son of Irish immigrants. Mack worked in a shoe factory and played baseball for the local team until 1886, when at age twenty-four he entered professional baseball as a catcher. As a player he wasn't much of a hitter, compiling a batting average of just .249 in an eleven-year career. He was better known for his excellent skills as a catcher. Often he would rag an opposing hitter or call for a quick pitch, and was even known to "tip the bat" on occasion. It is questionable, however, whether Mack resorted to these tactics to win ball games or simply to survive. At six foot one and 160 pounds, there wasn't much of an alternative.[4]

He began managing in 1896 with the Pittsburgh Club of the National League but quickly became disgruntled with ownership over the administration of the franchise.[5] Three years later Mack left to help establish a new league on the condition that he be given absolute freedom in running his own team. Together with two enterprising businessmen, Ban Johnson and Charles Comiskey, Mack organized the Western League and managed his own franchise in Milwaukee. A year later the Western League became the American League and entered professional baseball as a rival to the National League. The timing of the venture could not have been better.

By 1900 there was room for competition in major league baseball, since National League teams were losing money at the gate and their owners were divided into two warring camps over players' salaries and other administrative expenses. For its economic survival the National League was forced to drop four teams from its organization, teams that were quickly assumed by the new American League. The Philadelphia Athletics went to Connie Mack, who held 25 percent of the club's stock.[6]

Almost from the moment that he set foot in the City of Brotherly Love, Mack created controversy. He persuaded Benjamin F. Shibe, a business partner of sporting goods dealer Al Reach, to invest in his club. The offer wouldn't have seemed so conspiratorial if Reach hadn't been a part owner of the National League's Phillies, but Mack persisted. He even sweetened the deal by arranging to have the Reach company's baseballs selected as the official ball of the new American League. After clearing the offer with Reach, Shibe purchased 50 percent of the A's stock and became president of the club.[7] But Mack didn't stop there.

Fig. 9 Benjamin F. Shibe, president of Reach Sporting Goods, purchased 50 percent of the Philadelphia Athletics and assumed control of all business matters.

Stating that the purpose of the new American League was "to protect the players," unlike the National League, which sought "to protect the magnates," the brash baseball entrepreneur proceeded to raid the roster of the rival Phillies by offering sizeable pay increases to their stars.[8] Not only did Mack land a pitching staff for his team by signing Chick Fraser, Bill Bernhard, and Wiley Piatt, he captured a real prize when the Phillies' All-Star second baseman, Napoleon Lajoie, defected to the A's for $5,500.[9] Lajoie showed his appreciation by hitting .422 in 1901. He also drove in 125 runs and 14 homers to lead the American League in all three categories. The other bright spot for the A's was a twenty-five-year-old collegiate recruit, pitcher Eddie Plank, who won seventeen games fresh from the diamond of Gettysburg College. Unfortunately for the A's, it wasn't enough to defeat the Chicago White Sox for the league's first title. The Mackmen finished fourth with a record of 74–62, though they played the best ball in the A.L. during the final two months of the season.[10]

Roster raiding was made easier by the National League's refusal to pay any individual player more than $2,400 a season. American League clubs promised no salary cap and made more lucrative offers, and a total of seventy-four National Leaguers jumped to the new circuit.[11] When Phillies president John I. Rogers discovered Mack's scheme, he took him to court, arguing that the reserve clause prevented players from jumping to another team or league unless they were first released by their original club. The case was thrown out in common pleas court on the grounds that National League contracts "lacked sufficient mutuality." But the Phillies appealed the decision to the Pennsylvania Supreme Court, which ruled in their favor. The Phils obtained court injunctions against Lajoie, Fraser, and Bernhard, preventing them from playing for any club except theirs.[12]

John McGraw, the feisty manager of the National League champion New York Giants, was so enraged by Mack's efforts that he spited the A's by predicting they would turn out to be a money loser, the "White Elephants" of the new league. Mack countered by adopting the animal as his team's mascot, attaching a small white elephant to the left breast pocket of each player's dark blue warm-up sweater.[13] Nor did he have any intention of giving in to the National League on the Lajoie ruling. Since the Pennsylvania Supreme Court's decision could be enforced only within the state, American League president Ban Johnson, with Mack's blessing, transferred the contracts of Lajoie and Bernhard to the Cleveland Americans so the National League would be deprived of their services. Whenever Cleveland played against the A's in Philadelphia, neither player was permitted to take the field in accordance with the injunction. Instead they spent a paid vacation in Atlantic City.[14] Shortly after the arrangement had been sealed, Mack spitefully declared to the press: "The American League and the Athletics are here to stay, whether Lajoie is with us or not."[15].

Mack was as good as his word. After the court injunctions, several American League clubs transferred players to the A's. Catcher Ossie Schreckengost, better known as "Schreck," came to Philadelphia from Cleveland along with second baseman Frank Bonner. Boston sent pitchers Fred Mitchell and Howard "Highball" Wilson to the A's, and Milwaukee sent pitcher Bert Husting to Philadelphia. Mack also added second baseman Danny Murphy from the Connecticut State League. His biggest catch, however, was a zany lefthander by the name of George "Rube" Waddell.

Waddell was a farm boy who was raised near Bradford, Pennsylvania. He spent most of his youth fishing, playing ball, and chasing fire engines. After pitching for town teams, Waddell, at age twenty-one, signed his first professional contract with Louisville in 1897. Over the next few years he earned a reputation as a classic country yokel, being nicknamed "Rube" for his eccentric behavior. By 1900 Waddell was pitching for the Pittsburgh Pirates, but his free-spirited ways did not sit well with the rigid discipline of manager Fred Clarke. When Rube jumped the club, Clarke, who had grown tired of his flakiness, let him go. Mack, then manager of the Western League's Milwaukee club, "borrowed" Waddell from the Pirates. Rube's first start came in the opener of an August 19 double header against the Chicago White Sox. Not only did he pitch all seventeen frames of the extra-inning contest, he sealed the game for himself by tripling in the winning run, 3–2. After the managers agreed that the second game would go no more than five innings, Mack, realizing that Waddell was an avid fisherman, made a bargain with the wacky southpaw: pitch the second game and he could go fishing for three days instead of traveling on to Kansas City with the team. Delighted by the proposition, Rube proceeded to throw a five-inning shutout. In 1902 Mack, believing he could mentor the incorrigible pitcher, signed Waddell to fill the void left by Fraser's and Bernhard's departure.[16]

Through the first half of the 1902 campaign the A's hovered around the top of the standings, but in August they went on a tear, winning sixteen of seventeen contests. The offense was powered by third baseman Lave Cross (.339, 108 RBI) and right fielder Socks Seybold (.317, 16 HR, 97 RBI). There were also four other .300 hitters in the lineup: Schreckengost (.324), Murphy (.313), first baseman Harry Davis (.308), and outfielder Dave Fulz (.302). The pitching was just as effective. Waddell went 24–7 with a league-leading 210 strikeouts, and Plank chalked up another twenty victories. Although the Boston Pilgrims and St. Louis Browns made the pennant race closer in late September, the A's prevailed by sweeping a three-game series from the Orioles in Baltimore on September 25. It was also Philadelphia's first pennant since the Athletics of the old American Association won the flag in 1883. Unfortunately, there would be no World Series that year.

Fig. 10   In 1901 the Philadelphia Athletics finished the season with a record of 74–62. Among the players who defected from the National League's Phillies were pitchers Chick Fraser *(back row, first from right)*, Bill Bernhard *(back row, third from left)*, and Wiley Piatt *(back row, fourth from left)*; and All-Star second baseman, Napoleon Lajoie *(front row, second from right)*.

Barney Dreyfuss, owner of the National League champion Pittsburgh Pirates, refused to allow his team to compete in the Fall Classic. Dreyfuss was undoubtedly angered by Waddell's success after he watched Mack steal him away from the Pirates. Having lost many of his star players to the American League, the Pittsburgh owner refused to acknowledge the circuit's legitimacy by playing against any of its teams—especially the A's—in the postseason.[17] The dispute would finally be settled the following year, when a "peace agreement" was reached. According to the so-called "National Agreement of 1903," organized baseball would be governed by a three-man National Commission consisting of the presidents of the two major leagues and an owner of one of the clubs as chairman. The National Commission would regulate all business affairs as well as settle disputes between the two leagues and/or the several clubs. It also paved the way for an annual postseason World Series between the winners of both major leagues.[18]

During his early years in Philadelphia, Mack's reputation for controversy was exceeded only by his remarkable ability to discover and harness the talent of collegians and dim-witted roustabouts alike, molding them into a productive team. He was the first to use college ball as a proving ground for the majors at a time when other managers limited their scouting to the sandlots. His discoveries included two of the game's greatest pitchers, Eddie Plank from Gettysburg and Charles Bender from Dickinson.

Plank had never played baseball before college, which probably accounted for his finesse on the mound. He didn't have the chance to develop any bad habits and became a serious student of pitching. Quiet by nature, Plank had superb control. His effectiveness, however, came from an exceptional ability to mix a fastball with a sidearm curve that froze the hitter, and from his annoyingly deliberate habit of taking his time between pitches. Signed by Mack in 1901 at the advanced age of twenty-five, "Gettysburg Eddie" quickly became the left-handed ace of the Athletics.[19] Bender, a right-hander, was similar in temperament and pitching style, but much less confident of his abilities.

Shortly after signing the Carlisle product, Mack touted his rookie hurler to the press, believing that he would "solve any remaining weakness" in his team's pitching.[20] But Bender admitted that he was "at sea, both literally and figuratively from the first day of spring training." "If it hadn't been for Harry Davis, who took me in tow and looked after me like a father," he said, "I don't think I would have made it. I took his advice on *everything* and almost worshipped him."[21] Davis, a native Philadelphian, was the captain and first baseman of the A's and managed the team whenever Mack was absent. He was also a prodigious hitter who went on to lead the American League in home runs for four straight years between 1904 and 1907. Davis's mentoring was a blessing for Bender, who had much to learn about the professional game as well as its colorful lifestyle.

These were the days before ball clubs lodged in fancy hotels and instead sought any accommodations they could find. The A's, who

Fig. 11 George "Rube" Waddell led the A's to their first American League pennant in 1902 with a 24–7 record, 210 strikeouts, and a 2.05 earned run average. A classic country yokel, he was known for his colorful behavior. (National Baseball Hall of Fame Museum and Library, Cooperstown, New York)

trained in Jacksonville, Florida, boarded in an old barn, which doubled as a gambling hall. The structure slept five or six players in a make-shift room separated by partitions. They slept on cots and bathed using water pitchers and washbowls. Meals were taken at Wolfe's Café, known for its "baseball steaks," which tasted more like leather than meat. "One evening, Ossie Schreck and Rube Waddell nailed their steaks to the wall," Bender remembered. "It created quite a com-motion and for a time looked as if we might lose our eating place. But Mr. Mack smoothed things over as only he could do."[22]

Waddell was in especially rare form that spring. Schreck, his room-mate and partner in crime, knew it too. The A's catcher got along fine with Rube most of the time, applauding Waddell's penchant for wrestling alligators and waving teammates off the field in exhibition games just to strike out the side. Schreck didn't even complain when Waddell disappeared for two full days, only to return as a bandleader for a minstrel show. But there was one thing he simply couldn't tolerate, and that was Rube's habit of eating animal crackers in bed. His loud chomping resulted in many sleepless nights for the A's catcher. Schreck finally took his complaint to Mack, who had Waddell sign a contract promising to eliminate the bad habit.[23]

One of the most amusing incidents that occurred that spring, however, involved Rube's attempt to capture the affections of a Jacksonville bar wench. "One night after practice, he looked her up in his usual café and found her sitting at a table with someone else," explained Bender. "Rube told her he was heart-broken and started to cry. Leaping dramatically to his feet, he declared that he was going to kill himself by jumping off a dock and drowning. He then rushed out of the place with Schreck at his heels. Rube raced to the dock and jumped in. But the tide was out and instead of the usual five feet of water there was only six inches of water and two feet of muck. Rube hit the muck head-first, buried himself, and almost choked to death before Schreck and some dock hands could drag him out. He didn't threaten to commit suicide by drowning for some time after that!"[24]

In 1903 the A's would slump to a distant second-place finish, largely due to poor hitting. Topsy Hartsel was the only regular to bat better than .300, as the team watched its offensive production drop to a .264 clip, twenty-three points below the previous season's team average.[25]

Bender proved to be a bright spot in an otherwise unimpressive season. "We opened at Boston on April 20th," he recalled. "It was a double-header, one game in the morning and another in the afternoon. Waddell pitched the morning game and lost, 9–4. Rube was a poor fielder who couldn't get out of the box and Boston beat him by bunting. Eddie Plank started against Cy Young in the afternoon game and Boston knocked him out in the fourth inning with six runs. Mr. Mack called for me. Golly, I was scared—my first major league game and against Cy Young!"[26] Bender pitched brilliantly, surrendering just three hits.

The A's began to chip away at Boston's lead, pulling ahead in the eighth when Seybold tripled and outfielder Ollie Pickering singled him home for a 7–6 lead. The A's tacked on three more runs in the ninth on singles by Bender, Topsy Hartsel, and Davis and a triple by Lave Cross. With a 10–6 lead, Mack lifted Bender in the bottom of the inning and put in Weldon Henley, who promptly surrendered another run. But the A's held on for a 10–7 victory, giving Bender his first major league win.[27] "I felt like I was walking on air," recalled the Chippewa hurler, "especially after Mr. Mack came up to me and said: 'Nice work, Albert!'"[28]

Bender followed his initial appearance with a brilliant performance against the New York Highlanders a week later, on April 27. It was his first major league start as well as his debut at Columbia Park in Phila-delphia. Located at Columbia Avenue and Oxford Street between Twenty-ninth and Thirtieth streets in the northern section of the city, the ballpark had a seating capacity of 9,500. A semicircular single-decked grandstand hugged the infield, providing fans with a close view of the game and players with an earful of criticism when they weren't performing up to the hometown crowd's high expectations. Open bleachers were situated alongside both foul lines, with another, smaller, bleacher section running across left field. A twenty-five-foot-high chicken-wire fence extended from the right field bleachers to center field, making for the only open side of the ballpark.[29] When Bender took the field, the jeers from the stands were deafening.

Because of his dark complexion and coal-black hair, which gave the twenty-year-old rookie the distinctive appearance of an American Indian, Bender was taunted with war whoops and such jeers as "Back

Fig. 12   Columbia Park, located at Columbia Avenue and Oxford Street between Twenty-ninth and Thirtieth streets in North Philadelphia, was the A's first home ballpark. The small wooden "bandbox" stadium seated only 9,500 spectators and was often filled to capacity during the pennant-winning seasons of 1902 and 1905.

to the Reservation!" Some of the 7,000 fans who attended that day called him "Chief," in mock derision of his Native American ancestry. By the end of the afternoon, though, few of the fans were taunting him. Bender surrendered just four hits and three walks to defeat pitcher-manager Clark Griffith and his Highlanders, 6–0.

Dubbed the "artful aborigine" by the Philadelphia press, Bender was lauded in the local newspapers for "making good on all the predictions made of him," for "pitching with little or no seeming effort," and for "using splendid judgment" in his pitch selection.[30] Still, Philadelphians didn't know what to make of him. At best, the A's new hurler was considered a novelty by an urban society unaccustomed to Indian athletes. At worst, he was an object of scorn by the white working-class immigrants who frequented the ballpark as a release from the ethnic discrimination they themselves encountered in the workplace.

Despite the city's many colleges, museums, and liberal-minded reformers, Philadelphians were still quite narrow-minded in their view of race. The so-called "City of Brotherly Love" had produced such cranks as the self-styled "anthropologist" Samuel George Morton, who reinforced popular notions about the intellectual and social inferiority of Native Americans. Morton had a special passion for collecting and analyzing human skulls. After measuring the interior cranial capacity, he compared the results by race and ranked them on a scale beginning with the Caucasian race, which he believed was the most superior.[31] In 1849 he published his results in *Crania Americana; or, A Comparative View of the Skulls of Various Aboriginal Nations of North and South America*. According to his findings, the white race was "distinguished by the highest intellectual endowments," whereas Native Americans were "restless, revengeful, and fond of war." Since they were "averse to cultivation and slow in acquiring knowledge," Morton concluded that Indians were "among the lowest grade of humanity."[32] In fact, Morton's data were completely unsound. Using only the skulls and whatever information their donors provided, he had no way of checking the reliability of his racial findings. He also failed to factor gender and overall body size into his calculations, and, worse, he generalized about the different races from the extremely limited information he found in other biased anthropological writings and travel literature. Nevertheless, Morton's racial theories became even more popular at the turn of the century, as they were reinforced by students like Louis Agassiz.[33] Considering the circumstances, only time and a winning record would tell if Bender would be accepted by Philadelphia's baseball fans.

On May 7 Bender defeated Washington's Al Orth in a runaway 19–5 game. Five days later he suffered his first defeat against Roy Patterson of the White Sox in Chicago. The extra-inning loss was a 3–2 heartbreaker.[34] "The White Sox had the winning run on second with two out in the eleventh," Bender remembered. "Eddie McFarland, a .200 hitter, was at bat. I got two strikes on him—and you know what the next pitch had to be—a duster. That was the first thing that Harry Davis taught me when I joined the A's. He said, 'Kid, whenever you get two strikes on a batter and no balls, throw the next one at his bean. Don't be afraid. You'll never hit anyone when you throw at 'em. But don't throw behind 'em or you will surely hit 'em.' I thought it was good advice. So I threw the next one at McFarland's head. He ducked and the ball hit his bat and shot over first base for the cleanest single you ever saw, beating me!"[35]

Hard-luck losses weren't the only trying part of that season. Bender also became a popular object of derision on the Philadelphia sports pages, where he was often caricatured throughout his career. The most deplorable of these cartoons appeared on June 28, 1903, in the *Philadelphia North American*. It accompanied a story written by sportswriter Charles Dryden, who re-created Bender's misfortune of losing his wallet on a sleeper train the A's were taking en route to a game in St. Louis. "Big Chief Bender of the Chippewa's has lost his wampum belt valued at $100 and the mishap entailed no end of trouble," wrote Dryden. "The Indian's wealth got away from him in a Wabash sleeper early on the morning of June 2nd. All hands were routed from sweet dreams while the train was passing through the district of East St. Louis. Bender tumbled out of a top bunk, left his coat hanging on the rail that supports the curtain, and went to the washroom. A purse containing $100 in $10 bills was left in the inside pocket of the coat for safekeeping. Despite an exhaustive search, the wampum belt was never found."[36] In fact, Bender, not wanting to interrupt his teammates' rest, asked the train's conductors not to disturb them. But when St. Louis detectives boarded the train they searched all the Pullman passengers.[37]

As if Dryden's racist account wasn't bad enough, cartoonist Charles Nelan portrayed a "savage" Bender dressed in buckskin, moccasins, and feathers, searching for his "wampum belt" on the floor of a sleeper car while other passengers feared for their safety.[38] Such a caricature might have been intended as humor by the white press, but in exploiting Bender's Native American ethnicity it was, in fact, a deeply offensive racial slur. Somehow the young hurler refused to allow the negative press and racist taunts of the fans influence his pitching performance.

In 1903 Bender completed twenty-nine of the thirty-three games he started. He appeared in more ball games (36) and hurled more innings (270) than he would in any other season for the rest of his career. At season's end he had posted a 17–15 record with 127 K, and a

Fig. 13   Racist cartoon of Bender searching for his lost wallet on the floor of a sleeper car. The cartoon was drawn by Charles Nelan and appeared in the June 28, 1903, edition of the *Philadelphia North American.*

very respectable 3.07 ERA for a team that finished second, 14 1/2 games behind the pennant-winning Boston Red Sox. Together with Waddell (21–16, 302 K, 2.44 ERA) and Plank (23–16, 176 K, 2.38 ERA), Bender formed the core of a pitching staff that would contend for the next few years.[39] Their success on the mound can be attributed to remarkable control, which they worked hard to perfect. "Practice, constant practice gave me great control," insisted Bender. "If you look back at the records, you will see that Plank and Waddell also had fine control. Every day, Schreck would line the three of us up together, give each of us a ball, and hold his mitt at different spots. Each man would throw. Schreck would catch the ball in his glove hand and then place

Fig. 14   A rare photograph of the A's 1905 pitch staff in civilian clothes. Clockwise from bottom center are George "Rube" Waddell, Charles Albert "Chief" Bender, "Gettysburg Eddie" Plank, and Andy Coakley. Manager Connie Mack was so pleased that his team had captured their second pennant in four years that he had the photograph taken for posterity. (Robert D. Warrington)

it in his bare hand. He would wait until he had all three balls and then throw them all back at once. Never did he miss making a return throw."[40] With that kind of pitching staff, the A's were favored to capture another flag in 1904.

The team got off to a quick start with Waddell blazing his way to a new strikeout record that would culminate at 349. Both he and Plank also posted identical 26–17 records that year. Bender struggled, though. After reeling off four straight victories, his performance went into a tailspin. By August the A's were out of contention and Bender was in poor health. He also had his mind on other things. During a road trip to Detroit the previous season, he had met an attractive young woman by the name of Marie Clement. Their attachment grew during the '04 season, as she became a "constant visitor to the Tigers' ballpark whenever the Carlisle graduate pitched." They decided to marry on October 3 during the A's final visit to Detroit. The marriage raised eyebrows among the sportswriters in that Clement was Caucasian and, by the social etiquette of the time, an unsuitable match for a Native American.[41] Together with his poor health, later discovered to be appendicitis, public disapproval of the marriage probably contributed to Bender's mediocre 10–11 record that season.[42] Boston won the pennant and the A's finished a disappointing 12 1/2 games behind in fifth place.[43]

Although the American and National Leagues had agreed to coexist, John T. Brush, president of the National League champion New York Giants, refused to participate in a World Series. Echoing the sentiments of his manager John McGraw two years earlier, Brush insisted that the National League was "the nation's premier baseball organization" and refused to "jeopardize that prestige" by playing a postseason contest against the inferior American League. There would be no World Series in 1904, and Boston proclaimed themselves "world champions" by default.[44]

The A's returned to form in 1905. Although Chicago's strong pitching and Cleveland's heavy hitting allowed those two teams to dominate the first three months of the season, the A's paced themselves in a close third-place berth. Harry Davis's team-leading .284 batting average carried the A's through the season, while Philadelphia's pitching remained solid. Waddell and Plank were on pace to win another twenty games, while young right-hander Andy Coakley was developing into a reliable starter who would go on to post a 20–7 record that season. Bender also got off to a strong start, winning his first seven decisions before being hampered by kidney troubles.[45] The success of the pitching staff was due, in part, to the curfew that Mack imposed on Waddell.

The A's manager was convinced he could get more productivity from his ace pitcher as well as Rube's drinking pals if he hired a former constable to police the big oaf. "The plan worked, at least for the first two weeks of the season," according to Bender. "One night Harry Davis and I were sitting in front of the Euclid Hotel in Cleveland. It was about 11 o'clock. A cab drove up and Rube stepped out. He reached into the cab, pulled out the constable and tossed him over his shoulder. Rube then carried him into the hotel.

"'Getting in a bit early, aren't you, Rube?' asked Davis.

"'Getting in, hell!' replied the Rube. 'As soon as I put down this drunk, I'm startin' out for the evening.'"[46]

When Nap Lajoie, Cleveland's player-manager and leading hitter, was sidelined in July with blood poisoning, the Indians cooled off and the A's filled the void. On August 2 the A's moved into first place, ahead of the White Sox. With Cleveland fading, the A's widened the gap over the next few weeks. But on September 1 the A's lost Waddell to a freak injury. On that day the Rube declared war on straw hats, which according to the fashion etiquette of the era were popular headwear during the spring and summer but considered "out of season" beginning on the first of September. Waddell enforced the standard by punching his fist through the top of any straw skimmer he spotted. Apparently pitcher Andy Coakley was not aware of the tradition and wore his straw hat on the train carrying the team to Providence, Rhode Island. When Rube went after him, a scuffle broke out and he fell on his left shoulder, injuring it severely. Waddell worsened the problem by sleeping next to an open window in his Pullman berth. The cold air stiffened his arm so badly that the next morning he couldn't raise it above his shoulder. Although Mack tried to pitch him on two separate occasions in the heat of the pennant race, Rube proved ineffective and was benched for the remainder of the season.[47]

With Waddell lost to injury, the A's began losing ground to Chicago. On Thursday, September 28, the White Elephants were in first place by three percentage points, with the White Sox coming into Philadelphia for a critical three-game series. Mack was forced to pitch Plank in the first and third games and Bender in the second. Plank won, 3–2, on Thursday, and Bender increased the A's first-place lead to two games with an 11–1 whitewashing on Friday. On Saturday Plank lost, 4–3, but the A's still held a one-game lead with eight left to play in the season. When the A's defeated the last-place St. Louis Browns, 5–0, on October 1, and the White Sox lost to Washington, 3–2, Philadelphia's lead increased to two games.[48]

On October 5 the A's needed to sweep a doubleheader from Washington to clinch the flag. Bender pitched the opener and won, 8–0, scattering seven hits. Andy Coakley, the A's twenty-two-year-old right-hander, started the second game but struggled, surrendering three runs during the first two innings. Bender went to bat for Coakley in the top of the third and smashed a three-bagger and later scored on a triple by Topsy Hartsel. Before the inning was over the A's had tied the score at three runs apiece. When Bender came into the dugout he asked Mack if he could finish the game. Though he wasn't as sharp as in the opener, the Indian hurler won, 9–7. He also collected an RBI double in the eighth to seal the victory. By the end of the afternoon, Bender had collected two victories, six hits, and eight RBIs.[49] "It was a red letter day in the career of our noble red man, Charles Albert Bender," wrote Charles Dryden in the *Philadelphia North American*, once again playing on the young pitcher's Native American ancestry.[50] The A's clinched the pennant the following day when the Browns defeated the White Sox, 6–2.[51]

New York repeated as the National League champions. The Giants boasted the most powerful offense in the league with Mike Donlin (.356, 7 HR, 80 RBI), Sam Mertes (.279, 108 RBI), and Roger Bresnahan (.302). The pitching staff was more impressive and included thirty-two-game winner Christy Mathewson (206 K, 1.27 ERA), twenty-game winners Red Ames (198 K, 2.74 ERA) and Joe McGinnity (125 K, 2.87 ERA), and solid performers Dummy Taylor (15–9, 91 K, 2.66 ERA) and Hooks Wiltse (14–6, 120 K, 2.47 ERA).[52] After a one-year cancellation, the World Series resumed and proved to be the first of ninety-nine consecutive Fall Classics, the majority of which were the most widely popular event in American sports history.

In the early twentieth century, baseball was transformed into the national pastime, as Americans by the millions embraced the game. The World Series, which pitted the best teams in the American and National Leagues against each other, created a national frenzy. More people than ever before were involved in the games even if they didn't attend them, thanks to improvements in communication, like the telegraph and the proliferation of newspapers. The intensity of rivalries and the rapid urbanization of America also helped to transform baseball into a spectator sport where fans had fierce loyalties to the hometown team. At a deeper level, baseball was becoming an integral part of the national culture. The World Series, in particular, was a celebration of American democracy itself, since the games were undetermined and any outcome was possible. Even an underdog could prevail in the best-of-nine-game Series, giving the fullest expression to the American Dream that was so revered by the fans. At least that was the operating assumption.

But baseball was no longer an amateur pastime as it had been during its formative years in the mid-nineteenth century; it was now a professional sport. Winning was the major objective because it generated capital, not only for the owners of the more successful clubs, but for the businessmen and gamblers who attended the games as well as the players who cavorted with them. Rumors of a connection between gambling and baseball became common. Albert G. Spalding, president of the Chicago Cubs, admitted that "betting on the result of games naturally begot collusion between those who bet their money and some of those who played the game." But he also insisted that "throwing games" was a "stage in baseball's past." The issue had been resolved in 1877 with the expulsion of four players of the National League's Louisville team for "crookedness" in consorting with gamblers to "throw games."[53] Despite the claim, rumors of betting continued to swirl around the national pastime.

In 1904, for example, former Cubs pitcher John W. Taylor was accused by the club's owner, James Hart, of not giving his best in the previous year's city series against the Chicago White Sox. Hart, in a hearing before the National Commission, claimed that Taylor had told him he had been paid $500 to lose the game. After investigating the matter, the Commission, unable to find any direct evidence, dismissed the case against Taylor. Nevertheless, the incident suggested a disturbing precedent, namely, that if no one came forward with documented evidence of game fixing, the National Commission wouldn't take action against the suspected player for fear of a lawsuit. Since it was unlikely that anyone involved in a fix would come forward with incriminating information, and since evidence of a poor performance was not of itself sufficient to incriminate a suspected player, the Commission's position actually encouraged cheating.[54]

Not surprisingly, the 1905 World Series was tainted by rumors of a fix. The suspicions surrounded A's pitcher Rube Waddell, who had allegedly been approached by New York gamblers during the last month of the regular season and offered $17,000 to stay out of the Series. Waddell could invent his own excuse not to play, which he did by initiating a train brawl with Andy Coakley and injuring his pitching arm on September 1. The Rube allegedly was paid $500 up front with a promise to collect the balance after the Series had ended.

Waddell, according to the story, was then double-crossed, being cheated out of the $16,500 even though the Giants won the Series.[55] Mack quickly dismissed the rumor as "ridiculous," stating that "anyone who knew Waddell knows that money meant little to him" and that he was "always loyal to me."[56] Nevertheless, suspicions of a fix persisted for years afterward.

The 1905 World Series opened in Philadelphia at Columbia Park on October 9. McGraw, in an arrogant effort to intimidate the A's, dressed his Giants in special black uniforms with white "N.Y." lettering. Not to be outdone, Mack sent his outfielder Lave Cross out to home plate before the game with a lineup card and a package for the Giants' manager. Surprised by the "gift," McGraw unwrapped it on sight. It was an effigy of a white elephant, a reference to the spiteful remark he had made four years earlier when he predicted that the A's would become the money losers of the new American League. The crowd of 17,955 roared its approval. Unfortunately, the Giants got the last laugh when Mathewson defeated Plank, 3–0, to take Game One.[57]

Bender was slated to pitch Game Two in New York the following day. When the news reached the White Earth Reservation, a small band of Chippewa traveled more than a hundred miles to find a town where they could listen to the play-by-play unfold. Bender was one of their own, a symbol of Indian pride. He didn't disappoint them, either, much to the chagrin of the 25,000 Giants fans who packed the Polo Grounds to jeer him that afternoon. To be sure, New York squandered their scoring opportunities. Bresnahan opened the Giants' first with a double, but Bender regrouped to get George Browne and Mike Donlin on fly balls and struck out McGann to retire the side. The A's hurler experienced another close call in the second, when, with just one out, he issued back-to-back walks to Bill Dahlen and Art Devlin. But when the two runners attempted a double steal, A's catcher Ossie Schreck gunned down Dahlen at third and Bender retired Gilbert on a grounder to short. After that, the only real difficulty Bender faced came in the ninth. Giants outfielder Mike Donlin led off the inning and reached first base on an error by second baseman Danny Murphy. McGann, who had already fanned in his three previous plate appearances, walked. But instead of panicking, Bender refocused to retire Mertes on an infield pop-up and Devlin and Dahlen on routine grounders to second to end the game. The A's won, 3–0, as outfielder Bris Lord drove in two of the three runs off pitcher Joe McGinnity to even the Series at one game apiece.[58]

Mack was forced to call on Andy Coakley to pitch Game Three against Mathewson. Again, the A's were blanked by the Giants ace, who threw a four-hit shutout en route to a 9–0 victory. Coakley wasn't nearly as bad as the score suggests. Only one of New York's runs was earned; all the others came on five costly errors. The Giants also stole five bases on catcher Ossie Schreck, who was pulled by Mack midway through the contest. Game Four, played in New York on October 13, was closer, but the A's still lost, 1–0. Plank, making his second start, surrendered only four hits. The Giants' sole run was a gift, compliments of a Lave Cross error.[59] New York clinched the world championship the next day when Bender was defeated by Mathewson, 2–0, though by all accounts he "pitched as good a game as one could desire."[60]

To be sure, Bender's regular season record of 16 wins and 11 losses, 142 strikeouts, and a 2.83 ERA was not as impressive as those of Waddell, Plank, or Coakley. But his performance in the heat of the pennant race and in Game Two of the Series established him as Connie Mack's "money pitcher," the hurler the A's skipper would use in the single most critical game of a series over the next decade. The press also began to acknowledge Bender's exceptional talent, though they did it with a mixture of Indian wordplay and backhanded compliments.

Charles Dryden of the *Philadelphia North American* wrote that "Big Chief Bender is the greatest Indian since Tammany," referring to the New York political machine that took its name from the great Delaware chief.[61] The *Philadelphia Inquirer* ran a cartoon showing Bender with a large feather protruding from his cap and a tomahawk attached to his belt. He was staring into the eyes of a Giants player and hypnotizing him with an Indian sign. Lauding the "big copper-skinned athlete" for the victory, the accompanying story reported that Bender "possessed the speed of an arrow shot from the bow of an Eskimo in a snow hut, and his aim was as good as Davy Crockett when he was wont to hit a squirrel between the eyes."

The newspaper also noted repeatedly Bender's "exceptional cool-ness," a characteristic it attributed to his "Indian background" and a point that sportswriters would make a defining feature of his pitching

THE BIG CHIEF HAD THEM HYPNOTIZED

Fig. 15   Another racist cartoon of Bender, with a large feather protruding from his cap and a tomahawk attached to his belt. He is staring into the eyes of a New York Giants player and hypnotizing him with an Indian sign. The cartoon appeared in the October 11, 1905, edition of the *Philadelphia Inquirer*, a day after Bender shut out the Giants, 3–0, at New York's Polo Grounds in the second game of the World Series.

performance for the remainder of his career.[62] But no writer was more insulting than Charles Zuber of the *Sporting Life*, who wrote: "Bender, according to reports, is a typical representative of his race — being just sufficiently below the white man's standard to be coddled into doing anything that his manager might suggest — and to the proper exercise of his influence on the part of Manager Connie Mack much of the Indian's success as a twirler is due. Like the Negro on the stage, who 'will work himself to death if you jolly him,' the Indian can be 'conned' into taking up any sort of burden."[63] While some of this "praise" can be dismissed as cultural prejudice against a pitcher who lived differently from the white ballplayers he played with and competed against, Zuber's words reflect an overt racial prejudice toward Bender because he *looked* different.[64] In that sense, the burden Bender would shoulder throughout his professional career went well beyond the challenge of a single World Series game, or even the demands of a 154-game season. It was a racial burden that would never be lifted, no matter how successful he was on the mound, and no matter how hard he tried to change his lifestyle to accommodate white society. It was a burden that no other player on the Athletics carried, and only a few others knew in all of major league baseball.

4

CHIEF,
1906-1909

Charles A. Bender was not the first Native American to crack the majors. That distinction belongs to James Madison Toy, a mixed-blood of Sioux extraction who came from Beaver Falls, Pennsylvania. Toy was a catcher and utility infielder with the National League's Cleveland Spiders for 109 games in 1887. He played another forty-three games with Brooklyn in 1890 before a serious groin injury ended his career. But Toy, who sported a thick handlebar mustache, did not look like an Indian and purposely tried to hide his Native American ancestry.[1] Accordingly, most historians credit Louis Sockalexis, who starred for the Spiders in 1897, as the first Indian ballplayer.

Sockalexis, a full-blooded Penobscot from Old Town, Maine, possessed great natural ability and tremendous potential. He first attracted attention playing in a New England summer league in 1894. But his two-year career at Holy Cross College, which boasted one of the finest baseball programs in the country at the turn of the century, made him a major league prospect. Sockalexis's offensive exploits carried the team in 1895, when he hit .436, and again in 1896, when he hit .444. When he wasn't playing the outfield, the young Penobscot pitched and, remarkably, tossed three no-hitters during the same two-year span.[2]

Signed by the Spiders in 1897, Sockalexis became an instant success in Cleveland, both on and off the playing field. During the day, he

Fig. 16   Louis Sockalexis, who starred for the Cleveland Spiders in 1897, is widely credited as the first Native American baseball player. (National Baseball Hall of Fame Museum and Library, Cooperstown, New York)

played a seemingly effortless right field and hit at a .400 clip. At night he indulged in the urban nightlife. Sockalexis could run, throw, field, and hit for power as well as average, making him the prototype for the "five-tool players" of the future. His performance was so captivating that he allegedly provided the inspiration for renaming the Spiders the "Indians," a mascot the team still embraces today, to the dismay of many Native American organizations.[3] Legendary manager John McGraw, then a third baseman for the Baltimore Orioles, insisted that Sockalexis was the "greatest ballplayer he ever saw."[4] When the "Cleveland Indian" injured his leg in July, however, his performance tailed off, though he somehow managed to finish the '97 season with a .331 average. The sportswriters were quick to attribute the decline to "trysts with pale-faced maidens" and a "dalliance with the potent grape juice," alcohol.[5]

Sockalexis tried to make comebacks in 1898 and '99. But plagued by alcoholism, he saw little playing time. By 1903 he was out of the game for good and returned to New England, where he worked sporadically as a laborer until his death in 1913. Occasionally the national press would write about the "tragedy" of Sockalexis's promising baseball career, attributing the decline of the "drunken Indian" to alcoholism.[6] In the process, they cultivated a negative stereotype of Indian ballplayers that threatened to end whatever chances Native Americans had for making the majors. Fortunately, Bender's star was rising as Sockalexis's was flaming out.

Some baseball historians believe that Bender used the game as "a means of cultural resistance and a source of pride" in his Native American background.[7] However, there is greater evidence to suggest that Bender pursued a major league baseball career in order to distance himself from his Indian heritage. It was his way of becoming part of the white mainstream and achieving the coveted "American Dream." "The reason I entered baseball," he admitted to one interviewer, "was that it offered me the best opportunity both for money and advancement," and because "there was so little racial prejudice in the game that there has been scarcely a trace of sentiment against me on account of birth."[8]

While Bender was certainly attracted by the "money and advancement" baseball could offer, his remark that there had been "scarcely a trace of sentiment against [him] on the account of [his] birth" was probably meant to curry favor with teammates and opponents who otherwise might have treated him just as poorly as the fans and the press did. To be sure, he was discriminated against whenever he stepped onto a ball diamond. His dark features gave him the unmistakable appearance of an Indian, who was at best an object of fascination and at worst a target of racial prejudice. At the same time, Bender was an important pioneer for Native American ballplayers, a figure who would open doors for others if he could discipline himself to ignore the war whoops, catcalls, and jeers and let his pitching speak for itself. After all, major league baseball had a significant stake in attracting Native American talent because of its undeserved reputation as a "genuinely democratic" sport. The game's professed indifference to the ethnic makeup of its players reinforced baseball's symbolic role as a melting pot where everyone had equal access to the American Dream.[9] Once African Americans were barred from the game, in the 1890s, by a "gentleman's agreement" among the owners, Native American ball-players became even more attractive. Their presence in the game would show that baseball was, indeed, the American national pastime.[10]

Realizing the importance of perception, manager John McGraw of the Baltimore Orioles tried in 1901 to sign Charlie Grant, a second baseman for the Columbia Giants of the Negro Leagues. McGraw gave him the pseudonym "Charlie Tokahoma"—a play on the words "poke a homer"—and attempted to pass him off as a "full-blooded Cherokee." But Charles Comiskey, owner of the Chicago White Sox, foiled the plot once he discovered that "this Cherokee is really Grant, the crack Negro second baseman, fixed up with war paint and a bunch of feathers." He then threatened to "get a Chinaman and put him on third" if McGraw tried to keep "this Indian."[11] The failed scheme was revealing in two ways. First, McGraw's effort to disguise Grant as an Indian was based on the understanding that organized baseball accepted Native Americans. White prejudice toward Indians was not as severe as it was toward blacks, who were viewed in more absolute terms as "racially inferior." In general, whites saw Indians as having many of the same cultural tendencies as themselves and there-fore as having the potential to become "civilized." Second, Comiskey's discriminatory remark about Grant being "fixed up with war paint and a bunch of feathers" reflects the fact that while organized baseball tolerated Native American participation in the game, it still operated on cultural stereotypes that suggested the Indian's lack of civility. Those stereotypes were publicly displayed by rowdy fans who spewed forth "war whoops," "ki-yi-yis," and such catcalls as "Back to the Reser-vation!" whenever an Indian ballplayer took the field.

The most common form of discrimination, however, was the nick-name "Chief," which was applied to any player of Native American ancestry. To be sure, nicknames have always been common in baseball. At the turn of the century, nicknames often served as an indicator of ethnicity. German-American players, for example, were called "Dutch" or "Heinie" (a variation of Heinrich). Similarly, the nickname "Rube" might be given to a player who hailed from the farms, or the nickname "Dummy" to a player who wasn't very bright. While such nicknames were considered "colorful" by the fans and "endearing" by some of the players, Native American players felt quite differently about the use of the nickname "Chief." In Native American culture, "Chief" is a term of honor reserved for one selected to lead a tribe. To use the term as a generic reference to all Indian ballplayers, regardless of their talent, professional success, or potential, was insulting to all Native Americans. Such a reference assumed the same patronizing overtone as the term "boy" when applied generically to all African American males.[12] "Most Indians do not want to be called 'Chief' because it demeans the significance of the tribal chief," explains Joseph Oxendine, a Lumbee and author of *American Indian Sports Heritage*. "It's used by non-Indians as a constant reminder, as if to say, 'Hey, you're an Indian! That's how I can define you and keep you in your place.' You don't mind being known as an Indian, but you don't want it to be your whole identity."[13]

Early in his career, Bender, who was mistakenly referred to as a "full-blooded Indian" in press accounts, disdained the nickname "Chief," whether it was used by heckling fans or as a term of endearment by his own teammates. When asked for his autograph, he would sign it "Charles Bender" or "Charley Bender."[14] When fans at opposing ballparks mocked him with the nickname, Bender, with a sharp but humorless rebuke, would walk over to the stands and suggest that the "foreigners should either quiet down or return to Europe."[15] No wonder he tried to put an end to the treatment when, after pitching the A's to victory in the second game of the 1905 World Series, he requested that the sportswriters "not present his name to the public as an Indian, but as a pitcher."[16] Of course, the sportswriters refused to comply, because Bender's Indian ancestry made an otherwise shy, unremarkable personality "colorful." It was "good copy," just like the sensationalist press accounts of the other, more rowdy players on the team. Bender had no choice but to tolerate the nickname. But there were times when he lashed back.

Once, when Clark Griffith, pitcher-manager of the New York Highlanders, tried to intimidate Bender with racial insults, the A's hurler charged the mound and threatened to "make a gentleman" out of him. After Bender was ejected from the game, he went to Mack and pleaded that he be allowed to pitch the following day in order to "erase the blot on his character." Mack agreed and was rewarded with a 9–3 victory. Bender was so inspired he even hit an eighth-inning home run to aid his own cause.[17] His hot hitting continued later that week, when Mack, short-handed owing to injuries, played the Indian hurler in left field against the Boston Red Sox. Not only did Bender collect six hits in the A's 11–4 victory, but two of them were home runs, including an inside-the-parker against BoSox hurler Jesse Tannehill.[18] Mack, always one to make a mental note about player motivation, learned that he could rely on Bender to pinch-hit or play another position whenever necessary. As a result, the Indian hurler, early in his career, made a total of fourteen appearances in either the infield or outfield, and was regularly called on to pinch-hit. More important, Mack discovered that Bender burned to win, especially if his character was called into question.

While Bender eventually learned to channel his anger into a constructive performance on the playing field, it was very difficult for him to control his feelings when his family was criticized. When the *Philadelphia North American* referred to his wife, Marie, as a "fair Hiawatha," the A's right-hander demanded a retraction.[19] Apparently the sportswriter who wrote the story was unfamiliar with Longfellow's poem, mistaking Hiawatha for a female when in fact he was a man! However, the miscue did not go unnoticed by editor of the *Sporting Life*, who added insult to injury by publishing the following paragraph: "Charles Albert Bender feels that a gentle kick has arrived at his domicile, and he proceeds to register the same. In an account of the opening game he pitched, it was stated that a 'fair Hiawatha beamed down upon Mr. Bender from the pavilion.' Inasmuch as the late Mr. Hiawatha was a male Indian and Mrs. Bender is a beautiful young white woman, Charles Albert failed to appreciate the well-meant compliment. Ugh! The Big Chief has spoken."[20] To be sure, Bender was insulted by the reference because he was sensitive about the public response to his interracial marriage. He desperately wanted to keep his professional and home lives separate. The incident made him very wary of the press. He was already, by nature, a very introverted person when he came to the big leagues. But his distrust of sportswriters made him even more cautious, if not intimidating. According to one St. Louis scribe, Bender was "taciturn and non-talkative to a fault, having all the unemotional qualities of his race. When he is interrogated, he will look at you penetratingly with those brown-black eyes as if pondering over in his mind the answer he is going to give you. Sometimes you will wait for as long as 30 or 40 seconds for a response and the pause becomes embarrassing. Then will come the answer, slow, terse and couched in immaculate English—the language of a gentleman and a scholar. He talks quietly and slowly, his voice being modulated at a very low pitch."[21]

Bender's distrust of the press seemed to grow with each season. Nor was he any more forthcoming with teammates. While he was "well-liked by his fellow players," he kept a certain distance from them.[22] If anyone knew his innermost thoughts, it was Marie, who was the most important person in his small support system. He gave her his unconditional loyalty and pampered her without much consideration for the expense. "Charles is a fine husband," insisted his mother-in-law. "He spoils Marie. When they started housekeeping at Carlisle, he gave her more than $1,000 to buy the furniture, and he buys her all the soft silks she wants." Marie was easy to "spoil." She was much more outgoing than her husband and able to pry him out of his shy disposition. She understood his likes and dislikes and made an earnest effort to make his home life as relaxing as possible, especially during the season, when he "didn't like to talk over the ball games" after he returned home.[23] While Marie kept her husband's mind off baseball at home, Rube Oldring, Bender's roommate, kept him grounded psychologically when the A's were playing on the road.

Reuben Henry Oldring, an infielder with Montgomery of the Southern League, was acquired by Mack at the end of the 1905 season. A product of the New York City sandlots, Oldring went on to play for semipro teams in Orange and Hoboken, New Jersey, before joining the minor leagues. He was originally a third baseman, but Mack moved him to center field because of his tendency to overthrow first base. Oldring began to play regularly for the A's in August 1906 and proved to be a mainstay of the team for the next decade.[24] Rube's remarkable ability to get a good jump on the ball, along with his sure-handedness and speed, made for some exciting play in the outfield, much to the enjoyment of the fans. He would go on to lead the American League in fielding percentage in 1910, '11, and '15. His was also a respectable hitter, completing his thirteen-year major league career with 1,268 hits and a .270 batting average.[25] Accordingly, *Baseball Magazine* once called Oldring "as good a fielder as Ty Cobb, a better batsman than Joe Jackson, and a heavier hitter than Clyde Milan," quite a compliment for a player who never made it to Cooperstown.[26]

As far as Bender was concerned, Oldring was a perfect companion on the road. Because of his reclusive disposition, the Indian hurler remained at the hotel when he didn't have to be at the ballpark. While his teammates caroused in the bars and brothels of the city, he chose to "immerse himself in a book." On those rare occasions when he found himself in the company of teammates, Bender preferred to "sit in a chair and listen to them chat." "Very seldom" did he join in.[27] That was just as well. According to Oldring, who came to know the Indian hurler better than anyone else on the team with the exception of Mack, when Bender "got into one of his moods, he would just sit around, silent and looking glum." That kind of behavior "caused those around him to wonder what he was mad about, thereby casting a wet blanket on a gathering." Mack, who knew his players to a fault, realized that Bender could be a moody, temperamental individual, and selected Rube for his roommate on road trips. It was a stroke of psychological genius.

Oldring had an easygoing disposition, a welcome change from some of the gruff veterans who never really accepted Bender as a teammate. According to Rube Oldring Jr., the Indian pitcher had "already been with the A's for a few seasons when my dad broke in. I've heard that there were some hard feelings against Bender, either because he was an Indian or because he was a young player on a veteran team. But my dad and him just clicked. Dad was the kind of guy anyone could get along with. He wasn't a glory seeker or a 'show-boater.'" If Bender wanted to talk, Oldring would oblige him. If he wanted his privacy, the outfielder left him alone. Over the twelve years they roomed together, the two teammates reached a quiet understanding based on mutual support and trust that whatever was discussed stayed between them.[28]

While Bender was adjusting to life in the majors, the A's were struggling to field a contender. The 1906 season was an especially disappointing one. After being the frontrunners through the first four months of the season, the Mackmen were displaced by Fielder Jones's Chicago White Sox, a team known as the "Hitless Wonders" until they went on a nineteen-game winning streak. With the A's fading fast, the New York Highlanders and the White Sox battled through the September pennant race, with Chicago prevailing on the final weekend of the season. The White Sox went on to upset the heavily favored Chicago Cubs in a six-game crosstown World Series.[29] The A's, on the other hand, finished in fourth place, twelve games behind Chicago. Although the A's hit only .241 as a team, the poor performance was largely due to pitching. There was not a twenty-game winner on the staff. Waddell, who won twenty-six games for the 1905 pennant-winners, dropped to 16–16. Plank, who compiled twenty-five victories in '05, replaced him as the ace, posting a 19–5 record. Coakley contributed just seven wins, thirteen less than the previous year. Of all the pitchers, Bender's numbers were the most consistent. His 15–10 record and .600 winning percentage in 1906 was actually seven percentage points better than the 16–11 performance he turned in the previous year. In addition, his ERA dropped from 2.83 in 1905 to 2.53 in 1906.[30]

Mack would get one last hurrah out of his veteran team in 1907. Plank and Waddell rebounded from their lackluster performances of the previous season and eventually posted twenty and nineteen victories, respectively. Twenty-two-year-old Jimmy Dygert was the surprise of the pitching staff. In his two previous seasons in the majors he had won just eleven games, but in '06 he chalked up twenty. Bender, who had a slow start, got hot in July, winning eleven straight games before being defeated, 1–0, by Chicago on August 21. No more than two runs were scored off him during that eleven-game streak.[31]

As of late September the A's were locked in a tight pennant race with Detroit, Chicago, and Cleveland. With the A's and Detroit tied for first place on Saturday, September 27, the Tigers traveled to Philadelphia for a critical three-game series. Detroit was led by their young star outfielder, Ty Cobb, veteran Wahoo Sam Crawford, and pitchers Wild Bill Donovan, Ed Killian, and George Mullin. Donovan

Fig. 17 The 1906 Philadelphia Athletics. After capturing pennants in 1902 and 1905, *Sporting Life* magazine predicted that Connie Mack's A's would repeat as American League champions in 1906. Instead, the White Elephants dropped to fourth place, with a 78–67 record.

out-pitched Plank in the first game, 5–4. The following day's game was rained out and a double-header was scheduled for Monday the twenty-ninth.

A crowd of more than 24,000 packed Columbia Park in the hope of seeing the hometown A's take sole possession of first place. Detroit sent Donovan to the mound once again, this time against Dygert.

The A's took an early 7–1 lead, but when Dygert booted a couple of ground balls in the second inning, Mack replaced him with Waddell. Detroit tagged Rube for four runs in the seventh inning, narrowing the score to 7–5. The Mackmen scored another run in the bottom of the inning, but the Tigers came back to match it in the top of the eighth. Waddell was pulled from the game in the ninth after Crawford led off with a single and Cobb socked a homer over the right field fence to tie the game. Plank came in to pitch for the A's, while Donovan continued to hurl for the Tigers.

The game was still deadlocked when Harry Davis led off the bottom of the fourteenth with a long fly ball to center field. The ball landed in the spillover crowd, which had been cordoned off from the outfield by a rope. The hit should have been ruled a ground-rule double. But when Crawford, the Tigers' center fielder, collided with a policeman in his effort to make the catch, umpire Silk O'Loughlin ruled Davis out on account of fan interference. Outraged by the call, the A's charged the playing field and a melee broke out. Cobb, always one to instigate trouble, worsened the free-for-all by telling his teammate, first baseman Claude Rossman, that A's shortstop Monte Cross had called him a "Jew bastard." Rossman went after Cross, and Waddell, now in street clothes, went to his teammate's aid. Donovan followed suit and all four players traded punches. When order was finally restored, Rossman had been arrested by police and hauled off to jail, Davis was still out, and the game was still tied. "If ever there was such a thing as crooked baseball," declared an infuriated Mack, believing that the umpires had conspired against him, "this game would stand as a good example." Finally, after seventeen innings, the game—and the nightcap—were called on account of darkness, and the Tigers left Philadelphia in first place. Later that week, Detroit clinched the pennant with a four-game sweep of Washington and the A's finished in second, 1 1/2 games behind the Tigers.[32]

The A's dropped to sixth place in 1908, largely because of their mediocre pitching. Mack, having grown tired of Waddell's antics, traded the eccentric pitcher to the St. Louis Browns and replaced him with a journeyman right-hander named Rube Vickers, who led the A's staff that season with an 18–19 record. Plank (14–16, 46 K, 2.17 ERA) and Dygert (11–15, 97 K, 2.86 ERA) were the only other A's hurlers to post eleven or more victories. Bender suffered his worst season in the majors, posting an 8–9 record. Somehow he mustered the courage to ask Mack for a pay raise nevertheless. Berating him for being "out of condition," the A's skipper refused the request. "Bender is, in my opinion, the greatest pitcher in the big leagues when working right, and I certainly would not sell him for any amount," Mack told the press. "But I do not care to pay him a fancy figure till he shows me he can deliver the goods."[33] Bender would learn to be more accountable for his performance before making a similar request in the future.

With the decline of his veteran players, Mack also began to give more playing time to his youngsters. Catcher Ossie Schreckengost (.222, 0 HR, 16 RBI) was sold to Chicago late in the season, and twenty-three-year-old Jack Lapp split time with veteran Michael "Doc" Powers behind the plate. Simon Nicholls (.216, 4 HR, 31 RBI) was platooned at shortstop with rookie Jack Barry, a twenty-one-year-old collegian out of Holy Cross. Barry, who was adept at turning the double play, would become one of the finest defensive players of the Dead Ball Era. Thirty-eight-year-old Jimmy Collins (.217, 0 HR, 30 RBI) split time at third base with Frank Baker, a shy, twenty-two-year-old Maryland farm boy who swung a fifty-two-ounce bat. Baker would go on to become the premier power hitter of the Dead Ball Era, earning himself the nickname "Home Run." Predictably, he led the American League in that category for four straight seasons, from 1911 through 1914, and compiled a total of ninety-three round-trippers during his thirteen-year career. He also led the league in RBIs in 1912 with 133, and in 1913 with 126, and was still able to compile a .307 career batting average, unusual for a hitter who swung for the fences. Thirty-one-year-old Danny Murphy, who still had some offensive punch left with a .265 average, split time at second base with twenty-one-year-old Eddie Collins.[34]

Mack discovered Collins in the spring of 1905 while he was playing second base for Columbia University. That summer he sent Andy Coakley to pitch at Plattsburg, New York, where Collins was playing for a semipro team. When Coakley returned with a rave review, Mack, trusting his pitcher's judgment, went after the prospect. To be sure, the A's manager realized that if Collins played so much as a single out at the professional level, his amateur status could be revoked and he would be unable to participate in collegiate sports. Accordingly

Fig. 18   Eddie Collins debuted with the A's in 1906 under the pseudonym "Sullivan" because he had a year to complete at Columbia University. His aggressive, confident manner earned him the nickname "Cocky," and he was considered the most intelligent player in the game during the Dead Ball Era. (National Baseball Hall of Fame Museum and Library, Cooperstown, New York)

Mack insisted, in public, that he "was afraid to sign [Collins] to a professional contract" because he "did not want his amateur status affected."[35] In private, however, the Spindly Strategist coaxed the nineteen-year-old Collins into using the pseudonym "Sullivan" and played him at shortstop for six games during the 1906 campaign.[36]

Collins's aggressive, confident manner earned him the nickname "Cocky," and indeed he had much to be cocky about. For ten seasons he batted better than .340. An extraordinary base runner, he led the American League in stolen bases four times, his highest season totaling 81 in 1910. What's more, Collins had a way of getting on base. He served as Mack's number-two hitter in the lineup and drew 60 to 199 walks a year, giving him an exceptional on-base percentage of .400 in his eight seasons with the A's.[37]

Collins, Baker, and Barry were just three of the remarkable players discovered by Mack's impressive scouting network, recruited largely from his former players. Some were on the A's payroll. Others coached in the minor leagues or at the college level. Still others, known today as "bird dogs," were retired from the game, but still attended amateur contests for the simple pleasure of watching the event. This network put the Tall Tactician in contact with prospective talent from across the nation, mostly through written correspondence. Although he sometimes received as many as twenty letters a day, Mack "always replied," believing that "there may come a time when the man who has taken the trouble to write may be able to turn a fine young player my way." The corresponding scout might receive one of several replies. If there was a need at a particular field position, Mack would "make further inquiries about the player by contacting a baseball expert" in the prospect's home territory. That report determined Mack's subsequent action. If the "baseball expert" issued a favorable report, he would send one of his own players or scouts to watch the player perform in a game. If that scout's report was "satisfactory," Mack would "enter into negotiations with the youngster."[38]

While the scouting system identified some remarkable talent, it also yielded some of the most incorrigible, foul-mouthed players in the game. Among the most outstanding in both categories was Joseph Jefferson Jackson, from Brandon, South Carolina. As an outfielder for Greenville of the Carolina League, the nineteen-year-old acquired the moniker "Shoeless Joe" for having played one game in his stocking feet, the result of poorly fitting new spikes.[39] In the midsummer of 1908, Mack, looking for a young outfielder to replace the unproductive bat of veteran Topsy Hartsel, queried his scouting network. Within a few weeks the scouts found Jackson, and the A's signed him for $325 on August 22, 1908. The illiterate left-handed hitting outfielder made his debut three days later, on August 25, and went 1 for 4 while playing a flawless center field.[40] But Jackson missed his family so much that later in the week he hopped a train to Greenville without Mack's permission. When the A's manager discovered his young prospect missing, he ordered one of his coaches to "go down to Greenville and get this fellow's brothers and sisters and whole family to come with you if necessary, but bring him back!"[41] Later that season, Jackson— on his way to the ballpark for a game—was "seized" as he put it, with a "gripping desire to go to the theater." Letting his desire get the best of him, he forfeited the game to spend the afternoon at the burlesque.[42] Taken with his great hitting ability, Mack stayed with Jackson, hoping that he could reform his incorrigible behavior. Regardless of whether they were dim-witted roustabouts like Jackson or more refined collegians like Collins, Mack, over the next few years, harnessed the aggressive instincts of his players, shaping them into a championship dynasty.

Just as important, the A's enjoyed a large fan base. Philadelphia was a baseball town. The players lived in the same North Penn neighborhood as the fans, ate at the same diners, drank at the same taverns, and attended the same churches. In fact, outfielder Amos Strunk was born, raised, and continued to live in the neighborhood during his playing days. He dated his childhood sweetheart, who lived around the corner from their elementary school, and the two married at the local Lutheran Church. Chief Bender, Harry Davis, Eddie Collins, and Wally Schang lived within walking distance of Columbia Park, as did the rookies who boarded on Twentieth Street. Even Connie Mack lived at 2932 Oxford Street, across from the ballpark.[43] "They weren't strangers to us," said Emil Beck, who grew up in the North Penn neighborhood that surrounded Columbia Park. "Chief Bender, Rube Waddell and a lot of others lived in the area. You could often see Connie Mack and some of the players walking through the neighborhood.

We used to chase after them as they walked to the ballpark."[44] With that kind of an emotional tie to the team, the fans turned out en masse to support their hometown heroes.

With the exception of the A's inaugural season of 1901, when the team drew just 206,329 fans—an average of 3,330 per game—the club had excellent attendance figures. In 1902, 442,473 spectators passed through the turnstiles at Columbia Park. In 1907 the attendance rate peaked at 625,581, despite the fact that the A's finished in second place.[45] But their small wooden bandbox park, which had a seating capacity of 12,000, simply couldn't hold the crowds. Fire was also a constant threat in the days before steel-reinforced concrete. Envisioning higher profits based on even larger crowds at a bigger ballpark, majority owner Benjamin Shibe decided the time was ripe for a new, up-to-date ballpark. In 1908 he created the "Athletics Grounds Company," which would become the owner of the park. The company issued one hundred shares of capital stock worth $50 each. All of the A's existing shareholders took stock in the company: Shibe claimed thirty-six shares and made himself chairman; Mack was awarded twenty-six shares and became secretary; and newspapermen Hough and Jones were given twelve shares each. In addition, Shibe's son Thomas was awarded twelve shares and another son, John, was given two shares in the company. All six men were members of the board of directors.[46]

On December 31, 1908, Shibe purchased from city contractor Joseph M. Steele a six-acre plot at 21st and Lehigh for $141,918.92. Although the area was just a mile and a half to the northeast of Columbia Park, it was mostly vacant lots and woods. But the presence of several nearby trolley lines made the location accessible to the public and convinced Shibe to build there.[47]

Completed in less than a year by the William Steele and Sons Company, Shibe Park—named after the A's principal owner—cost $315,248.69. Located at 21st and Lehigh Avenue in North Philadelphia, the structure was the first steel-and-concrete ballpark in the nation. It was a handsome facility, giving the appearance of a French Renaissance castle from the outside. Two roofed double-decked grandstands hugged the infield from first base to third base and were joined at 21st and Lehigh, where the domed tower of the main entrance stood. Uncovered single-decked bleachers continued the rest of the

Fig. 19   Groundbreaking for Shibe Park took place on April 13, 1908.
Principal owner Benjamin Shibe is located fourth from left and Connie Mack
is sixth from left.

way down both foul lines. The first base line ran parallel to Lehigh
Avenue; right field to center field, to 20th Street; center field to left
field, to Somerset; and the third base line, to 21st Street. The dimensions of the park were formidable by contemporary standards: the
right field wall was 340 feet from home plate; left field, 378 feet; and
center field, an intimidating 515 feet. These were Dead Ball Era
dimensions, which discouraged the home run and catered to the base
hit, the stolen base, and the hit-and-run.

At the turn of the century, the game was played with a heavier,
rubber-centered ball. It was also a thinking man's game in which
strategy and pitching mattered more than power hitting. By today's
standards, which favor the home run, the Dead Ball days are a happily
forgotten era. But to those who followed the game at the turn of the
century, the tactics and pace of the game were enthralling. To accommodate popular demand, Shibe nearly doubled the seating capacity
of Columbia Park at his new stadium, which boasted 23,000 seats. An
additional 10,000 fans could stand behind ropes on the banked terraces
in the outfield if necessary.[48]

Fig. 20   Shibe Park, completed in 1909, was the first concrete-and-steel stadium in the nation and gave the appearance of a French Renaissance castle. (National Baseball Hall of Fame Museum and Library, Cooperstown, New York)

    Shibe Park opened to the public on April 12, 1909. Fans began lining up for tickets at 7:00 A.M., five hours before the gates were to open at noon. It was a scene of controlled pandemonium. The clanging bells of the street trolleys, oo-gahs of automobile horns, and piercing shrills of the traffic cops' whistles cut the air. People scurried to buy tickets — 50 cents for bleachers, $1.25 for grandstand seats, and $2.00 for box seats — and poured through the turnstiles at the main entrance. Eventually, a crowd of 35,162 made its way into the park — the largest ever to watch a baseball game to that point. Those who couldn't purchase a ticket crowded onto the rooftops on 20th Street or stood outside the park. Some, who had waited for hours in line only to be informed that all the tickets had been sold, became so angry that they tried to storm the gates, or threw rocks at the ticket windows until the police subdued them.

    Inside the park vendors made their pitch — "Getchur scorecard lineup!" "Roasted Peanuts, here!" — while the First Regiment Band

under the direction of Samuel H. Kendle serenaded the crowd. At
2:30 P.M. fans rose to sing "America," and shortly thereafter the Athletics
and visiting Boston Red Sox marched to the center field flagpole to
raise Old Glory while the band played "The Star-Spangled Banner."
Just before 3:00 P.M., Philadelphia mayor John E. Reyburn threw out
the first ball and home plate umpire Tim Hurst cried, "Play ball!"
Eddie Plank delivered the first pitch to Amby McConnell, Boston's
lead-off hitter, and the game was under way.[49]

The A's took a 1–0 lead in the first inning and never looked back.
Plank scattered six hits, while striking out eight batters and walking only
four. Inspired by their new surroundings, the White Elephants pounded
out thirteen hits off Boston starter Frank Arellanes, four by second
baseman Danny Murphy. But Simon Nicholls was the hero of the game,
collecting three hits and scoring four runs in the A's 8–1 victory.[50]

The game provided a rare occasion for the highly critical Philadelphia press to applaud the Athletics, which it did in superlative terms.
William Weart of the *Evening Telegraph* praised the A's for building a
ballpark "for the masses as well as the classes," noting that Shibe Park
had "more room for the poor man than for the rich one." "That is as
it should be, for baseball is the people's sport." Not to be outdone,
Horace Fogel of the *Evening Bulletin* gushed, "It was a great day for
Philadelphia in the baseball world, it was a great day for the fans, a
most profitable one for the owners of Shibe Park and a grand start for
the Athletics."[51] Unfortunately, the high spirits generated by the new
park were dashed two weeks later when "Doc" Powers, the A's opening-
day catcher and a favorite of the fans, died of an intestinal infection.
Rushed to Northwestern General Hospital after going 1 for 4 in the
game, Powers's condition declined steadily as peritonitis developed.
Despite three operations to arrest his worsening condition, Powers
died on April 26.[52]

The Athletics were able to put the Powers tragedy behind them and,
despite the prognosticators, turned out to be a contender. The heavily
favored Detroit Tigers under manager Hughie Jennings provided the
toughest competition. Led by seasoned stars such as Cobb, Crawford,
Donie Bush, and George Mullin, the Tigers were especially aggressive in 1909. Having lost the World Series the previous two years,
Detroit was determined to make it back to the Fall Classic and clinch

the elusive championship. But the revamped A's were also a fairly determined bunch.[53]

Mack switched Danny Murphy to the outfield to make room at second base for Eddie Collins. The young Columbia University product didn't disappoint him either, hitting .346 and leading all American League second basemen in put-outs (373), assists (406), double plays (55), and fielding percentage (.967). Nicholls was replaced at shortstop by Barry, a more reliable fielder who hit in the clutch and was a threat on the base paths. Baker took over at third base and hit .305 and led the league in triples with 19. Harry Davis continued at first base, with the catching duties split between Ira Thomas and Paddy Livingston.

The pitching was outstanding. Plank (19–10, 132 K, 1.70 ERA) was the ace of the staff, while Bender (18–8, 161 K, 1.66 ERA), Morgan (16–11, 81 K, 1.65 ERA), and left-handed rookie Harry Krause (18–8, 139 K, 1.39 ERA) turned in impressive performances. Together, the four pitchers composed the American League's best pitching staff, with Jack Coombs (12–11), another collegian from Colby, and Dygert (9–5) filling in when necessary.[54]

The A's held first place into late August, when the Tigers displaced them with a three-game sweep in Detroit. Detroit won the first game, 7–6, the second, 4–3, and the finale, 6–0. To add insult to injury, Tiger fans mercilessly taunted the A's young outfielder Joe Jackson for his illiteracy. Despite Mack's offer to pay for a tutor, Jackson stubbornly refused the help. Fans throughout the American League, aware of his problem, capitalized on the shortcoming. Exasperated by the all heckling, Shoeless Joe finally lashed back. Standing on third base after hitting a bases-clearing triple, the young outfielder heard a raucous Tiger fan jeering at him: "Hey, Jackson! Can you spell cat?" As the crowd laughed at his expense, Shoeless glared at the offending spectator, spit out a stream of tobacco juice, and retorted, "Hey mister, can you spell shit?"[55] Even worse, Cobb, who was known to sharpen his cleats before the game, spiked Baker, cutting him on the forearm. Mack, infuriated by the incident, called him a "back-alley artist" and the "dirtiest player in the game." A's fans were more subtle, sending Detroit's volatile star anonymous death threats.[56]

By the time the Tigers traveled to Philadelphia on September 16 for a four-game series, the acrimony between the two teams had reached

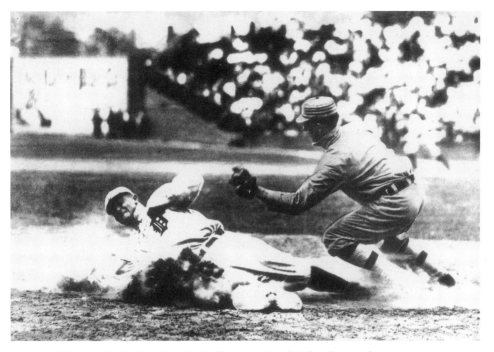

Fig. 21   Ty Cobb spikes A's third baseman Frank Baker during a late August 1909 contest. Mack called the Detroit outfielder a "back-alley artist" as a result of the incident. A's fans were more subtle, sending Cobb so many anonymous death threats that he required his own entourage of policemen when the Tigers traveled to Philadelphia in mid-September.

a fever pitch. Cobb required a police escort to and from the ballpark. Plank won the first game for the A's by a score of 2–1. Krause lost the following day as the Tigers stole seven bases. When Cobb stole third, Baker shook his hand in an effort to ease the tensions between the two teams. Bender, ever the big-game pitcher, came to the rescue on September 18. Before a crowd of 35,409—the largest ever to see a baseball game to that date—the Indian hurler shut out Bill Donovan and the Tigers, 2–0, to keep the A's pennant hopes alive. Plank's 4–3 win in the final game of the series cut Detroit's lead to two games. But the Mackmen would get no closer, finally finishing second, 3 1/2 games behind the pennant-winning Tigers.[57]

Not all was lost, though. The Athletics had served notice that they would be perennial contenders in the near future. Not only did they

Fig. 22   Connie Mack became a father figure to Bender during their
early years together in Philadelphia. (National Baseball Hall of Fame
Museum and Library, Cooperstown, New York)

field a lineup of young, highly talented players, but the team could boast of the best pitching staff in the American League. Mack, who believed that pitching was "ninety percent of the game," realized that his team's hurlers—and Bender in particular—held the key to the A's future success.[58]

At the end of the 1909 campaign Bender had compiled a 100–71 record over the seven seasons he had pitched for Mack.[59] While his record may not have been as outstanding as Plank's, who was widely acknowledged as the ace of the team, Bender was a more intelligent pitcher. "The Chief takes advantage of every hitter's weakness," observed umpire Billy Evans. "Once a hitter shows him a weak spot he is marked for life by the crafty Indian."[60] Bender's talent for learning and capitalizing on the opposing hitters' weaknesses was reflected by the fact that his ERA dropped every year from 1903, when it was 3.07, to 1910, when it was 1.58.[61] This is why Mack considered him his "greatest money pitcher," the hurler he would rely on in the single most critical game of a series.[62] Predictably, the Tall Tactician learned quickly to protect his investment.

Ever the "father figure" to his players, Mack referred to Bender as Albert, not Chief. Aware that the Indian hurler could be temperamental, Mack handled him with great care. He even admitted that his biggest challenge with sensitive players like Bender was to "simply remind them that the ball field was no place for troubles." "No matter what a man's troubles were off the diamond, he must leave them behind when he goes out on the field so he can attend strictly to business."[63]

Mack's careful handling of Bender allowed him to blossom into a star performer at the major league level, but it couldn't eliminate the painful sting of racism to which the Indian hurler was constantly exposed. Only Bender could address that issue, and it would eventually consume him, destroying his patience as well as his health.

5

DYNASTY,
1910-1914

At the dawn of the twentieth century, baseball was not the most reputable profession, but it did embody the "rags-to-riches" myth of the American Dream. Played on rural sandlots and in urban alleys, the game was respected just a bit less than vaudevillian theater. But the young man with playing ability was able to rise from his modest beginnings to the green cathedrals of the big leagues. With a little luck and a lot of determination, he might even go on to stardom and fame. Such was the case with Charles Bender, who by 1910 had achieved his American Dream.

Bender's success on the playing field and the novelty of his Native American background made him one of the most prominent pitchers in major league baseball and the focus of popular attention whenever and wherever he stepped onto the mound. The baseball season generated a special excitement he had not known in his youth, traveling from city to city and competing at a sport he loved, while the off-season was spent indulging in his favorite hobbies: hunting, fishing, trap shooting, and bowling.[1] Happily married, Bender and his wife, Marie, lived in a comfortable two-story redbrick home at 3515 Judson Street in the Tioga section of Philadelphia.[2] In addition, the A's hurler owned 160 acres of land in his native Minnesota on the White Earth Reservation.[3] At the age of twenty-six, Charles Bender enjoyed the kind of material success that few, if any, Native Americans would ever realize in their lifetime.

The success had not come easily, though. Bender acknowledged that fact in a questionnaire he completed for the Carlisle Indian School during the winter of 1909–10. Instead of responding directly to the question, "Have you done anything for the betterment of your people?" Bender crossed out the query and gave a brief outline of his life since leaving the Indian school. The capsule biography ended with the counsel: "Wouldn't advise any of the students at Carlisle to become a professional baseball player. It's a hard road to travel. Many temptations along the way."[4] To be sure, Bender believed that baseball, with its poor reputation for alcoholism, gambling, and philandering, was not a suitable occupation for Native Americans. But the hard road he had to travel was also paved with both overt and subtle forms of racism, which tempered whatever personal satisfaction he took in his professional achievement. Nor did he seem to believe that he had made any significant contribution to the "betterment" of the Native American race through his pitching exploits. Despite his personal reservations, Bender's was a charmed life that only promised to get better with the coming baseball season.

During the preceding five years, Connie Mack had molded a group of budding young stars and some aging veterans into a championship dynasty that would capture three world championships and four pennants between 1910 and 1914. The cornerstone of the team was the famed "$100,000 Infield," a term that captured the financial value of the four players who composed it: Stuffy McInnis, an extraordinarily gifted first baseman credited as the inventor of the "knee reach"; second baseman Eddie Collins, a remarkable base runner and consistent .300 hitter; shortstop Jack Barry, whose ability to turn the double play was unparalleled in the American League; and third baseman Frank "Home Run" Baker, a premier power hitter of the Dead Ball Era.[5] Mack also refashioned his outfield.

Topsy Hartsel, an aging veteran who had been with the A's since 1902, was beginning to slip. Mack began platooning him with youngsters Shoeless Joe Jackson and Heinie Heitmuller in left field and moved Danny Murphy, formerly a second baseman, to right field. Murphy had also been with the club since 1902 and proved to be a good hitter

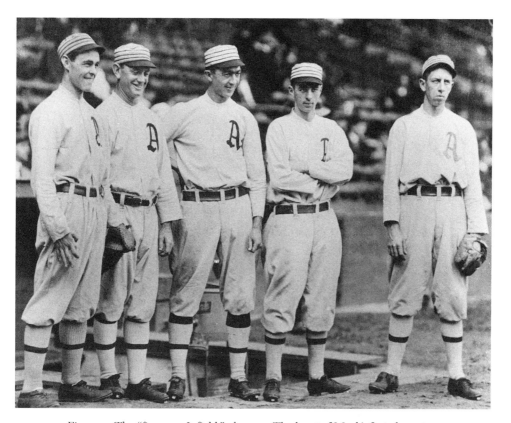

Fig. 23 The "$100,000 Infield," plus one. The heart of Mack's first champion-
ship dynasty was the famed "$100,000 Infield," a term that captured the financial
value of the four players who composed it. Pictured, from left to right, are first
baseman Stuffy McInnis, second baseman Danny Murphy, third baseman Frank
Baker, shortstop Jack Barry, and Eddie Collins, whose exceptional playing ability
forced Murphy into the outfield when Collins took over second base in 1909.
(National Baseball Hall of Fame Museum and Library, Cooperstown, New York)

and reliable infielder. But Mack's need to make room for Eddie Collins,
his promising youngster, left Murphy without a position. Ever the
team player, Murphy agreed to try the outfield so Collins could take
over at second and the team could still benefit from his productive
bat.[6] Rube Oldring anchored the defense in center field.

The key to Mack's success, however, was his pitching staff. Bender
and Plank were joined by Harry Krause, a young southpaw who had
burst into the majors the previous season with ten straight victories.

During that streak, Krause pitched ten complete games and six shut-outs, and surrendered a total of just five runs. Mack also acquired another winning pitcher, Cy Morgan, a wild but effective spitballer who had hurled for the Boston Red Sox.[7] But Jack Coombs proved to be the most effective pitcher in 1910.

Coombs had been discovered by Mack's brother, Tom, an innkeeper at Worcester, Massachusetts. Tom McGillicuddy, who scouted the local sandlots, was impressed with the twenty-three-year-old Colby College product and tipped off his brother. Mack signed the young pitcher and sent him to the mound against Washington on July 5, 1906, with no minor league experience. Coombs won the game, 3–0, scattering six hits and striking out six batters. He went on to win another nine games that year, the most memorable being a twenty-four-inning contest against Boston in which he struck out eighteen batters. During the next two seasons, however, Colby Jack was able to win a total of only thirteen games.[8] "Jack had a lot of arm trouble after his first fine season with us," recalled Mack, years later. "Then, about the middle of the 1909 season, I had him finish a game; he worked six beautiful innings and showed a little curve ball. It didn't break much, but I saw that it could be developed into a most effective delivery."[9] Mack, who had been toying with the idea of converting Coombs to the outfield, met with the beleaguered pitcher after the game and encouraged him to develop the curve ball. Coombs agreed. By the spring of 1910 he was throwing a devastating curve that broke so sharply that it almost hit the ground after crossing home plate. Opposing hitters were paralyzed by the pitch. Even those who knew the curve was coming couldn't hit it.[10] That curve ball would carry Coombs and the A's, in 1910, to the first of three world championships over four years.

Since the A's finished in sixth place in 1908 and second, 3 1/2 games behind the Detroit Tigers, in 1909, the prognosticators dismissed them as "too suspect in the outfield and too inexperienced as a team" to make a run at the pennant. Instead, the Tigers were favored to capture their fourth straight American League title. Others favored Boston, which finished third during the 1909 campaign and strengthened its offense with some off-season acquisitions. But Mack believed other-wise. "I have a feeling of what we can do," he said as the A's broke spring training camp. "I feel we are pennant-winning material."[11] To ensure success, or perhaps to feed the superstitious egos of his players, the Tall Tactician hired Louis Van Zelst, a hunchbacked dwarf, as the A's mascot and batboy. Following the tradition of other teams who hired dwarfish mascots, many of the A's hitters would rub Van Zelst on the back for good luck before stepping up to the plate. A base hit would reinforce the superstition and a home run would remove all doubt that the dwarf made the A's a team of destiny.[12]

The A's opened the season at Washington and witnessed history in the making as President William Howard Taft, better known to history for his love of baseball than for his mediocre political career, became the first chief executive of the United States to throw out the ceremonial first pitch. Photographers were on hand to capture the moment for the next day's sports pages. After removing his new kid gloves, Taft made an awkward throw to Washington's opening-day pitcher, Walter Johnson, who was forced to reach down and grab it. Johnson kept the ball and eventually asked the president to sign it. Taft's unwieldy throw not only solidified baseball's budding reputation as the "national pastime," it also began a popular custom among American presidents. Ever since, chief executives, with the exception of Jimmy Carter, have made at least one appearance to throw out the ceremonial first pitch at a ball game.[13]

Johnson defeated Eddie Plank and the A's that day, 3–0. Philadelphia's only hit was a ground-rule double that came off the bat of Frank Baker in the seventh inning.[14] But the loss didn't dampen the club's spirit, and the A's quickly rebounded. Coombs, Plank, and Bender pitched brilliantly, and the team enjoyed some heavy hitting from Baker, Collins, and Murphy through the first month of the season.

In May the Mackmen reeled off a thirteen-game winning streak, which included a 4–0 no-hitter by Bender. The contest was played against the Cleveland Indians at Shibe Park on May 12. Bender was hurling a perfect game until the fourth, when he walked Terry Turner. On the next pitch Turner broke for second base, but catcher Ira Thomas threw him out. No other Cleveland hitter reached base for the remainder of the contest.[15] "There was nothing that looked like a base hit that day," recalled Rube Oldring. "Our third baseman, Frank Baker, handled a hot drive by George Stovall in the eighth inning

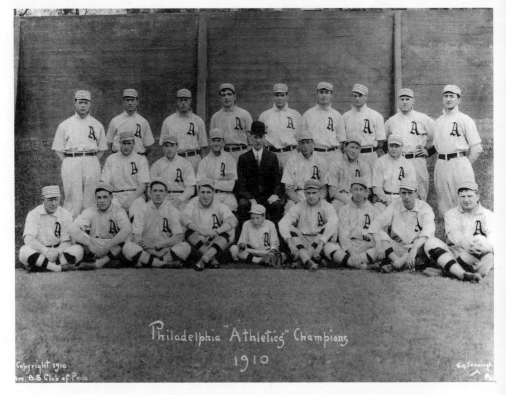

Fig. 24 The 1910 Philadelphia Athletics played winning baseball all season, capturing their first pennant in five years and defeating the Chicago Cubs, four games to one, in the World Series. Some of their luck was attributed to a small hunchback, Louis Van Zelst *(seated in front of Connie Mack)*, who was the A's mascot. (National Baseball Hall of Fame Museum and Library, Cooperstown, New York)

and that was the hardest chance. The most spectacular play came in the sixth when Bris Lord sent a long foul fly in the direction of right field. Danny Murphy went after the ball at full speed and after catching it had to vault the wall into the stands to avoid a crash."[16]

Bender didn't realize he was throwing a no-hitter until the seventh inning. When he came into the dugout one of the A's players happened to mention it to another teammate, who quickly discouraged any more talk of it. "Shut-up!" he said, in an effort to avoid jinxing Bender. "You'll break the spell."[17] Although the A's hurler overheard the conversation, he "didn't give it much thought" until the final inning.[18]

"Elmer Flick was the last man to face me," Bender recalled after the game. "He worked the count to two balls and two strikes, and then I turned loose with all I had on a fastball on the outside. He took a good cut, but lifted a foul behind the plate. [Catcher] Ira [Thomas] circled around it like a drunken sailor, but finally caught it—and I breathed a big sigh of relief."[19]

Bender following his no-hit performance with a 3–0 shutout against the Chicago White Sox on May 17. He went on to post a 23–5 record and a 1.58 ERA, leading the American League with an .821 winning percentage that year.[20] There were several keys to his success. First, Bender developed a pitch that he identified as the "nickel curve," which appeared to the hitter like a fastball but at the last second dropped sharply as it crossed home plate. The predecessor of the modern-day slider, the nickel curve confounded some of the game's best hitters.[21] Ty Cobb, considered to be the very best hitter of the Dead Ball Era, called the pitch "wicked" because of its deceptiveness.[22] Whereas a batter with good timing could hit the fastball, the nickel curve was unpredictable because of a split-second drop in the trajectory of the pitch. Often, fooled by what they thought was a fastball, hitters simply froze, like deer caught in the headlights of a car. Predictably, Bender used the nickel curve as his "out pitch" whenever he fell behind in the count and needed a strike. The nickel curve defined his success on the mound. Without that pitch, Bender would have been one among many "good" hurlers, but not a Hall of Famer.

Second, Bender enjoyed an exceptional ability to place the ball where he wanted it to go. Dividing the strike zone into four quadrants— inside high, inside low, outside high, and outside low—Bender aimed to keep the pitch off the center of home plate at all costs, since anything "down the middle" was easiest for the batsman to hit. Instead, he threw at the corners, sometimes alternating opposite corners and at other times throwing consecutive pitches at an area that proved difficult to hit for a particular batter. Because of his exceptional control, Bender kept the hitter guessing. "Control is the greatest requisite for a pitcher," he insisted. "Without control you are like a ship without a rudder. No matter how much power or speed you may have, you are unable to get results. Speed and power with control, however, will make you a great pitcher."[23]

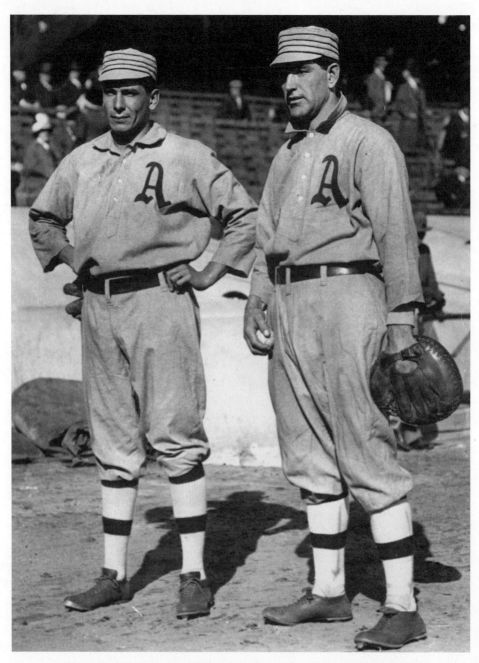

Fig. 25   Bender poses with catcher Ira Thomas in 1910, his most productive
year with the A's. That season he posted a 23–5 record, including a no-hitter
against Cleveland. The Chippewa hurler also earned the victory in the deciding
game of the World Series that year. (National Baseball Hall of Fame Museum
and Library, Cooperstown, New York)

Third, Bender was an *intelligent* pitcher who studied carefully the idiosyncrasies of the hitters. If a particular batsman stood deep in the batter's box and away from home plate, for example, Bender would throw his pitches on the outside corner to make him reach for the ball, limiting the power of the swing. Another hitter might hold the bat high in the air above his head. Then Bender would throw him nothing but low pitches, forcing him to swing like a golfer, which usually resulted in a routine fly out. According to American League umpire Billy Evans, "the crafty Indian takes advantage of every weakness. If a hitter shows him a weak spot he is marked for life."[24] To prove the point, Evans recalled a game the A's played against Washington in June 1910. Bender was being hit badly during the first inning. After the frame ended, he walked by Evans on his way to the dugout and asked about his speed, "Have I got anything on the ball, Bill?"

"To me, it looks as if you have a world of speed," replied the umpire, "but evidently your stuff doesn't look that way to the Washington boys."

Bender thanked Evans for the remark and added, "I'll have to slip them something different next inning."

In the second, Bender returned to the mound and baffled the Washington hitters by changing speeds and alternating his fastball with the nickel curve and changeup. He went on to win the game, 8–5.[25] Bender's remarkable ability to study the hitters and take advantage of their weaknesses allowed him to lower his earned run average every year from 1903 to 1910.

Finally, and just as important as the other three qualities, Bender possessed a healthy confidence in his pitching ability and a positive attitude whenever he stepped onto the mound. He had learned to ignore the catcalls and jeers from the stands and to concentrate fully on the game. Whether he won or lost, Bender stayed on an even keel emotionally, never letting his true feelings show. Once, when a younger pitcher, Harry Krause, was brooding about a tough loss, the Indian hurler advised, "It's a matter of record now, Harry. Forget about that game. Win the next one."[26] At the same time, Bender did not take his abilities for granted. His philosophy on motivation can be summarized in one of his favorite clichés: "If what you did yesterday still looks big to you, then you haven't done much today!"[27]

With Bender on pace to win twenty-three games and Coombs in the midst of a remarkable 31–9 performance, the A's took over first place from Detroit on June 21. If there was a weakness in the lineup it was Topsy Hartsel in left field. Balls he had once fielded with ease were getting away from him, and his batting average had dropped to .220. Not wanting to take any chances, Mack, on July 25, traded Morris Rath, a utility infielder, and his promising young outfielder, Joe Jackson, to the Cleveland Indians to bring Bris Lord back to the Athletics.[28]

Jackson had never caught on in Philadelphia. He was homesick and uncomfortable in the big city. His teammates only made matters worse by playing pranks on him. Once, after an exhibition game in Reading, Pennsylvania, Jackson was standing on a train station platform gazing intently at a nearby row of milk cans labeled with red tags. "I wish I had one of those labels on me, and that I would be sent away somewhere," he confided to another teammate.

Mack overheard the remark and asked, "Do you really mean that, Joe?"

When Jackson admitted that he wanted out of Philadelphia, Mack obliged him. He farmed Jackson to the Savannah club, where he hit .358 in 1909. Promoted to Philadelphia the following season, Jackson continued to suffer the abuse of teammates. "My players didn't seem to like him," said Mack, "though I told them at the time he was going to make one of the great hitters of baseball." Once again Mack farmed him out, this time to New Orleans.[29] When the need for a more productive outfielder arose in midseason, Mack, realizing that he had to risk the future to secure a pennant, traded Shoeless Joe. Ever since, there has been speculation that had Jackson remained under the paternalistic watch of Mack he might not have succumbed to the temptations of game fixing during the 1919 season, when he played for the infamous Black Sox.[30] It's a moot point. Those who second-guess Mack for trading away the greatest natural hitter in the history of the game are also missing the point: the A's were in the thick of a pennant race and under those circumstances the manager must make the trades he believes are necessary to clinch the flag.

"I knew exactly what I was doing when I let Jackson go to Cleveland," Mack said, defending the deal years later. "I knew Joe had great possibilities as a hitter. But Bris Lord would help me more at the time."[31]

Mack was right. When Lord joined the A's in late July, he was placed in center field and Rube Oldring was moved to left. Lord proceeded to hit at a .280 clip and strengthen the once suspect outfield. By August 1 the A's boasted a 60–30 record and held first place by six games. The club went 22–7 that month, extending their lead to eleven games.[32] The A's clinched the pennant with more than two weeks remaining in the season. Now they set their sights on winning one hundred games.

On October 1 Mack sent Clarence "Lefty" Russell, a twenty-year-old rookie, to the mound. Russell pitched the A's past the Boston Red Sox to clinch the hundredth victory of the season, the first time a major league team accomplished that feat. The A's finished the 1910 campaign with a 102–48 record, 14 1/2 games ahead of second-place New York.[33]

The A's were scheduled to face Frank Chance's Chicago Cubs in the World Series. Having defeated the Detroit Tigers for the world championship in 1907 and '08, Chicago was heavily favored to capture its third world title in four years. Because the American League season ended a week earlier than the National, Mack arranged a series of exhibition games against a team of American League All-Stars, including Ty Cobb, Tris Speaker, Walter Johnson, and Ed Walsh. "Mr. Mack wanted us to stay sharp for the World Series against the Cubs," explained Rube Oldring.[34] But the A's took such a beating that the usefulness of the matches was questionable. In addition, Oldring fractured his knee during one of the contests and had to watch the Series from the sidelines in a cast. With Oldring out, Mack was forced to play Amos Strunk, a veteran utility man, in left field. Worse, sore-armed Eddie Plank was also unavailable, and Mack had to squeeze five complete games out of Bender and Coombs.

Game One of the World Series was played on Monday, October 17, at Philadelphia's Shibe Park before a crowd of 26,691. The start of the game was delayed by an argument over whether motion-picture photographers could remain on the field in an effort to film the World Series for the first time in history. It was nearly 3:45 P.M., and Bender, who was slated to pitch the opening contest, had been warmed up since 3:00 P.M. Although it was a sunny day, the temperature had dropped to fifty degrees and Mack was worried that his pitcher would cool off. It didn't matter, because Bender had something to prove. He was motivated by the insulting remark of a Chicago sportswriter who claimed that he was "built for the Cubs to hit."[35] Bender took his damaged pride to the mound and proceeded to hurl a gem. Through eight innings only two batters reached base, one on a hit and another on a walk. On both occasions catcher Ira Thomas threw them out when they tried to steal second. Bender lost his shutout in the ninth on two errors by Strunk and Thomas. Frank Baker provided all the offense he needed, though, knocking in all of the A's runs for a 4–1 victory.[36]

Afterward, Jimmy Isaminger of the *Philadelphia Inquirer* noted the war whoops that rained down upon Bender from the stands throughout the game. In a rare and insightful column, Isaminger wrote that the Indian pitcher's success was due to a "constant effort against the scoffing word," and that his life was "set apart by race distinction and by nerves hardened by many slights cast upon a sensitive spirit."[37] Another scribe, this one from the *Chicago Daily News*, was also astonished at the hometown crowd's shameful treatment of Bender and asked him why he decided to pursue a major league career in spite of it. "I adopted the game because I played it better than I could do anything else," he replied. "The life of a baseball player appeals to me and there has been scarcely a trace of sentiment against me on account of my birth. I have been treated the same as other men."[38] It was a cautiously worded response. After seven years in the majors, Bender knew how to handle the press, and he was not willing to reveal his true feelings about the mocking derision he suffered at the hands of the spectators each time he took the mound. Nor was he willing to risk the comfortable relationship he had established with his teammates, who otherwise might have been just as spiteful as the fans. Instead, Bender chose the path of least resistance, solidifying his reputation as a gentleman-athlete.

The example was not lost on those who were rooting for him back at Carlisle, either. "Baseball lovers in Carlisle have watched with interest the career of Charles Albert Bender, the Indian pitcher of the Athletics," editorialized the *Carlisle Evening Sentinel*. "On Monday he won the greatest victory in his career when his pitching secured a victory for his team in the championship series with Chicago. We believe that Bender's success may be attributed to hard work and correct habits of life, both of which are all too often not found among professional ball players. In this, his career is a lesson not only to members of his own race, but to all who hope to be a star in the world of sports."[39]

Game Two pitted Jack Coombs against Cubs ace Mordecai Brown. Coombs was plagued by control problems, walking nine batters and surrendering eight hits. The A's fielders didn't help matters much, making four errors. But luck was with Philadelphia. The Cubs stranded fourteen base runners, hitting into three double plays, and Brown, who was shaken by a car accident on his way to Shibe Park, pitched even worse, giving up nine runs in seven innings of work. The A's did manage to pull off a fourteen-hit assault, six of their nine runs coming in the seventh inning. Collins led the offensive attack with two doubles, a single, and two stolen bases, and the A's won the game, 9–3, to enjoy a two-game lead in the Series.

When the Series moved to Chicago on Thursday, October 20, Cubs fans greeted their hometown team with the kind of vitriolic treatment usually given by Philadelphia fans. Manager Frank Chance was heckled so badly that he attacked one of the instigators. It was a preview of the nasty reception that awaited the Cubs at West Side Park. When the team took the field for Game Three, they were greeted with a chorus of boos. The jeers became louder in the third inning, when, with the score tied at 3–3, the A's knocked Cub pitcher Harry McIntire out of the box and continued their assault on reliever Jack Pfiester. The A's pounded out five more runs, three coming on a homer by Danny Murphy. When the ball hit a sign on a distant right-field fence, Chance darted out of the dugout to argue a ground-rule double. But the umpire refused to listen and ejected him from the game, the first ejection in World Series history. The A's added another four runs in the seventh, sealing the 12–3 victory for Coombs.

Bender faced "King" Cole in Game Four on Saturday, October 22. Cole was the Cubs' second-best pitcher, having posted a 20–4 record during the regular season. The A's rapped him for eight hits, but the Cubs defense held the Mackmen to just three runs. Bender struggled this time out. He took a 3–2 lead into the ninth but surrendered the tying run on triples by Schulte and Chance. The Cubs went on to win the game, 5–4, in ten innings. Coombs clinched the championship for the A's the following day when he defeated the Cubs, 7–2. Using only two pitchers, Philadelphia had overcome the odds to defeat a heavily favored Chicago Cubs team, outscoring them 35–15. Not only did Coombs prove to be the star pitcher, notching a perfect 3–0 record, but his .385 batting average was higher than any Cubs hitter's. Charles Comiskey, owner of the Chicago White Sox, was so thrilled with the defeat of his crosstown rivals that he sent the A's players two cases of champagne and 1,000 cigars as a token of his appreciation.[40]

Of all the teams Connie Mack managed, the 1911 Athletics was his favorite. The players were a rough-and-tumble bunch that loved the camaraderie of the game and never missed an opportunity to pull a prank. Occasionally they chose the wrong audience, though. Once, Eddie Collins and Stuffy McInnes decided to conspire against an umpire who had an infamous reputation for calling the play before it was made. Collins, at second base, fielded a hard grounder and faked the throw to first while actually holding on to the ball. McInnes, at first base, pounded his mitt as if he caught the ball. True to form, the offending umpire called the runner out. No sooner had he done it than Collins produced the ball and showed the arbiter the error of his ways. While Collins and McInnis had a good laugh for themselves, the umpire was much less amused and tossed them out of the game for embarrassing him. It was one of the very few times Collins was thrown out during his twenty-five-year career.[41] On another occasion, during the eighth inning of a hot summer's afternoon game, Mack wanted to make a pitching change. Going to the top step of the dugout, he began waving his trademark scorecard down the left-field line where the bullpen was located, indicating that he wanted a relief pitcher. After a few minutes he could see that no one was getting up. Angry that he was being ignored, he sent one of his reserve players out to the bullpen to find out what was wrong. It turned out that all the pitchers had left the ballpark through the bullpen exit onto 21st Street and Lehigh Avenue and gone down to the corner bar for some afternoon refreshment.[42]

The 1911 A's were also the first truly great team in the American League and one of the greatest of all time, featuring four future Hall of Famers: Frank Baker, Charles Bender, Eddie Collins, and Eddie Plank. The A's finished 13 1/2 games ahead of second-place Detroit and twenty-two games ahead of third-place Cleveland. But the Mack-men did not get off to an auspicious start. In fact, the Tigers began

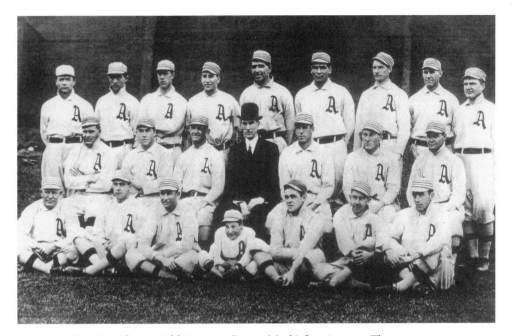

Fig. 26   The 1911 Athletics were Connie Mack's favorite team. They were a rough-and-tumble bunch of pranksters who put winning above everything else. The team finished 13 1/2 games ahead of second-place Detroit to clinch the American League pennant, and defeated the powerful New York Giants in the World Series.

the season by winning thirty-one of their first forty games and were entrenched in first place for most of the season. The A's, on the other hand, dropped six of their first eight games and started the season in the cellar. They closed the gap to one game by going 19–6 during the month of June, and took over first place on August 4, though they didn't clinch the pennant until September 26.[43]

The slow start may have been due to Mack's tendency to take it easy on his players during spring training. "There is no good in putting a team of ball players right on edge for the opening of the season," he believed. "The players should be conditioned slowly. The race is so long that, no matter how carefully the men are worked, the players individually and collectively are certain to go stale at some stage of the campaign. For this reason I do not believe in working players too hard down south. A complete rest of a day or two does them more good than harm, for when they return to the field they go at their work with more zest than if they had to do many hours exercise each day."[44]

No longer an inexperienced team with an average age of twenty-five, the A's featured a lineup of proven talent, with some powerful hitters. Bris Lord played left field and hit .310. Oldring returned to center field and hit .297. Murphy, a .329 hitter, remained in right. But the A's big batsmen were second baseman Eddie Collins, who hit an impressive .365, and third baseman Frank Baker, who emerged as the American League's home-run champion, with eleven round-trippers, while also driving in 115 runs and batting .334.[45] Baker's eleven homers— a new record during the Dead Ball Era—probably reflected the intro-duction of a cork-centered baseball that year.[46] But the third baseman's use of a fifty-two-ounce bat also helped. "Up until I got too old to get around on good fastball pitching, I used a 52-ounce bat," Baker once admitted. "Honest! You had to hit that ball fair and square and with some weight and power back of it to make it go over the fence. I swung with all my might at a good fastball, hit it fair and square and was lucky if it bounced against the fence. I hit the fence in Shibe Park 38 times in one year. Eddie Collins told me that if I had been hitting the livelier ball that Babe Ruth hit in the 1920s, every one of those 38 balls would have gone over the fence."[47]

Together with shortstop Jack Barry (.265), Baker and Collins anchored the $100,000 Infield, which now included twenty-year-old John "Stuffy" McInnis, who replaced Harry Davis as the regular first base-man. Although McInnis hit an impressive .321 and proved to be a defensive mainstay, he couldn't help but be in awe of the A's other infielders. "Gosh, those fellows were great ballplayers," he gushed. "Collins at second and Barry at short teamed up marvelously. Prac-tice, practice, that's all they did. When they were off the field they talked about situations that might arise and what they'd do."[48]

Once again, the A's remarkable pitching put them into the World Series. Coombs enjoyed another sensational year, posting twenty-eight victories. Plank, after suffering through three below-par seasons, returned to form with a 22–8 record. Morgan and Krause combined for another twenty-six wins. Bender won seventeen of twenty-two deci-sions, though his performance tailed off after learning of the death of his younger brother, John, in September.

John Bender idolized his older brother and followed him into professional baseball in 1905, when he debuted as an outfielder for Charleston, South Carolina, in the Sally League. He moved on to Columbia of the South Atlantic League three years later. During his tenure there, he got into a heated argument with manager Winn Clark and slashed him with a knife. Blacklisted by the National Commission for two years, the ban was lifted in 1911 and John was signed by Edmonton of the Canadian League. On September 25 he agreed to pitch for the team, and during the sixth inning he suddenly collapsed and died, the victim of a massive heart attack.[49]

Although Bender had not seen his younger brother in years, John was the only member of his family with whom he was close. He took the loss hard and, for the first time, found solace in drinking. Near the end of the regular season, Bender reported to the A's clubhouse "unfit to pitch" and was suspended by Mack.[50] When the suspension was over, the Spindly Strategist summoned his money pitcher to his tower office at Shibe Park and said: "I'm counting on you to win the World Series."

Mack, a strict disciplinarian when he had to be, could also demonstrate a fatherly compassion toward his players. "Forgiveness" was one of the many methods he used to secure and maintain the allegiance of the young men he managed.

"I'll do the best I can," murmured Bender, noticeably moved by Mack's confidence in him. Embarrassed, the Indian hurler turned to leave. Just as he opened the door, Mack asked: "Albert, how much do you still owe on your house?"

The question took him by surprise. Bender was a proud person who would never think of disclosing such confidential information. But Mack persisted. Emotionally vulnerable, Bender told him that he still owed $2,500 on the mortgage and awkwardly excused himself.[51] He had work to do.

The defending world champion Athletics would get the opportunity for revenge in the 1911 World Series. Their opponents were John McGraw's New York Giants, a team that had defeated them in the Fall Classic six years earlier. The Giants stole the National League pennant that year, both literally and figuratively. A team of gutsy, dashing youngsters, the Giants stole a total of 347 bases to set a still unbroken major league record. McGraw had rebuilt the team with some classy talent, including Buck Kerzog at third base, Art Fletcher at shortstop, Larry Doyle at second, and Fred Merkle at first. There were four speedy youngsters in the outfield: Josh Devore, Fred Snodgrass, Red Murray, and Beals Becker. John Meyers, also called "Chief" because of his Native American background, did the catching. While Christy Mathewson, who posted a 26–13 record, was still the ace of the team, the Giants' pennant was largely made possible by the transformation of southpaw Rube Marquard from a hard-luck loser in 1910 to a 24–7 stopper in 1911. Leon Ames and George Wiltse, also leftovers from 1905, rounded out the starting rotation. Otley Crandall doubled as a relief pitcher and pinch hitter.[52]

With classic pitchers' duels, controversial plays, and dramatic home runs, the 1911 World Series is considered by most to be among the best ever played. Game One, on October 14 at New York's Polo Grounds, featured a rematch between Bender and Christy Mathewson. In an effort to intimidate the A's, the superstitious McGraw dressed his Giants in special black uniforms with white trim, like the ones that had brought them good luck six years earlier.[53] Undaunted, the A's began the scoring in the second inning when Baker singled, advanced to second on a sacrifice, and then progressed to third on a passed ball. Veteran Harry Davis, forced into action because of an injury to Stuffy McInnis, singled to left to score Baker. The run broke Mathewson's string of twenty-eight scoreless World Series innings.

The Giants tied the game in the fourth inning when Snodgrass walked and Murray advanced him to second on a hit-and-run. Herzog followed with a hard liner to second that glanced off Eddie Collins's glove for an error. Before Collins could retrieve the ball, Snodgrass crossed the plate, tying the game. The contest remained deadlocked until the bottom of the seventh inning, when Giants catcher John Meyers doubled off the left-field fence and was singled home by Josh Devore. The 2–1 loss was a heartbreaker for Bender, who surrendered only five hits while striking out eleven batters. Still, Mack considered the contest one of the "greatest games" Bender ever pitched. "The Chief was wonderful," he remarked afterward. "I don't think he ever was faster or had more stuff. Of course, Mathewson was good, too, but the breaks gave him the game." Giants second baseman Larry

Doyle agreed, insisting that Bender's fastball "looked the size of a pea as it came over the plate."[54]

Worse than the A's defeat, however, was Giants president John Brush's attempt to swindle the players of both teams out of additional bonus money by purposely reporting low attendance rates for the game. Since bonus shares for the players of both teams were calculated by a percentage of the gate, Brush's tally of 38,281 accounted for significantly less money than that generated by the 50,000 seating capacity of the Polo Grounds. It was clear to anyone who attended the game that there was standing room only. Angered by the deception, New York catcher John Meyers convened a committee of Giants and A's players, including Bender, and met with the National Commission to discuss the matter. Ultimately their charge of a "short count" was unceremoniously dismissed by both league presidents, Garry Herrmann and Ban Johnson, and the players were forced to settle for less bonus money.[55] But the incident left a deep impression on Bender, who began to look more critically at the white baseball establishment and its treatment of the players, especially Native Americans like himself and Meyers.

Like Bender, Meyers, a Cahuilla Indian, was also called "Chief" and was forced to shoulder the burden of racism because of his dark complexion from the time he joined the Giants in 1908. Because McGraw had made an earlier attempt to sign Negro League star Charlie Grant and pass him off as an Indian, many teams and their fans believed Meyers was the New York manager's latest attempt to "pull a Negro over on them." Accordingly, the Giants catcher was forced to endure racist jeers and was called "Nigger" whenever he came to bat. Also like Bender, Meyers was college educated, having attended Dartmouth before signing to play minor league ball, first in Butte, Montana, and later in St. Paul, Minnesota.[56] When he first came up to New York, McGraw platooned Meyers at catcher but quickly came to trust his abilities and talent for handling pitchers. By 1910 Meyers was the Giants' regular backstop. He became a reliable hitter, averaging .285 or better over the next five years, and a close friend of ace Christy Mathewson, whose success was due, in part, to Meyers's brilliant pitch calling.[57] Meyers was also a proud individual who resisted, whenever possible, the discriminatory treatment of owners, players, the press, and fans. He talked candidly—even boldly—about

Fig. 27   John "Chief" Meyers, a Cahuilla Indian, was the New York Giants'
catcher. Unlike the mild-mannered Bender, Meyers was outspoken. He talked
openly about his Native American background as well as about the discrimination he suffered because of it. (National Baseball Hall of Fame Museum and
Library, Cooperstown, New York)

his Native American background and Indian rights as well as about the discrimination he suffered because of his cultural identity. Bender liked and respected Meyers because he challenged the white baseball establishment, something he had been unable to do up to that point in his career.

When the Series resumed in Philadelphia on Monday, October 16, Eddie Plank faced Rube Marquard. With the game deadlocked at 1–1 in the sixth inning, Collins doubled down the left-field line and Baker followed with a blast over the right-field fence. According to Francis Richter, who covered the game for the *Sporting Life*, Baker's dramatic homer "sent the great multitude howling, cheering, and stamping for fully five minutes, in the conviction that the hit settled the game."[58] Indeed, that belief proved to be correct as the decisive blow gave the A's a 3–1 victory.

The two teams traveled back to New York on Tuesday, October 17, for a game that has been described as both the "most exciting" and the "oddest" in World Series history. It would be another pitchers' duel, this one pitting New York's Mathewson against the A's Jack Coombs. Before the game Mathewson, in a ghostwritten newspaper column supposedly written by him, criticized teammate Rube Marquard's poor pitch selection in the previous day's game. It provided wonderful theater when, in the ninth inning, Matty, clinging to a 1–0 lead, faced Baker himself. Since Baker had homered off of a Marquard fastball in Game Two, Mathewson decided to throw him a curve ball. "I figured that Baker could not hit a low curve over the outside corner, as he is naturally a right-field hitter," said Mathewson, explaining his pitch selection. "I got one ball and one strike on him and then delivered a ball that was aimed to be a low curve over the outside corner. Baker refused to swing at it, and Brennan, the umpire, called it a ball. I thought it caught the outside corner of the plate, and that Brennan missed the strike. It put me in the hole with the count two balls and one strike, and I had to lay the next one over near the middle to keep the count from being three and one. I pitched a curve ball that was meant for the outside corner, but cut the plate better than I intended."[59] In fact, Baker was expecting the curve and blasted the pitch into the right-field stands to send the game into extra innings. Together with his prodigious shot the previous day, the homer earned him the nickname Frank "Home Run" Baker.[60]

In the bottom of the tenth inning, Baker became the object of one of the most controversial plays in the history of the Fall Classic. New York's Fred Snodgrass, trying to leg out a triple, slid into third base with his spikes high. Baker, trying to block the bag, was spiked in the thigh as the umpire called Snodgrass safe. While Snodgrass insisted that the spiking was unintentional, Mack accused the New York out-fielder of deliberate "back alley tactics." Snodgrass was even booed by the hometown Giants fans for the act.[61]

New York's defense yielded to the A's offense in the top of the eleventh inning when Collins stroked a single to left field and Baker, with a bandaged thigh, legged out an infield hit. Both runners advanced on a wild pitch. When shortstop Art Fletcher misplayed Danny Murphy's grounder, Collins scored and Baker limped to third. Davis followed with another single, scoring Baker, and the A's led, 3–1. The Giants came within six inches of tying the game in the bottom of the eleventh. Herzog led off the inning with a base hit, bringing Meyers to the plate. Meyers ripped a Coombs fastball deep into left field, but a gust of wind caught the ball and blew it just inches foul. Given a reprieve, Coombs retired Meyers on a harmless ground ball before surrendering a second Giants run. He escaped any further damage and the A's won, 3–2.[62]

Game Four, scheduled to be played in Philadelphia, was delayed by six days of rain. "There is nothing but mud and water at Shibe Park," reported the *Philadelphia Inquirer*. "The field is absolutely flooded now and a good, hot sun and strong wind are needed to sop up the wet spots."[63] Because of the Blue Laws prohibiting baseball on the Sabbath, no game was slated for Sunday, October 22, and on Monday the field was still too wet to play. With all the spare time, accusations between the two teams began to fly. Snodgrass's spiking of Baker had already created bad blood between the two teams and their fans. When the Giants outfielder arrived at the hotel, he was greeted with a bushel basket of hate mail, including several threats against his life. McGraw made matters worse. In an effort to defend Snodgrass, he blamed Baker's "awkwardness in playing third base" for the spiking.[64] Meyers joined in, accusing Bender and Harry Davis of stealing his signs. "They knew what Matty and Marquard were pitching," he charged. "I went to Rube and Matty and said, 'Pitch whatever you want to pitch, and I'll catch you without signals.' And still Charlie and Harry Davis, who share third base coaching duties when they aren't playing, are calling our pitches."[65]

"I know a lot of people believe that the Chief has some way of getting the catcher's signs, but it's not true," insisted Cy Morgan, a fellow A's pitcher. "The Chief has wonderful eyes and he simply studies the pitchers. There are a lot of little things almost unnoticed about the motions different pitchers use in their delivery and most of those motions have meaning. When Bender gets up on the coaching lines he studies the pitcher's motion. If there's anything he detects, he comes back and tells the hitters."[66]

The Series finally resumed on Tuesday, October 24, with Bender facing Mathewson again. The Giants opened the scoring in the first inning when Devore singled and scored on Doyle's triple to deep center field. Snodgrass followed with a sacrifice fly, knocking in Doyle. But after those two runs, Bender shut down the Giants' offense.

The A's did all of their scoring in the bottom of the fourth inning. Baker, Davis, and Murphy hit consecutive doubles, as Mathewson's famous fade-away pitch failed him. After driving in Baker and Davis, Murphy advanced to third on a fielder's choice and scored on a sacrifice. The A's added a fourth run when Collins singled and then scored from first on Baker's second double of the game.[67]

Game Five, played at the Polo Grounds, was another close one. With two outs in the ninth, runners on second and third, and the A's ahead by 3–1, the Giants tied the game on a single by Josh Devore. Crandell held the A's in the top of the tenth and the Giants launched a comeback in the bottom of the inning. With one out and Larry Doyle on third base, Fred Merkle hit a deep but catchable fly down the right-field line. A's outfielder Danny Murphy knew that if he caught the ball Doyle would tag up and score the winning run. If, on the other hand, he let the ball drop, it might fall in foul territory, preventing Doyle from scoring. Murphy circled under the ball, made the catch, and threw home. Doyle easily beat the throw and the game was over. Fans stormed onto the field as the Giants and A's barely made their way into their respective clubhouses. In the middle of all the mayhem, umpire Bill Klem stood at home plate waiting to make a signal on the play. Doyle had never touched the plate! Nor did A's catcher Jack Lapp notice it! Since the players had already retired from the field, Klem had no choice but to count the run. Afterward, Mack and several of his players insisted that they noticed Doyle's failure to tag home but chose not to protest. "My players know that Doyle did not touch the plate," said the Spindly Strategist. "It was the most pleasing moment of my life when not one of them chose to take advantage of a technicality. It was a matter of prudence and good sportsmanship."[68] Mack must have had been convinced that his team would win the championship with a 3–2 game lead and the Series returning to Philadelphia for Game Six the following day. While he placed a high priority on "honor," he would have been foolish not to challenge Doyle's miscue under any other circumstances, especially if it meant losing the championship.

To guarantee victory, Mack pulled Coombs, who was scheduled to start Game Six for the A's, and gave Bender the ball.[69] The Chippewa hurler held the Giants to two runs on four hits en route to a 13–2 victory, giving the A's their second straight world championship.[70] Bender's pitching totals for the six-game Series were just as impressive, as he posted a 2–1 record with a 1.04 ERA, allowing just sixteen hits and three runs in twenty-six innings of work.[71]

After clinching the championship, Mack approached Bender in the dugout. "Do you remember that conversation we had before the Series started?" he asked his money pitcher.

"No, I don't," Bender demurred, embarrassed by the possibility that Mack might offer to pay off his mortgage.

"Well, be in my office tomorrow morning and I will refresh your memory," he said, then turned and walked away.

The next morning Bender went to Mack's Shibe Park office, where he was handed two checks—one for his $3,654 World Series bonus, the other for $2,500 to pay off his mortgage.[72] It was Mack's way of showing his appreciation to his money pitcher. Of course, Bender and his teammates reciprocated. As a sign of their appreciation, the team of pranksters purchased for their beloved manager a two-ton elephant—a real live mascot to complement the one they wore on their warm-up sweaters—shortly after they clinched the championship. They marched the beast the seven blocks from Shibe Park to Mack's house at 2119 Ontario Street, where they tied it to a post in the backyard so it could graze on the small plot of grass there.[73]

After winning two consecutive world championships, the Athletics believed that they would repeat in 1912. To be sure, most of the base-ball writers picked Philadelphia as odds-on favorites to capture their third title in as many years. But when the season began they played poorly and never managed to get on track. Although the A's won ninety games that season, they finished in third place, fifteen games behind the pennant-winning Boston Red Sox. "If ever a club suffered from overconfidence, it was my 1912 team," said Mack, explaining the down-fall. "Maybe I, too, was complacent and thought the boys would step up to the plate."[74]

Among the greatest disappointments was Bender, whose record dropped to 13–8. Mack attributed his star pitcher's decline to a "swelled head." He spent most of the season indulging in the nightlife, good food, and drink, and his "pitching suffered." Out of condition and strug-gling with a 2.74 ERA, his worst since 1905, Bender was suspended by Mack in late September and told to "get into condition" before reporting to spring training.[75]

Mack learned a painful lesson in 1912, namely, that talent wasn't enough. A team without competitive desire could not win the pennant. Never again would he allow the Athletics to lose because of compla-cency. He would break up the team before he would allow that to happen, and he reinforced his authority by becoming more vested in the club's ownership. After the season ended Mack purchased the shares of sportswriters Frank Hough and Sam Jones, who had owned a total of 25 percent of the A's stock since 1901. The Tall Tactician now owned 50 percent of the club and the ballpark, ensuring his con-tinued commitment to the organization.[76]

During spring training in 1913, at San Antonio, Texas, Mack worked his players harder than usual, constantly reminding them that a smug attitude had cost them a pennant during the previous season. He also realized that his 1913 edition was not as strong as his previous pennant winners. While Mack had retained the $100,000 Infield, which was the nucleus of the team, the rest of the squad had to be revamped. Catcher Ira Thomas was replaced by Wally Schang, who split the catching duties with veteran Jack Lapp. Schang would soon develop into a first-rate backstop and take over as the regular in 1914. The outfield also had to be reconfigured. Bris Lord was gone and Danny Murphy was nearing the end of his career. Rube Oldring would continue as the center fielder, but youngsters Eddie Murphy and Jimmy Walsh were called on to take over the corner positions, while Amos Strunk would continue to play an important role as a reserve.[77] The biggest question was pitching. Jack Coombs contracted typhoid fever in the spring and was lost for the season.[78] Cy Morgan, another veteran who had dropped to 3–8 the previous season, was released. Thus the fortunes of the A's rested in the hands of Plank and Bender, the anchors of the staff, and five young pitchers: Carroll "Boardwalk" Brown, who posted a 13–11 record in 1912; Byron "Duke" Houck, who went 8–8 the previous season; and Stan Coveleski, "Bullet Joe" Bush, and Herb Pennock, all of whom saw limited action in 1912.

With so many untested arms, Mack was forced to develop a new pitching strategy. In addition to using Bender and Plank as starters, he would also use them to relieve the youngsters in close games. It was a calculated risk. Bender and Plank were on the downside of their careers, each having pitched in the majors for more than a decade. The additional wear on their arms could result in serious injury and potentially end their careers. Bender appeared in a total of forty-eight games that season, twenty-one more than in the previous year. Still, he managed to post a 21–10 record, with six of the victories coming in relief. Plank pitched in a total of forty-one games, going 18–10, with four victories coming in relief. The youngsters also contributed. Boardwalk Brown went 17–11, including eleven complete games. Duke Houck and rookie Bullet Joe Bush posted identical records of 14–6, and Bob Shawkey, another rookie acquired by Mack in midseason, went 6–5. Capitalizing on the strength of their pitching, the A's moved into first place in late April and remained there for the rest of the season, finishing ahead of second-place Washington by 6 1/2 games.[79]

Once again the A's faced the New York Giants in the World Series. John McGraw, in a bold move, decided to start Rube Marquard instead of his ace Christy Mathewson in Game One against Bender. Since the opener was played at New York's Polo Grounds, Philadelphians flocked to the *Inquirer* building downtown to watch the huge, manually operated scoreboard record the action. Although Bender wasn't as effective as he had been in earlier Series openers, surrendering four runs on eleven hits, he was still good enough to defeat the Giants, 6–4. Baker hit a two-run homer in the fifth inning to knock Marquard out of the game, and Schang turned a timely triple play to preserve the win.

Despite Bender's subpar performance, Native Americans gloried in his triumph. Among those who gathered outside the *Inquirer* building were a band of Lenape Indians who had traveled 150 miles from northeastern Pennsylvania just to cheer on Bender.[80] The *Odanah Star*, the newspaper of the Bad River Chippewa Reservation in Michigan, hailed Bender as "one of our own," and boasted that he "pitched the entire game for the Athletics, striking out three of the Giants."[81]

Bender wasn't the only Indian who captured the attention of Native Americans. The 1913 World Series was the first to feature three Indian ballplayers: Bender of the A's, and John Meyers and Jim Thorpe of the Giants. Thorpe, who also attended the Carlisle Industrial School, was much better known for his Hall of Fame football career and winning gold medals in the pentathlon and decathlon at the 1912 Olympics. Stripped of his medals when it was discovered that he had played minor league baseball in 1909 in violation of the Olympic rule that all competitors be amateur athletes, Thorpe used his fame to sign a lucrative three-year contract with the New York Giants.[82] Although he didn't see any playing time in the 1913 World Series, his mere presence on the team showed that Native Americans had made important inroads into the national pastime. "If my race continues to devote the same attention to the diamond game that it has in the past few years, there will soon be a pretty large tribe in organized baseball," predicted Meyers. "The national pastime has opened a profession to the Indian in which he can best employ those natural senses that centuries of life in the open have endowed him with. I am thoroughly delighted with the fact that my race has proven itself competent to master the white man's principle sport."[83] Ed Goewey of *Leslie's Illustrated Weekly* agreed with Meyers, albeit in a patronizing, if not racist, fashion: "All arguments to the contrary notwithstanding, there *are* good Indians, and three of the greatest of these are Chief Bender of the Athletics and Chief Meyers and Jim Thorpe of the Giants. This trio represents

Fig. 28   Jim Thorpe, a Sac and Fox Indian better known for his gold-medal-winning performances in the pentathlon and decathlon at the 1912 Olympics, began his baseball career with the New York Giants. Although he didn't see any playing time in the 1913 World Series against Philadelphia, his presence in the game, along with that of Meyers and Bender, indicated that Native Americans had made significant inroads into the national pastime. (National Baseball Hall of Fame Museum and Library, Cooperstown, New York)

the highest type of red man, viewed from the standpoint of the athlete, in the public eye today."[84]

Mathewson faced Plank in Game Two at Philadelphia's Shibe Park. The contest was a classic pitchers' duel that was not decided until the top of the tenth inning, when the Giants scored three runs for a 3–0 victory. The Series shifted back to New York for Game Three. Mack started Bullet Joe Bush, who held the Giants to two runs on five hits. The A's offense, led by Collins, Schang, and Baker, hammered out eight runs on five hits for the 8–2 Philadelphia victory.[85]

Bender was on the mound for Game Four at Shibe Park, facing Al Demaree of the Giants. He pitched well through the first six innings and the A's gave him a six-run lead. Rube Oldring made a sensational catch in the fifth on a rapidly sinking line drive to center field to preserve the shutout. But the Giants rallied in the seventh to score three runs, all of which came on a home run by Fred Merkle. New York added two more runs in the eighth and put the tying run on base. With two outs and the A's clinging to a 6–5 lead, Giants outfielder Red Murray stepped to the plate. Bender remembered that Murray had singled up the middle his last time up. Repositioning infielder Eddie Collins closer to the second-base bag, the Chippewa hurler toed the pitching rubber and threw a low fastball to the outfielder, who grounded the ball directly to Collins for the final out of the inning. Bender retired the Giants in order in the ninth to preserve the 6–5 victory.[86] "I doubt if many spectators gave Albert credit for that splendid piece of strategy," said Mack after the game. "The Giants' rally was nipped in the bud by his foresight. It was the turning point of the game."[87] With the 6–5 victory, Bender's World Series record improved to 6–3, and he held the distinction of topping all major league pitchers in postseason wins.

After the game, sportswriter Grantland Rice observed that Bender's "sharp reflexes" and his ability to "take the game as it comes to him, rarely getting excited or off-balance," were tremendous assets. "Given the same chance," he added, "Bender has the white man lashed to the post."[88] While the inversion of Bender as a "master" of the "white slave" is intriguing, it does not change the fact that Rice, like the fans, players, and baseball establishment, continued to view Bender, like all Native Americans, as a "racial object" rather than a human being. No matter

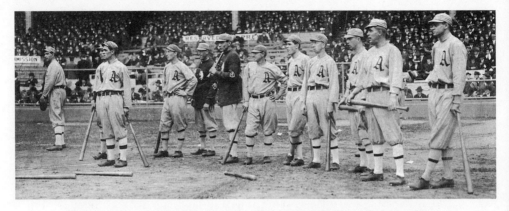

Fig. 29 Rare photograph of the A's at New York's Polo Grounds during the 1913 World Series. Pictured, from left to right, are Ira Thomas, "Bullet Joe" Bush, "Stuffy" McInnis, Jack Lapp, "Gettysburg Eddie" Plank, Charles Albert "Chief" Bender, Jimmy Walsh, Eddie Murphy, Eddie Collins, Jack Barry, Rube Oldring, and Amos Strunk. (Robert D. Warrington)

how successful he became, Bender would remain at best a fascinating specimen, at worst a threat to popular notions of white superiority.

Plank faced Mathewson in Game Five on Saturday, October 11, at the Polo Grounds. The A's got to Matty early, scoring three runs by the end of the third inning. Plank might have pitched a no-hitter had it not been for a mix-up in the fifth. With one out and the bases empty, Plank walked Tillie Shafer. Murray, the next batter, was given the hit-and-run sign. But he lifted a high fly ball directly over the pitcher's mound as Shafer broke for second base. Unable to locate the ball, Shafer made no attempt to return to first in order to prevent a certain double play. Meanwhile, the A's infielders gathered under the fly ball trying to decide who should make the catch. At the last moment, Baker lunged at the ball, knocking it out of Plank's glove. What should have been an inning-ending double play resulted in runners on first and second with just one out. Giants catcher Larry McLean came to bat and stroked a single into left field to drive in the Giants' only run. The A's went on to win the game, 3–1, and clinch the championship.[89]

The victory also made Mack the first manager to capture three world titles in the history of the game. Another pennant would follow in 1914, the sixth of Mack's illustrious career. After that, he would have to wait another fifteen years to reach the Fall Classic again.

Chief Bender had played a major role in the success of the Athletics' first championship dynasty. Between 1910 and 1914 he won a total of ninety-one games, leading the league in winning percentage in three of those years (1910, '11, and '14). Bender also compiled a very impressive 2.19 ERA, appearing in 164 games, both as a starter and a reliever. Prior to the 1914 World Series, the Chief was 6–2, with 43 strikeouts and a 2.32 ERA, the best postseason record among all pitchers in major league baseball.[90]

"Whatever success I've had I owe to Mr. Mack," admitted a grateful Bender early in his career. "His earnestness has aided me and I am well satisfied to remain with the Athletics as long as he wants me."[91] But the mutual admiration the two men once felt for each other had changed by October 1914 and would result in a bitter divorce between Bender and the Athletics.

6

CORRUPTED WORLD SERIES, 1914

The 1914 pennant race was another runaway for the Athletics, who finished 8 1/2 games ahead of second-place Boston. Since the A's clinched the pennant in late September, a full week before the close of the regular season, Mack ordered Bender to scout the National League's Boston Braves, who looked as if they would be their opponents in the World Series. Bender, embroiled in a season-long salary dispute with his manager, wasn't very happy with the directive and decided to ignore it. He had good reason to be angry.

At a time when baseball's premier players were making between $8,000 and $12,000 per year, Bender, considered one of the top pitchers in the major leagues, was never paid more than $2,500 a season.[1] Just once before, in 1909, had he challenged Mack for a pay raise and been denied on the grounds that the 8–9 record he posted the previous season was not deserving of an increase. Instead, Mack retained the pitcher's loyalty by telling the press that he considered Bender "the greatest pitcher in the big leagues when working right," and that he would "certainly not sell him for any amount."[2] Bender grudgingly accepted his manager's explanation. He admitted that his performance was below par because of appendicitis and agreed that he should be paid more money only if he "made good."[3] But the situation was different in 1914. That season Bender posted a 17–3 record, including a fourteen-game winning streak and a 2.26 ERA; he led the American League with an .850 winning percentage.[4] Those statistics, to his mind, demanded a pay raise. Anything less would be a sign of ingratitude.

Until 1914 Bender had no choice but to sign on the terms Mack offered him or not play at all. Under the reserve clause he was the property of the Philadelphia Athletics, unless Mack traded him, released him, or declined to offer him a contract. Nor would another team bid for his services because of the tacit agreement among owners not to raid one another's rosters.[5] But when a band of wealthy businessmen formed the Federal League in 1913, Bender saw his opportunity to get even. Lured by the promise of a higher salary and the possibility of free agency, he held out for a pay increase while being actively courted by the Baltimore Terrapins of the Federal League. The stalemate between Bender and Mack carried over into the postseason.

On September 30, when the Indian hurler was supposed to be in New York watching the Braves-Giants series, Mack ran in to him in Philadelphia near Shibe Park.

"I thought you were supposed to be in New York scouting the Braves," said Mack incredulously.

"Oh, I didn't give them a second thought," Bender replied. "I didn't see any need to scout that bush league outfit."[6]

To be sure, the Boston Braves were hardly a powerhouse. Perennial losers, they had finished last in the National League four of the past five seasons. The 1914 season began just as inauspiciously. Mired in last place in July, they staged an amazing turnaround, going 68–19 to end the season and beating out the New York Giants by 10 1/2 games to capture the National League pennant, earning themselves the name the "Miracle Braves." Still, they were hardly a force to be reckoned with. The remarkable parity that existed in the National League owing to player raids by the outlaw Federal League made it easier for Boston to move from last place to first than it might otherwise have been, especially for a team whose offense struggled to hit .250. In fact, only one regular, third baseman James "Red" Smith, batted over .300, and he broke his ankle during the last regular-season game, which sidelined him during the World Series. That the Braves made it to the Fall Classic was due, in part, to an outstanding manager, George Stallings, whose innovative platoon system got more offense out of eight weak outfielders collectively than he could have from them individually. The Braves also sported the best double-play combination in baseball in Johnny Evers and Walter "Rabbit" Maranville, and featured two of the National League's best pitchers in Bill James, who posted a 26–7 record, and Dick Rudolph, who went 26–10.[7]

Despite the Braves' "miracle" climb to the pennant, the A's were still 10-to-6 favorites going into the World Series.[8] Newspapers in Boston and Philadelphia echoed the odds. "In a short series," wrote John Taylor of the *Boston Globe*, "speed and hitting will win out and the A's have both. Philadelphia's team average of .268 is 20 points higher than Boston's. When it comes to speed, Philadelphia has stolen 220 bases to the Braves' 125. I do not think that the Series will even be close. The A's will win in five games."[9] Philadelphia sportswriter Frank Hough's prediction was haughtier. "Whoever said that 'there's no joy like the joy of anticipation,' certainly wasn't from Boston," he wrote in the October 5 edition of the *Inquirer*. "When the Braves have to anticipate facing Chief Bender and Eddie Plank, the chances are there won't be many outbursts of mirth from them. On form and past performances, the A's, victors in three World's Series, are logical favorites over Boston."[10] Even Ty Cobb, who gave the Braves' pitching a slight edge over the A's aging hurlers in a syndicated ghostwritten column, predicted that Philadelphia would be the "ultimate winner" because the A's hitting and defense "outclasses Boston's."[11] The Braves just laughed. "I am perfectly confident," said Evers before the Series. "The Athletics are destined to receive one of the biggest surprises of their lives." Braves manager George Stallings was gruffer, promising to "knock Mack's head off."[12]

Stallings's attitude and vocabulary didn't improve much as the Series opener at Philadelphia drew near. On October 8, the day before Game One, the Boston manager accused Mack of reneging on an agreement to allow the Braves use of Shibe Park for a final workout. Accusing the A's skipper of "unsportsmanlike conduct," Stallings threatened to "punch him on sight." When Mack learned of the charge, he protested his innocence and promised to address the "misunderstanding," adding that he believed Stallings "didn't mean to say" that he would punch him.[13] The next morning an A's fan by the name of Guy Callaghan began mocking the Braves manager in the lobby of the Hotel Majestic.

"Betcha any amount that your team will lose," said Callaghan when he spotted Stallings.

The Braves' skipper ignored him at first, but the heckler persisted.

"Get away from here, ya big stiff!" Stallings snarled.

"You can bluff about beating up Connie Mack," snapped Callaghan, "but you can't beat up me!"

Stallings had heard enough. He lunged at the loud-mouthed fan, grabbing him with both hands around the neck until two hotel attendants pulled the two men apart.[14]

Meanwhile, Philadelphians were buying up tickets at a brisk pace. Public sales began on Wednesday, October 7, at Gimbels Department Store, the only place in the city where tickets could be purchased. Tickets came in a series of three and were limited to two series per customer to ensure that every fan wanting to see a game would be able to do so. Box seats were set at $15 ($5 each), grandstands at $9 ($3 each), and pavilion seats at $6 ($2 each).[15] More than 6,000 people stood in line beginning at 6:00 A.M. on the first day of sales, waiting for Gimbels to open its doors at 9:00 A.M. The lines stretched for blocks as policemen tried to keep order. Plainclothes officers arrested scalpers who inflated the price of their newly bought tickets. Within six hours all the tickets had been sold and thirteen individuals had been arrested for violating an 1883 law barring the scalping of tickets along a public highway.[16] Each of the offenders made the $600 bail, however, just in time to scalp their remaining tickets for Game One, albeit in a more discreet fashion.[17] Uniformed patrolmen sold places in line, an action that stirred yet another investigation in an already scandal-ridden police department.[18]

Residents along 20th Street bordering Shibe Park's low right-field fence were just as ambitious as the corrupt patrolmen. They spent the two days before the opening of the Series constructing wooden grandstands on the rooftops of their homes once they learned that the police had rescinded their initial prohibition of rooftop seating. Many of those residents profited handsomely, charging two to three times the price of the legitimate tickets for the privilege of watching the games over the right-field fence.[19] Cops on the take, scalpers, and rooftop grandstands provided an interesting sideshow to the main event, which opened on Friday, October 9, at Shibe Park to an "inside-the-park" crowd of 20,562.

Bender, the hero of so many previous World Series, was the starter for the A's, and Dick Rudolph started for the Braves. True to form, however, Connie Mack provided some interesting theater when he sent Eddie Plank out for batting practice before the game. Stallings didn't fall for the ploy and waited to see Bender appear on the field before finalizing his lineup card.

Bender got through the first inning easily enough, retiring the Braves in order. Rudolph, for his part, had a shaky start. Eddie Murphy opened the A's half of the first with a single to right field and Oldring sacrificed him to second base. Rudolph issued an intentional walk to Eddie Collins in order to set up a double play. Baker followed with a pop-up near the Boston dugout. Murphy, trying to advance to third base after the catch, was doubled up, and the inning was over.

Then the tide began to turn in the Braves' favor. Bender opened the inning by walking on four pitches the Braves' cleanup hitter, outfielder Possum Whitted. First baseman Butch Schmidt followed, smacking a fastball into deep left field, where Oldring made a catch against the wall. Whitted, who thought the ball would land for extra bases, had to scurry to get back to first. Bender proved to be even more careless with the next batter, catcher Hank Gowdy. After working a full count, the Chief carelessly threw a fastball right down the middle of the plate and Gowdy smashed it against the fence in right center field for a double, scoring Whitted with Boston's first run. Rabbit Maranville stepped to the plate next. Again, with the count three balls and two strikes, Bender made the same mistake, grooving the ball down the center of the plate and allowing Maranville to smack the pitch into center field, scoring Gowdy.[20] Neither Gowdy nor Maranville had a regular season average over .246, but Bender's pitching made them look like dangerous batsman. Throwing the ball down the center of the plate on a full count once could be understood as a mistake, but not twice in the same inning to back-to-back hitters, not with Bender's control and intelligence.

Third baseman Charlie Deal, a .210 hitter, stepped to the plate next and hit a scorching grounder up the middle. Fortunately, A's shortstop

Fig. 30   Suspicions still exist that Bender "lay down" during Game One of
the 1914 World Series against the Boston Braves. (National Baseball Hall of
Fame Museum and Library, Cooperstown, New York)

Jack Barry cheated toward the second-base bag. He fielded the ball and flipped it to Collins at second, who turned a double play to end the inning. But the damage had been done.[21]

Sportswriter James C. O'Leary, who was covering the Series for the *Boston Globe*, sat in the press box, stunned by what had just occurred. But he was not as shocked as A's fans. "The Philadelphia fans, who had been deriding the Braves players in the previous inning, were thunderstruck," he wrote in that afternoon's account of the game. "They began to sit up and take notice. That the Braves could put over two runs on Bender seemed incredible."[22]

The A's scratched back in the bottom of the second. Rudolph walked McInnis, and Strunk followed with a single to right that went through outfielder Herbie Moran's legs for an error, allowing McInnis to score and Strunk to reach third. Barry struck out and Schang hit a hard ground ball to Evers. Strunk tried to score on the play but was thrown out at the plate. Bender came to the plate next and hit into a fielder's choice to end the inning. Still, the A's managed to score a run on one hit and one error and were back in the game, or so it seemed until the fifth inning.[23]

Gowdy, who had already doubled in the second inning, led off for Boston in the fifth. As a serious student of hitters, Bender knew that he would have to pitch more carefully to the Braves backstop than he had in his previous plate appearance. He also knew that he must, at all costs, keep the ball off the middle of the plate, the same spot that Gowdy had doubled off him in the second inning. It defies logic then as to why Bender threw his first pitch straight down the middle of the plate. The Braves' lanky catcher reciprocated by slamming the longest drive of the game, a triple to deep center field. Maranville, who knocked in the first run of the game, stepped to the plate next. Bender threw him a curve ball on the outside corner and the Braves infielder singled to right, scoring Gowdy for the Braves' third run of the game. Had Maranville not been doubled up off first base on Deal's bunted pop fly to Bender, the A's might have suffered even more damage. But Rudolph struck out to end the inning. Still, the Braves now led, 3–1.[24]

Rudolph, now more confident with a lead, held the A's hitless in the bottom of the fifth. Bender's fortunes, by contrast, diminished as the sixth inning unfolded. After retiring Herbie Moran on a short fly ball to left field, the Indian hurler was hit hard as the Braves sealed the game with a three-run rally. Evers singled to center, Connolly walked, Whitted tripled, and Schmidt singled.[25] "Bender had nothing," wrote George Young of the *Philadelphia Public Ledger*. "There was little speed to his curve and when he tried his 'fastball' there was no 'hop' to it to escape the walloping sticks of the Braves. The mighty Indian had fallen."[26] Mack had seen enough. With the Braves holding a commanding 6–1 lead, he motioned to young Weldon Wyckoff to come in from the bullpen and pulled his "money pitcher" from the game. Head down, the grim-faced Bender walked slowly toward the dugout, where Mack was waiting for him. "Pretty good hitting for a bush league outfit, Albert," muttered the A's skipper, making a sarcastic reference to Bender's earlier excuse for refusing to scout the Braves.[27]

The A's went on to lose the opener, 7–1. "Boston beat, whipped, licked, tormented, maltreated, belabored, walloped, smashed, gashed, bruised, mangled, and wrecked the A's, to say nothing of inflicting other indignities too multitudinous to be itemized," satirized James C. Isaminger of the *Philadelphia North American* after the game. "Now that we have broken the news gently, we will tell the score. It w-w-w-was, 7–1." Isaminger went on to mourn the fate of the once-great Bender. "The Boston vandals ruined Mack's masterpiece in bronze," he wrote. "Charles Albert Bender, with a record of six conquests in previous World Series, was sunk by a Boston submarine in the sixth inning. The official verdict of the press was that the Chief couldn't control his curve or fastball. Boston, however, seemed to control them. They plastered the curve and the fastball against the fence almost whenever they selected."[28] Never before had Bender been knocked out of a game in World Series competition. Even Braves manager George Stallings was surprised by his team's achievement. "I honestly didn't think we would ever drive Bender out of the box," he admitted after the game. "Inasmuch as the Indian had a long rest, we anticipated considerable trouble with him. His past record has shown him to most always deliver an unbeatable game at the start of the World Series."[29]

The following day Eddie Plank lost to Bill James and the Braves, 1–0. Boston scored the game's only run in the top of the ninth inning when, after a misplayed fly ball by outfielder Amos Strunk and a botched rundown had put a runner on third, Braves outfielder Herbie Moran smacked a run-scoring single just past the reach of second baseman Eddie Collins.[30] But the close score was deceptive. The contest was hardly the "pitchers' duel" anticipated by the press. While James pitched a wonderful game, scattering just three hits, Plank was much less impressive, surrendering seven hits, walking four, and hitting one batter. If not for the A's tight defense, which stranded eleven Braves on base, the score could have been much worse.[31] Plank, who was also courting the Federal League, showed only fleeting shades of the brilliant hurler he had been in past seasons. With Plank's defeat, the Athletics were down two games to none in the Series.

It staggers the imagination to think that the A's, a team that posted a 50–24–4 record at home, could lose two straight games to a team like the Boston Braves in Philadelphia, especially when Bender, their most reliable pitcher, was on the mound. Most astounding was Mack's decision to use only his younger, less experienced pitchers—Joe Bush, Bob Shawkey, and Herb Pennock—in the remaining games at Boston. He voluntarily made this announcement to the sportswriters before the A's boarded a train for New England.[32] It was Mack's way of sending the message that he had lost confidence in his top two pitchers, who were cavorting with the renegade Federal League: Bender, who was originally scheduled to pitch Game Four on four days' rest, and Plank, slated to pitch Game Five. It didn't really matter, though.

On October 12 the Series shifted to Boston's Fenway Park. The Braves received permission from the Red Sox to play at their brand-new stadium because their own field, the South End Grounds, was too small to accommodate the large crowds. The game was a pitchers' duel between Boston's George "Lefty" Tyler and the A's "Bullet Joe" Bush. With the score tied 2–2 in the top of the tenth inning and runners on second and third, Frank Baker hit a scorcher to second baseman Johnny Evers. The ball deflected off Evers's shin, scoring one of the runners. Apparently dazed, Evers had trouble locating the ball. After recovering it, he stood at second holding it, allowing the second runner to score. Boston, now down in the game by a score of 4–2, tied the game in the bottom of the tenth. Gowdy led off with a deep fly ball that bounced into the center-field bleachers for a home run. Moran followed with a walk and Evers singled him over to third. Then Joe Connolly tied the game with a sacrifice fly. Stallings brought in Bill James, who

Fig. 31   Mack relied on young pitchers like Herb Pennock to salvage the 1914
World Series after Bender and Plank, his veterans, had failed him. Pennock
would go on to become a Hall of Fame pitcher with the New York Yankees in
the 1920s. (National Baseball Hall of Fame Museum and Library, Cooperstown,
New York)

had already thrown nine innings in the previous game, to pitch the eleventh inning for the Braves. James held the A's scoreless for the next two innings, allowing the Braves to win, 5–4, on a fielding error by Bush.[33]

Mack, with his back to the wall, was forced to pitch another youngster—Bob Shawkey—in Game Four against the Braves' ace, Dick Rudolph. Boston began the scoring in the fourth on a walk and a costly error. Shawkey doubled in the tying run for the A's in the top of the fifth. Johnny Evers regained the lead for Boston in the bottom of the inning when he knocked in two more runs. Mack called on Herb Pennock to pitch the next three innings and Pennock shut down the Braves' offense, scattering just two hits. But Rudolph held the A's hitless over the final four innings to preserve his second victory by a 3–1 score and clinch the title for the Braves.[34]

Boston's four-game sweep not only ended Philadelphia's championship dynasty but astonished the baseball world. The Associated Press declared that the "Miracle Braves" had "scored the greatest sports upset of the first half of the twentieth century."[35] Ty Cobb, who offered his analysis of the Series in a syndicated ghostwritten column, attributed the outcome more to the A's "spirit of overconfidence" than any "miracle" by the Braves.[36] A's pitcher Rube Bressler agreed. "Overconfidence was the thing that did us in more than anything else," he said. "We thought Boston would be a pushover because they were the weakest of all the teams we faced in the World Series [in the past five years]. And we lost in four straight games!"[37] Benjamin F. Shibe, the principal owner of the A's, chalked up his team's defeat to "just plain hard luck."[38]

But rumors of game fixing also surfaced, suggesting that the A's "lay down," or at least failed to play up to their full potential.[39] Even Mack entertained doubts about the legitimacy of his team's effort and said as much to the Philadelphia sportswriters after the Series ended. "I really am glad that in losing we were beaten in four straight games," he said, trying to restrain his anger. "It is the best thing that could have happened to baseball. It proves the honesty of the game, which comes before everything else."[40] His reference to the "honesty of the game" is especially pertinent, considering the rumors about possible gambling influences on some of the A's. While there is no documentary evidence to support a fix, questions still linger about the legitimacy of the A's playing efforts in the 1914 World Series.[41]

First, how could Philadelphia, winner of three world championships in the previous five years, fall to the Braves, a statistically inferior team, in four straight games? For a team that led the American League in hitting (.272), slugging (.352), hits (1,392), runs (749), and home runs (29), Philadelphia's offensive totals for the Series were strikingly low. The A's batted just .172 and scored just 6 runs on only 22 hits.[42] With Wall Street placing 10-to-6 odds in favor of Philadelphia, anyone betting on the Braves at the outset of the Series would have realized a handsome profit on his investment. Second, what role did the outlaw Federal League play in the poor performance of the A's in the 1914 World Series? To be sure, Danny Murphy, who enjoyed a twelve-year career with the A's, jumped to the renegade league for the 1914 season and was recruiting his former teammates. According to Connie Mack, Murphy found a receptive audience. "Our team was divided into two factions: one for jumping to the rich Federal League, and the other for remaining loyal to the American League," he admitted years later. "I knew we could walk away with the Series if only we had been united. I was especially hurt as we were paying our players the highest salaries in our circuit [but] we were being outbid by the Federal money-bags."[43] During the regular season, the A's skipper acknowledged that some players came to him and admitted that the Federal League was recruiting them, including Bender, Collins, Coombs, and Plank. While they promised to play out the 1914 campaign with the A's, they told Mack that they planned to jump to the new league for the following season. In an effort to retain some of these players, Mack "tore up some contracts" to write more lucrative long-term ones. Still, the Federal League owners "kept raising their offers, giving two and three times what [the A's] were paying" their players.[44] At the very least, then, Mack believed that the Federal League's entreaties to his players had a distracting influence on his team during the World Series. At most, the Federal League served as an insurance policy against expulsion from organized baseball for those A's who signed with it and might have conspired with gamblers to throw the World Series.

Finally, the National Commission's reluctance to pursue allegations of game fixing without direct evidence only served to encourage the practice. While organized baseball insisted in 1911 that "the evil of players consorting with gamblers to throw games" was a stage in baseball's past and that baseball was "united in [its] conviction that the game was clean, that the gamblers had been kicked out," the statement appeared to be little more than inflated rhetoric.[45] Between 1877, when four players from the Louisville team were expelled from the game for "crookedness," and the 1919 Black Sox scandal, there were at least three incidents of game fixing in major league baseball.[46] But in each case the Commission was deterred from taking any firm action against the suspected players for fear of a lawsuit, and none of the suspects volunteered any incriminating information. As noted earlier, since evidence of poor play on the field was not of itself sufficient to incriminate, those incidents "actually served to encourage cheating."[47] Under the circumstances, those members of the A's who might have cavorted with gamblers to throw the Series had the confidence of knowing that they would be able to escape punishment.

At the center of the game-fixing controversy was Bender. How, for example, could he have been knocked out of Game One with his remarkable previous performance in World Series competition? Did he conspire with gamblers to throw the Series, or did he simply lie down for the Braves in order to spite Mack for refusing to pay him a higher salary? Why did Mack pull Bender, his so-called "money pitcher," from the rotation shortly before the Series moved to Boston for Game Three? Why was Bender the first to be released in Mack's fire sale of the team after the A's dropped the World Series?

Bender was one of the players accused of breaching their contracts by engaging in salary negotiations with the outlaw Federal League. He allegedly signed a two-year contract with the Baltimore Terrapins during the World Series.[48] Mack was "especially hurt" by Bender's action since he had brought him to the majors and mentored him. "It was," as Mack later said, "as if the Federal League waved the 'long green' in front of him and stole him away from me."[49] The irony here is that Mack, for all of his paternalism, had pulled the same ploy thirteen years earlier when he came to Philadelphia and raided the Phillies' roster. He was, above all, a shrewd businessman and understood that loyalty was given only to those who paid top dollar for the services of the players.

At the same time, if Bender wanted to get even with Mack for refusing to pay him a higher salary, there was no better opportunity than to sign with the Federal League, which offered him a two-year contract worth $15,000.[50] The figure was three times the value of what Mack had paid him for the same duration. To be sure, Bender was bitter about that fact. He realized that, without a contract, Mack would most likely ask for waivers on him at the end of the season. Therefore, before other clubs had a chance to bid on him, Bender signed with the Baltimore Feds, admitting that he "didn't want Mack to profit by his sale even to the extent of the waiver price."[51] Bender had little incentive to do anything more in the World Series than show up for his starting assignment. Besides, with each A's player receiving $2,031.68, just $781.40 less than the winner's share, Bender would stand to benefit financially from the Series regardless of how he performed.[52]

Of course, Bender, in his only start of the 1914 Series, pitched terribly. He was knocked out of the game in the sixth inning trailing by a score of 6–1. It was the only time he did not go the full nine innings of a World Series start. What raised suspicions about his performance, though, was the fact that during the regular season Bender posted a 17–3 record, winning his last fourteen starts. If he was suffering from arm troubles, which has been suggested, how could he have won that many consecutive games?[53] It is doubtful that his condition could have deteriorated so rapidly in the week that intervened between the end of the regular season and the opening game of the World Series, especially given the extended rest. What's more, Bender had always risen to the occasion in postseason competition. He boasted a 6–3 record with an ERA under 2.00 in nine previous World Series starts. Those who had played with the Indian hurler since his earliest days in Philadelphia were stymied by his dismal performance.

"Bender has at least three more good years in him," teammate Eddie Collins told sportswriter Grantland Rice shortly after the A's lost the Fall Classic. "I can hardly figure out his sudden slip in the Series. It must have been that he lost interest, and when Bender loses interest, he finds it hard to drive himself."[54] Collins's statement that Bender had "lost interest" undermines the fundamental assumption upon which baseball operates, namely that *all* players give their absolute best to win each time they take the field. Interestingly, Collins never again made a public statement about Bender's performance in the 1914 World Series or offered another opinion about the Braves' four-game sweep of the A's. "I think he was deeply hurt by the outcome of

Fig. 32   The 1919 Chicago White Sox, more infamously known as the "Black Sox" for throwing the World Series that year, featured former Philadelphia Athletic Eddie Collins *(pictured in middle row, fourth from right)*. Collins was haunted by the 1914 and 1919 World Series for the rest of his life. (National Baseball Hall of Fame Museum and Library, Cooperstown, New York)

that World Series," said his son, Eddie Collins Jr. "I don't know if he thought the games were played on the level or not because he kept his thoughts to himself on controversial matters. But I do know two things. First, of all the World Series my father played in, there were two he never discussed—1914 when he played for the A's, and 1919 when he played for the Chicago White Sox, who of course are better known to history for the Black Sox scandal. The other thing I know is that my Dad was as honest as the day is long and he would rather die than to tarnish his name by throwing a World Series."[55]

 If Bender did conspire with gamblers to throw the Series, it might have been because of his own financial circumstances. Money was an issue for him. At age thirty he was among the oldest players on a team with an average age of twenty-six. He had never made more than $2,500 a season pitching for Connie Mack, and in 1914 his career was winding down. He had to make as much money as he could before his playing days ended. Perhaps that is why Bender was one of six Philadelphia Athletics called in by the Internal Revenue Service for failing to report their World Series bonuses.[56] Under the circumstances, it is not too much of a stretch to suspect that he might have cavorted with gamblers to enhance his World Series earnings. As we know, corruption was growing rapidly in baseball. Rumors of game fixing abounded during the early years of the twentieth century, and the laissez-faire attitude of the National Commission in prosecuting scandals would lead to the infamous Black Sox scandal just five years later.

While it would be extremely difficult to prove that Bender or any of his teammates threw the World Series along the same lines of that scandal, the suspicion that the 1914 Fall Classic was "corrupted" by those players unhappy with the tightfisted Mack is not too far-fetched. At least four players—Bender, Collins, Coombs, and Plank—were entertaining offers from the Federal League. All four had upstanding reputations. But that does not mean that their intrigues with the Federal League might not have destroyed team chemistry, distracted significantly from the team's focus on the Word Series, and forced Mack to dilute his starting rotation by benching his experienced star pitchers. Mack's public acknowledgment after Game Two that only younger pitchers would be used from there on out seems to reinforce the theory of a "tainted" World Series. It defies logic that Mack would remove from the rotation his two star hurlers, Plank and Bender, just because the team was down two games, unless he believed that they were not putting forth their best effort.

Finally, Mack's decision to break up the championship dynasty shortly after the A's lost the Series reinforces the suspicion that the Series was corrupted. Aware that he would do irreparable damage to the game if he went public with his suspicions, Mack engaged in a cover-up. In explaining his decision to the sportswriters, the A's skipper insisted that he was breaking up his championship dynasty because the fans had become too complacent about winning and were no longer turning out to see the A's play.[57] Indeed, there was some truth in this explanation. The A's home attendance, even with a pennant winner, had plummeted from 571,896 in 1913 to 346,641 in 1914, leaving Mack with a $60,000 deficit.[58] Under the circumstances, he either

Fig. 33   Disgruntled by the renegade Federal League's attempt to steal his star players with promises of higher salaries, Connie Mack broke up his championship dynasty after the A's lost the 1914 World Series. "If the players are going to cash in and leave me holding the bag," he said, "there's nothing for me to do but cash in too." (National Baseball Hall of Fame Museum and Library, Cooperstown, New York)

had to unload his star players or cut their salaries. Inside the baseball establishment, though, the A's manager confided that his players were concerned more about money than about the game. Mack, always fussy about his integrity, intended to punish his corrupt players by breaking up the team. "If the players were going to cash in and leave me to hold the bag," he admitted years later, "there was nothing for me to do but cash in too."[59]

Regardless of the reason, Mack broke up the team. Among the very first players to go were Bender and Plank, both of whom jumped to the Federal League. By 1916 all the high-priced stars were gone, and Mack began the rebuilding process with a team that dropped 117 games and is still widely regarded as the worst team ever to have played baseball. The A's would finish in last place for the next five seasons.[60]

When he learned that Mack and some of his A's teammates questioned his desire to win Game One of the 1914 World Series, Bender exploded. "If they really said that," he told the *Philadelphia Inquirer,* "then I stand convinced there is no gratitude in baseball. I worked faithfully twelve years for the Athletics, gave them the best there was in me. I do not think the summary way I was treated was the right kind of treatment for my years of labor."[61] Bender's remark about his "summary treatment" was a reference to Mack's refusal to tender him a pay increase. While the two men remained estranged for the next two decades, the Indian hurler continued to insist that his performance in the 1914 Series was on the level and that he was just as upset about the loss as Mack. "Mr. Mack thought I was the coolest pitcher he ever had," Bender explained years later. "I was cool—on the outside. On the inside, I burned up. I couldn't eat for three hours after a game. After the 1914 season, my nerves reached such a pitch that I broke out in hives and spent hundreds of dollars on doctors and lost two big years on my career."[62]

Bender's nervous condition might well have been caused by his intense approach to the game, but it could just as well have been caused by the insecurity he felt as a Native American in a white society that treated him like a second-class citizen, both socially and financially. He may not have taken any money from gamblers to throw the 1914 World Series, but losing Game One and then jumping to the renegade Federal League in order to double his salary seemed like a personal vindication.

7

FEDS, PHILS, AND BUSHES, 1915–1930

On the morning of November 1, 1914, Charles Bender was on a hunting trip near Williamsport, Pennsylvania, when he stopped at a local diner for breakfast. As he took a seat at the counter, he glanced at the sports page that had been left behind by a previous patron. There, staring him in the face in bold black print, was the headline: "Mack Asks Waivers on Bender and Plank."[1]

"I felt as if someone had hit me with a sledge hammer," Bender recalled days later, when asked for his reaction to the news. Dismissing charges of a conspiracy with the Federal League, he insisted that he had never made contact with officials from the renegade circuit until *after* the season, when they offered him a two-year contract for $15,000. He accepted the offer, he said, because he "thought the waivers meant that Connie Mack was through with [him]."[2] Like Mack, Bender was also involved in a cover-up.

During the World Series, Detroit manager Hughie Jennings leaked the news to the press that Bender, Plank, and Coombs had been waived by the A's because they were "engaged in negotiations with the Federal League and promised to jump if satisfactory terms were not received from Mack." The A's skipper verified the rumor and added that he "would not have asked for waivers on the three pitchers but for the fact that one of them had told [him] that he was talking business with the Federal League" and that he had been offered "big money" to jump. Mack admitted that he couldn't match the offer but encouraged the player to see if "some of the other clubs in the American League would meet the demand." Mack also expressed his anger at Jennings for leaking the news to the press, when waivers are "supposed to be treated in confidence by owners and club managers."[3]

On December 8, after losing Bender, Plank, and Coombs to the Federals, Mack sold Eddie Collins to the Chicago White Sox for $50,000. While the three pitchers were aging veterans, Collins, at age twenty-seven, was still in his prime, so the move came as a surprise to Philadelphians, especially since Mack had signed the second baseman to a three-year, $42,000 contract prior to the 1914 season.[4] The A's manager planned to build his team around twenty-eight-year-old Frank Baker, who still had two years remaining on a three-year, $20,000 contract. But on February 17, Baker, who was also entertaining offers from the Federal League, told Mack that he would return in 1915 only if he was paid more money. Not only did the Tall Tactician reject the pay increase, he also refused to trade or sell him. On March 2 the Yankees offered the A's $25,000 for Baker, but Mack's demand of $50,000 ended the negotiations.

Just before opening day, Baker met with Mack and informed him of his decision to sit out the 1915 season and play semiprofessional ball in the Delaware County League outside Philadelphia. Mack told his star third baseman that he wouldn't blacklist him for leaving, but that he was "through with him." He finally sold Baker, in February 1916, to the New York Yankees for $37,500.[5]

To be sure, Mack's decision to unload his star players was due, in part, to his financial losses. But the question still remains: "Why didn't he rebuild the A's by retaining those members of his team who were loyal, like Eddie Collins?" "When a team starts to disintegrate," he explained to the press, "it is like trying to plug up a hole in the dam to stop the flood. The players who are left have lost their high spirits and wanted to go where the future is brighter."[6] Mack was trying to dismiss the subject by engaging the press in the kind of doublespeak that would become a routine ploy for him in subsequent years. In fact, Collins was *extremely* loyal to Mack and would have gladly remained with the team. Mack felt the same personal loyalty toward him. Sending

Collins to the White Sox, a budding contender, was Mack's way of rewarding his star second baseman for his loyalty and looking out for Collins's professional interests.[7] Ironically, Collins's new team would fall victim to the biggest scandal in baseball history five years later, when the White Sox threw the 1919 World Series to the Cincinnati Reds.

If Mack really wanted to field a contending team, he could have done so by retaining Collins's services and investing the money he saved on the salaries of Baker, Bender, Coombs, and Plank on one of the game's greatest prospects—Babe Ruth. Ruth, then a pitcher for Baltimore of the International League, was offered to Mack by Orioles owner Jack Dunn for just $23,000. But Mack, crying poverty, turned him down.[8] Instead, Babe Ruth went on to stardom with the Boston Red Sox and, later, the New York Yankees. Mack's decision to break up his championship dynasty, then, was made to spite those stars who betrayed him, and perhaps to teach any of his remaining players not to challenge his authority when it came to the reserve clause. It was a foolish decision that sent the A's plummeting to the cellar of the American League. Mack would learn to be more careful two decades later, when he dismantled a second championship dynasty, doing so more gradually over the course of four years rather than in a single off-season.[9]

In 1915 the Athletics finished in last place with a record of 43–109 and saw their attendance plummet from 346,641 in 1914 to 146,233 in 1915. It was the first of seven straight last-place finishes for the A's, who developed a reputation as the worst team in major league baseball.[10]

Bender's fortunes had changed just as dramatically. When he signed with the Baltimore Terrapins of the Federal League at the end of the 1914 season, Bender believed that he had finally achieved financial security. According to the "square-deal" contract established by the new league, the player was guaranteed a salary and a position for the term of the agreement. Bender signed a two-year contract worth $15,000, or $7,500 a season.[11] The "square deal" was the Federal League's incentive to attract prominent stars from both the American and National Leagues to fill its eight franchises—Baltimore, Brooklyn, Buffalo, Chicago, Kansas City, Newark, Pittsburgh, and St. Louis—and pose more direct competition in the majors. In the end, the Federal League was little more than an exalted minor league, consisting mostly of retired ball players and those with no previous big-league experience.

Some stars, like Walter Johnson, were tempted by the Federal League's overtures but remained in the American League. Others, like Bender, Plank, Coombs, Three Finger Brown, and Joe Tinker, fell victim to the big-money offers. Officially, the Federal League respected major league contracts, but as National and American League owners began to enter into salary disputes with their stars, who played the renegade league against them, open warfare spilled over into the courts. A close pennant race in 1914 resulted in fair attendance for the Federal League in most of its cities. But large financial losses were also sustained thanks to extensive litigation by the American and National Leagues, which accused the Feds of raiding their rosters in violation of the reserve clause. In January 1915 the Federal League filed an antitrust suit against Major League Baseball, hoping for a ruling against the reserve clause and hence any subsequent lawsuits. The case was entered before Judge Kenesaw Mountain Landis, known for his stringent stance against monopolies.[12]

In the meantime, Bender found himself in the midst of a bitter rivalry between the Balt-Feds and Jack Dunn's minor league Orioles. Dunn had been hit hard by the expansion of the new league into Baltimore. The Terrapins, who finished third in 1914, were wildly popular, since six hundred citizens, including everyone from bankers to construction workers, held stock in the team. Among the stockholders were Harry Goldman, a successful Baltimore insurance man, and Ned Hanlon, former owner of the Orioles and a prosperous urban landholder. Goldman and Hanlon were the primary sponsors of the Terrapins, contributing $74,000 to the operation of the new franchise. Together with the $164,400 raised by Baltimore's citizen-stockholders, the revenue paid for a brand-new stadium across the street from the Orioles ballpark.[13] Intent on stealing away fans from the Orioles, Caroll W. Rasin, president of the Balt-Feds, signed Bender as a major drawing card, along with the team's shortstop and manager, Mike Doolan.[14] Shortly after Bender's signing, Dunn, who had recently sold his star pitcher, Babe Ruth, to the Boston Red Sox, realized that his minor league Orioles were no competition for a third major league. Accordingly, he pulled his team out of Baltimore and relocated to Richmond, Virginia.[15] It was a premature decision.

The Terrapins went 47–102 in 1915, dropping to last place, and Bender wasn't much help at all. After losing his first six games, he explained that he was "slow in rounding to form" but insisted that he was in "better shape and [had] better stuff" than he did with the A's. His excuse for an inflated 3.99 ERA was the "exceptional hitting of the Federal League's batsmen."[16] Bender went on to win just four games that season, while losing sixteen. It was the worst performance of his professional career. "I had nothing but bad luck," he said after the season ended. "My arm was so weak I couldn't get anyone out."[17] But there was more to Bender's troubles than bad luck.

For more than a decade he had been the object of racial and cultural discrimination. While he learned passive strategies of resistance, there was no way to ignore completely the humiliation and pressure he experienced in the white man's world. In 1915 Bender suffered an emotional and physical breakdown. He would not be able come to terms with that fact for another decade, when he finally admitted, "I was always nervous like anyone else—maybe twice as nervous—only I couldn't let it out. Indians can't. After I left the A's my nerves got worse. The acid in my stomach made it impossible to eat. I got thinner and thinner. I broke out in a rash. If only I had learned before how to relax. Every athlete has to relax. If he doesn't, he goes into a slump."[18] Jeff Powers-Beck believes that Bender's inability to release the tension he felt as a Native American player in a white society was misinterpreted by the press, which assumed that all Indians were "naturally impassive and unfeeling." Powers-Beck also contends that Bender was caught in an impossible position, aware that if he did demonstrate his anger and frustration outwardly it would only "exacerbate the abuse" of the fans and opponents because of the popular stereotype of the "savage Indian."[19] Instead, he turned increasingly to alcohol.

Between November 1914 and February 1919 Bender was involved in three car accidents and charged with "reckless driving." Although the last of the accidents resulted in the death of another driver, Bender was "absolved of negligence by a coroner's jury."[20] The incident might have convinced him that he needed help. By that time, however, his professional baseball career had unraveled.

The Federal League folded after the 1915 season. Major League Baseball partially compensated the debt-ridden owners in exchange for their agreement to withdraw their lawsuit. Plagued by the financial losses, Federal League president James Gilmore, who was responsible for compensating all of the players, reneged on the second year of Bender's contract after he was unconditionally released from the Terrapins on August 30, 1915. Carroll Rasin, president of the Balt-Feds, claimed that Bender "failed to keep in the condition necessary to give the club his best services." Rasin also insisted that Bender owed him payment on a $1,000 loan that the club advanced him when he signed his contract.[21] Infuriated by the charges, Bender filed a suit against the Federal League for breach of contract and asked for a judgment of $1,080, which he claimed was owed to him as the final payment for the first year of his contract, and another $7,500 for the second year.[22]

Bender, now a free agent, believed that he "still [had] several good years of pitching left" and vowed to be "back in the majors" the following season.[23] He was signed by the Philadelphia Phillies, who were coming off their first pennant-winning season and had high hopes for capturing a second straight flag. Bender became a spot starter and reliever for an impressive pitching staff featuring Grover Alexander (33–12, 167 K, 1.55 ERA), Eppa Rixey (22–10, 134 K, 1.85 ERA), and Al Demaree (19–14, 130 K, 2.62 ERA). In 1916 the Phillies' strong pitching kept the team in first place as late as September 8, but the club's light hitting led them to falter down the stretch. Despite a valiant effort, the '16 Phils finished 2 games behind the pennant-winning Brooklyn Dodgers. Bender completed the season with a 7–7 record, with 43 strikeouts and a 3.73 ERA.[24] The following season he showed flashes of his former brilliance, compiling an 8–2 record in twenty appearances. He completed eight of the ten games he started and reduced his earned-run average to 1.67. But the Phillies finished a distant second to the New York Giants, who captured the pennant by ten games. When Alexander was drafted into service for World War I, Phillies owner William Baker used the excuse that he feared for his best pitcher's safe return from the battlefront and traded him to the Chicago Cubs. In fact, Baker needed the money to recoup his losses from a declining gate. He also saved some money by releasing Bender, who was considered past his prime at age of thirty-three.[25]

Fig. 34   Bender, at age thirty-four in 1916, played his final season in the major leagues with the Philadelphia Phillies. He is pictured in this rare photograph at far left during spring training at Coffee Pot Park, St. Petersburg, Florida, with *(left to right)* Erskine Mayer, George Chalmers, F. N. U. Rhodes, and Ben Tincup. (Robert D. Warrington)

When the United States entered World War I in 1917, Bender was thirty-four, too old to join the military. Instead he contributed to the war effort by going to work in the Philadelphia shipyards. "It was tough work," he admitted. "But it put me in great shape. I weighed 195 pounds and was as hard as nails."[26] While not the most favorable situation, the job allowed him to remain near his North Philadelphia residence and, in the autumn, play baseball, albeit at the semiprofessional level. Pitching on Saturday afternoons for the Chester Club, Bender became the main attraction of southeastern Pennsylvania's Delaware County League, one of the most respected semipro leagues on the East Coast.

He was paid $250 per game and led Chester to its second straight league championship with a 4–3 victory over Upland. There would be no "next year" for the Delco League, which "fell victim to the Great War." Since many of the younger players were drafted and the older ones were employed in defense jobs, the league suspended operation for the duration of the conflict.[27]

While Bender struggled with retirement from professional baseball, his sister, Elizabeth, was making a name for herself. Unlike her brother, Elizabeth retained and even gloried in her Native American heritage. After graduating from the Hampton Institute, she taught school for the children of Blackfoot Indians in Montana, and later at the Carlisle Indian Industrial School.[28] She married Henry Roe Cloud, the first Native American to graduate from Yale University and the founder of the American Indian Institute at Wichita, Kansas. The Roe Clouds would go on to become prominent Native American educators. In 1940, Elizabeth, chair of the Oregon Federation of Women's Clubs, would be named by President Franklin D. Roosevelt a delegate to a White House conference on children and education. In 1950 she would be voted "Mother of the Year" by a select national committee of women. Chosen from fifty-two candidates across the nation, Elizabeth was the first Native American to receive the honor. She was selected for her "success as a mother as shown by the character and achievements of her four daughters (all graduates of prominent Ivy League or state universities) and her own strong religious and spiritual honesty."[29] Another sister, Mrs. Emma Huff, was a private duty nurse at Philadelphia's Germantown Hospital. Although he had been distant from these two siblings earlier in his life, the former A's pitcher began to visit with them and their families more frequently after his release from the Phillies.[30]

Bender rekindled his professional baseball career in 1919 when Ben Wilson, owner of the Virginia League's Richmond Club signed him as a player-manager. Having been out of pro ball for two years, the former A's hurler was eager to return to the game. He joined Richmond, a last-place team, in late May of 1919, with only two weeks remaining in the first half of the season. Bender quickly turned things around, as both manager and pitcher. "I pitched Mondays, Wednesdays, and Saturdays," he recalled years later. "Ended up winning 29 and

Fig. 35   Bender made a cameo appearance with the Chicago White Sox at the age of forty-two in 1925. He is pictured here with former A's teammate Eddie Collins, who was Chicago's player-manager. (National Baseball Hall of Fame Museum and Library, Cooperstown, New York)

lost only 2 with an earned run average of 1.06. It was my biggest year in the way of victories and losses. We won the second half and the fans gave me a new auto and Wilson gave me a $1,000 bonus."[31] Anxious to shore up their pitching for the pennant race, the Cincinnati Reds and New York Yankees tried to purchase Bender's contract from Richmond, but the fans raised $2,000 to retain him as player-manager. When Wilson asked him what he wanted to do, Bender asked to stay with the team.[32] Perhaps he didn't want to return to the pressure of the major leagues, or perhaps he felt, for the first time in his career, that the fans and his teammates respected him for his pitching abilities rather than his Native American background. Since the historical record is silent on this issue, we can only speculate about Bender's decision. But one thing is certain — except for a cameo appearance with the Chicago White Sox in 1925, at the age of forty-two, and a brief stint as a pitching coach for the New York Giants in 1930, Bender stayed in the minor leagues for the next quarter century.[33] It wasn't a bad decision, either.

Between 1919 and 1950, the minor leagues achieved their peak popularity. While the major leagues struggled to survive the Black Sox scandal, the Great Depression, and World War II, the minors found creative ways to promote baseball and attract fans. Interest in minor league baseball grew dramatically during this time as teams proliferated in small cities and remote towns across the country, while the majors remained locked into ten cities in the East and Midwest. Even after the signing of the National Agreement in 1921, which subordinated the minors to the major leagues, minor league officials took advantage of the situation by creating higher classifications for their most successful circuits, like the Pacific Coast, International, and Eastern Leagues. The quality of play in these leagues was every bit as good as that in some major league clubs. In fact, some of the finest teams in organized baseball played in the high minors in Baltimore, Los Angeles, and Newark during this era. Local heroes emerged. Some went on to the majors, others spent their entire careers toiling down on the farm. Regardless of their destiny, minor league players tended to develop closer ties than major leaguers did to the fans in the towns where they played. In the process, the minor leagues became the true foundation of baseball as a national pastime.[34]

Bender enjoyed his minor league career tremendously. In 1920 he succeeded Danny Murphy, a former A's teammate, as player-manager of New Haven of the Eastern League. As much as he appreciated his stay in Virginia, Bender could not resist the one-year $8,500 contract he was offered by George Weiss, owner of the New Haven club. It was the highest salary he had ever made in pro ball. "I'll bet it was the highest salary ever paid an Eastern Leaguer," Bender said, years later. "It didn't seem quite fair to accept it since I had so much fun that year."[35] Signing with New Haven allowed him to play with John "Chief" Meyers, a former catcher for the New York Giants who had also discovered a more enjoyable career in the minor leagues. Together, Meyers and Bender would form the first "Indian battery" in the history of professional baseball.[36] With players like Jimmy Wilson and Frank McGowen, who went on to star with the Cleveland Indians, Bender found his managerial duties rather easy. He led New Haven to the Eastern League championship that year, and in the process almost threw a no-hitter.[37] On August 19 Bender found himself two outs away from a perfect game against Bridgeport. New Haven was leading the contest, 3–0, in the ninth inning, when Bridgeport manager Ed Walsh, once the pitching ace of the Chicago White Sox and an old nemesis of Bender's, inserted himself into the lineup. "I got two strikes on him, then cut loose with a duster," Bender recalled. Walsh ducked, but the ball hit his bat and sailed out as a high fly ball in short left field. Earl Stimpson, our left fielder, could have made the catch easily, but stumbled, fell, and the ball landed for a hit."[38]

During the next decade Bender continued to pitch and manage in the International League with Baltimore (where he posted a 6–3 record with a 5.03 ERA) and Reading, Pennsylvania (8–13, 2.41 ERA), as well as in the Mid-Atlantic League with Johnstown, Pennsylvania, (7–3, 1.33 ERA). After 1928, when he took a coaching job with the U.S. Naval Academy at Annapolis, Maryland, the former A's hurler focused more on managing than on pitching. He would spend the 1930s and early '40s piloting a variety of clubs, including Erie of the Central League, Newport News of the Virginia League, and Savannah of the Southern Association.[39] Wherever he managed, Bender was extremely popular with the fans. In fact, the Indian manager was so popular that when Ralph Kilby, president of the Erie Club, fired him for instigating a fight with an umpire, the fans forced Kilby to retract his decision and rehire Bender.[40]

As much as he enjoyed the minor leagues, Bender also used his minor league career to ensure his financial security. Having learned that white society values material wealth above most anything else, the former pitcher focused on making more money than he had earned during his major league career. At a time when America was suffering through the Great Depression, Bender made sure he was paid well for his services, and if the owners reneged, he took them to court to secure his full salary. In 1934, for example, Bender filed a suit in common pleas court against the House of David Baseball Club for $700 in back wages the club refused to pay him. He won the suit.[41] He also channeled his hobbies of trap shooting and hunting into a fairly lucrative sporting goods business.

For years Bender spent his off-seasons target shooting, live-bird shooting, and hunting. He enjoyed shooting because it was "a clean and inspiring means of recreation that not only provided a certain amount of physical exercise" but also "trained the eye and mind to develop self-control."[42] Such self-control was a prerequisite for effective pitching. Bender viewed his off-season trap and bird shooting as a way to prepare for the upcoming baseball season. Interestingly, he was not the only player who took this path. Among the others who participated in trap shooting were Ty Cobb, Christy Mathewson, Eddie Collins, Honus Wagner, Jake Daubert, and Frank Baker. But none of them was as successful as Bender. By 1915 he was one of the top sharpshooters in the United States. During one competition he hit a total of 1,658 clay targets out of 1,800 thrown, for a .9211 average.[43] Hunting was even more enjoyable. Bender, like other Chippewa, was a conservationist. He did not hunt game simply for the sake of killing animals. He had more respect for wildlife than that and had learned it at an early age. Bender loved the outdoors, watching the various animals in their natural habitat, and "communing with nature." "If a man thought only of killing when hunting deer or any other kind of game," he said, "he was wasting his time and should stay home. The most enjoyable part of hunting is being one with nature."[44]

While his enjoyment of hunting might have had its origins in his Native American background, Bender parlayed it into a successful sporting goods business. After working in sporting goods at Philadelphia's exclusive Wanamaker's department store during his earlier years in baseball, Bender opened his own center city store in 1915. Located at 1306 Arch Street, the store dealt in "high grade athletic goods," including rifles, hunting accessories, bats, balls, and baseball gloves.[45] Between the money he earned managing and playing in the minor leagues and from his sporting goods business, Bender accumulated enough income to purchase significant real estate in Cumberland County, Pennsylvania.

According to the deeds of sale for that county, he purchased eight properties in Carlisle, Hampden, and Camp Hill between 1914 and 1949.[46] In addition to the 160-acre-plot he still owned on the White Earth Reservation in Minnesota, Bender's real estate holdings indicate that he was fairly affluent by the time he reached his mid-fifties. At the very least he had learned that land was the only insurance a Native American could possess in the United States, and he acted as though he could never accumulate enough of it. That the land he purchased was located in or around Carlisle may have reflected his own difficulty in breaking completely with the past, and specifically with the Industrial School he called home for a significant portion of his youth. It was, after all, in Carlisle that he developed his athletic prowess, his understanding of the white man's society, and the game he would embrace as his professional occupation in later years.

For all that the Industrial School had taught Bender and other young Indians about white society (and for all it stole from them as Native Americans), the institution had fallen on hard times. Public concern about the school's overemphasis on sports and the exploitation of Indian athletes led to a congressional investigation of the school in 1914. Glenn Warner, the athletic director, and Moses Friedman, who replaced Captain Richard Pratt as superintendent, had already eliminated the baseball program in 1910 on the pretext that this would involve more students in the summer outing program and steer them away from the depraved life of minor league and summer league players. Many, however, suspected that Warner, never a strong supporter of baseball, abolished the program out of selfish motives. He wanted to promote greater interest in his own football and track-and-field programs.[47] Still, the criticism of "sports over academics" persisted.

On February 6, 1914, the investigation of abuses in Carlisle's athletic program and administration began. Many of the students called to testify blamed Friedman for the low morale at the school, but their testimony against Warner was more damning. They charged that Warner "continually used profane and abusive language," "used the football team for the purpose of gambling," and "abolished branches of athletics that he was not capable of coaching like baseball."[48] While

Friedman was exonerated on the charge of mishandling funds, he was still dismissed from the school along with Warner. Despite the appointment of a new superintendent, enrollment dwindled and the once nationally ranked football program declined. More nonreservation schools were established in the West, removing the necessity for Indian children to go east for an education. Without a convincing reason to keep the school open, the War Department, in the summer of 1918, closed the doors of the Carlisle Industrial School for good.[49]

Nevertheless, Bender returned to Carlisle on August 28, 1930, at the invitation of local civic groups, which hoped to honor him as a "native son."[50] The homecoming rivaled that of another great Indian athlete and Industrial School product, Jim Thorpe, years earlier. Arriving shortly after noon, Bender and his wife, Marie, registered at the Molly Pitcher Hotel, where he addressed a Rotary Club luncheon. A host of friends who had known him as a student greeted him. Changing into a Philadelphia Athletics uniform, Bender left the hotel for a parade down Main Street to Biddle Field. There, state senator Leon Prince welcomed him with the following words:

> Every town, great or small, shines in the reflected glory of celebrated persons or events associated with its history. Carlisle boasts of the prison of Major Andre, the birthplace of General Armstrong, the ancestral home of James G. Blaine, the burial ground of Molly Pitcher, and the school of Chief Bender. There is an ancient feud between his people and ours. But if the white man conquered the red man with the cannon balls, the red man has conquered the white man with the baseball. Chief Bender holds priority of place in sport as other world figures hold it in science, industry and art. There is only one Edison, only one Henry Ford, only one Douglas Fairbanks, and only one Chief Bender. We extend our heartfelt welcome to Chief Bender and the gracious lady who adorns his name and who shares his merited popularity of our affectionate pride in his native accomplishments.[51]

If the name of "Bender" had not already been synonymous with Carlisle, Prince hoped to ensure that the two would be forever bound together in the future. It was a touching—but rather dramatic—speech that admitted the injustices of whites against Native Americans as well as the ultimate triumph of Indian athletes like Bender over the white man's national pastime. What better way to underscore the point than to have Bender pitch for the Carlisle Athletic Association against the Philadelphia division team of the Pennsylvania Railroad in a game that occurred later that day. Although he lost the game, 1–0, Bender gave the fans a "wonderful exhibition for seven innings."[52] Afterward, he was asked how he felt about returning to Carlisle. Noticeably moved, Bender replied: "The visit brings back memories I've carried with me for twenty-eight years. It's also been that long since I pitched here. I'm afraid my legs are gone and my arm is gone, but my spirit is still good."[53]

Nearly three decades after leaving, Bender returned to Carlisle as a survivor. Perhaps that was his greatest accomplishment of all. Not only had he survived the cultural devastation of the Indian Industrial School, but also the emasculation of a white society bent on destroying the Indian through personal humiliation and financial exploitation. Ironically, baseball, once a primary vehicle for the process of cultural degradation, had been used by Bender to effect his own resurrection.

8

MENDING FENCES,
1931–1954

Charles A. Bender spent the last two decades of his life mending fences with Connie Mack and the Philadelphia Athletics. He returned to the organization as a scout in the 1930s and continued in that capacity through the 1940s. When J. G. Taylor Spink of the *Sporting News* asked Bender, in 1942, why he decided to remain in the game when so many of his contemporaries had long retired, he replied: "Thirty-eight years may seem long to you, but to me it has gone too fast. I love baseball. I love working with the youngsters. The game was good to me. It had its heartaches, but they were a drop in the bucket compared to the fun I had and the friends I made."[1] Bender was finally free of the demons that had haunted him throughout his playing career. He intended to enjoy his last years in the game.

These were hard times for the A's, though. Mack's glory days were clearly behind him. After crafting a second championship dynasty that captured three pennants and back-to-back World Series between 1929 and 1931, the A's once again sank slowly to the bottom of the American League. They performed more like a "gentle comedy of errors" than a contender, in the words of novelist John Updike, a big A's fan.[2] Outfielders ran into walls — or worse, into each other — in pursuit of a fly ball; quality players were constantly traded for unknowns; the team continued to lose, and nobody seemed to mind. By the mid-1940s Al

Simmons, a former A's star hired as a third-base coach, was really running the team.[3] Mack, in his eighties, was more of a figurehead who was slowly losing his memory. Through it all, the Tall Tactician remained optimistic, undaunted by the critics or the A's lack of success. There were a few bright spots, though.

In 1937 Mack was elected to the National Baseball Hall of Fame in Cooperstown, New York, being recognized for his many contributions to the game as a manager.[4] On August 4, 1944, Philadelphians celebrated his more than fifty years as manager as 29,166 fans crowded Shibe Park to honor him. Bender was among the former players who turned out to pay tribute to the Grand Old Man of Baseball, along with teammates Ira Thomas, Rube Oldring, and Bullet Joe Bush.[5] Four years later, in 1948, the A's managed to contend for the pennant until the final weeks of the season, when injuries and poor relief pitching cost them another World Series appearance. The following year, the infield combination of Eddie Joost, Pete Suder, and Ferris Fain set an American League record for double plays.[6] At the same time, however, contention for ownership of the A's was building within the Mack family.

Control and ownership of the club was divided equally between Mack and his three sons, Roy, Earle, and Connie Jr. Roy and Earle's desire to implement their own plans led to tensions between them and their father. Faced with a weak and unprofitable team, a deteriorating and inaccessible stadium, and poor health, Mack issued his two elder sons an ultimatum in 1950—buy him out or sell out to him and Connie Jr. When the brothers chose the former course, they forced their eighty-seven-year-old father to retire, ending his baseball career.[7] On October 18, 1950, Mack retired from baseball with the words: "I'm not quitting because I'm getting old, I'm quitting because I think people want me to."[8]

One month later the A's announced that the sixty-six-year-old Bender would return to the organization as a pitching coach for manager Jimmy Dykes. The "Money Pitcher" replaced Mickey Cochrane, who became the club's new general manager.[9] The following spring Bender reported to the A's spring training camp in West Palm Beach, Florida, where he began working with the team's pitching staff. He assumed his new coaching duties with the same serious-mindedness he displayed as a

Fig. 36   Bender returned to the A's in 1951 as the team's pitching coach. He quickly earned the respect of such hurlers as Sam Page. (National Baseball Hall of Fame Museum and Library, Cooperstown, New York)

pitcher. "Chief showed up at the field each day and went about his responsibilities with the pitchers," recalls shortstop Eddie Joost. "He wasn't a typical coach, though. He wasn't always talking to them. Instead, he preferred to stand by in the bullpen and watch. Of course, he was cognizant of any problems with a pitcher's delivery and wouldn't hesitate to talk with them about it and how to correct it. But I think that kind of easy-going approach was appreciated by our pitchers, especially Bobby Shantz, who was rather quiet himself."[10]

Shantz, a five foot six, 139-pound left-hander, had been with the A's for two years by the time Bender arrived as pitching coach in the spring of 1951. Although he had shown some promise, his statistics were not very impressive. In 1949, his rookie season, the twenty-four-year-old Pottstown native compiled a 6–8 record with a 3.40 ERA in thirty-three appearances, for a .429 winning percentage. Mack gave him more innings the following season and he actually performed worse, going 8–14 with a .364 winning percentage and a higher ERA of 4.61.[11] Mack would probably have given up on Shantz after that season had he not relinquished control of the team to his elder sons.[12] Under Bender's tutelage the young southpaw became the Most Valuable Player of the American League in 1952, when he posted a 24–7 record.[13]

"What I really appreciated about Chief Bender was that he gave me a chance," Shantz said years later. "He helped me a lot as a pitcher. He taught me how to prepare myself, mentally, for a game and how to pitch with better control. It wasn't that he forced his ideas on you. He'd just stand by and watch you throw. Then, when he had something to say, you'd listen. He took an interest in me off the field, too. During spring training, for example, we would often go fishing together. Since neither of us was much for conversation, we just enjoyed each other's company. Chief Bender was a heck of a nice guy."[14]

Shantz was so appreciative of Bender's mentoring that he wrote the following letter near the end of his 1952 MVP season as his mentor lay in Philadelphia's Graduate Hospital recuperating from abdominal surgery:

Dear Chief,
We all certainly do miss you and hope you can be back with us soon. I'd like to thank you for all the things you taught me

about pitching. I'll probably never be the pitcher you were, but I'll always be in there trying my best to do the things you taught me.

It sure is a great asset to the club to have a man of your caliber around. I couldn't say this if I had to speak orally, but I can write it pretty good. Guess I'll never learn to talk much.

Best of luck and health to you and to your wife, Chief. May God bless you,
Bobby Shantz[15]

The abdominal surgery was one of many health problems Bender suffered during the last years of his life. "I felt sorry for Chief," recalls Lester McCrabb, a batting practice pitcher for the A's and Bender's roommate. "He suffered from arthritis so bad. It really was a struggle for him to be with the team. Once, I remember brushing up against him and it really hurt him. He didn't like anyone to touch him because of his arthritis."[16] In addition, the former A's hurler fought a prolonged battle with cancer, but he kept it a secret.[17]

Despite his poor health, Bender appeared to enjoy his final years of life. He remained close to his good friend and roommate Rube Oldring, and often visited him on his southern New Jersey farm. "When I was a kid, Chief and his wife would visit us on our farm," Rube Oldring Jr. recalled. "It was a real treat for me. They were pretty classy people. Both of them had impeccable taste in clothing and jewelry. But I guess what impressed me more was the fact that Chief was an Indian. That dark complexion and pitch-black hair were so different than the other men my father knew. He'd entertain me by lighting up a cigarette and blowing smoke rings. I just loved to see that."[18] In fact, Bender loved children, probably because he and his wife were not able to have their own. Often he was the most popular person at the ballpark with the players' sons, whom he'd entertain with spellbinding tales of his experiences as a pitcher.[19]

Just as important, Bender returned to the organization that had given him his start in baseball and made him into one of the finest pitchers in the history of the game. Whatever ill feelings he once harbored against Mack or the A's had evaporated, and he seemed to relish the opportunity to give something back to the game. Bender went beyond his coaching duties as well. He conducted an annual tryout camp in North Philadelphia, hoping to discover some home-grown talent.[20] He worked behind the scenes on behalf of Native American athletes and Indian school athletic programs.[21] During the off-season he volunteered to be a public relations representative for the club, speaking to a variety of local civic organizations. Once, when A's publicity director Tommy Clark passed him over for a speaking engagement out of fear that it might tax Bender's fragile health, Bender became annoyed. "I never asked to be taken out of a game when I was a pitcher," he told Clark. "If I'm going to die, I can do it just as well on my feet, trying to make a few friends for the team!"[22]

Indeed, Bender was popular among the fans. On September 4, 1952, for example, the A's held a "Chief Bender Night" at Shibe Park. A scroll with some 150,000 signatures expressing admiration for the former hurler was presented to him, along with a check for $6,009.50—funds collected to help Bender with his growing medical bills. The event attracted 31,424 fans, who had finally come to appreciate Bender's fifty years of service to the game as a pitching great and coach instead of simply an "Indian."[23]

Occasionally an audience would ask Bender about rumors of game fixing in the 1914 World Series. The A's pitching coach, who was extremely sensitive about the subject, always dismissed the rumor by insisting that the team "tightened up," able only to "squeeze through the pennant." "By the time the Series opened," he would add, "we just couldn't win." If pressed on the subject of his own performance, the Indian hurler responded: "I did the best I could for five innings and the score was 1 to 1; then they hit everything I had." "It was a disgrace to get knocked out. When it happened, I felt like crawling into a cave to hide." Bender would go to his grave insisting that the Series was played on the level.[24]

On September 28, 1953, the Veterans Committee of the National Baseball Hall of Fame, at its very first meeting, elected Bender and five others to be enshrined at Cooperstown, New York.[25] Sid Keener, director of the Hall, congratulated the Chief on his election and informed him that induction ceremonies would take place on Monday, August 9, 1954.[26] Unfortunately, Bender did not live to see his enshrinement.

Fig. 37   Hampered by poor health, Bender's last spring training with the Athletics came in 1954 at Palm Beach, Florida. (National Baseball Hall of Fame Museum and Library, Cooperstown, New York)

Eddie Joost, the A's shortstop, was named manager at the end of the 1953 season and asked Bender to stay on as pitching coach. "I really wanted him to continue with us," recalled Joost. "Chief offered our players so much in terms of his knowledge of the game. He was, of course, a Hall of Famer. Just being around that kind of greatness would be an inspiration for our players, especially the younger ones."[27] Ignoring the advice of his physician, Bender traveled by car from his suburban Philadelphia home to Florida for the A's spring training in March 1954. The long drive and his already poor health made him so weak that he was confined to a wheelchair while coaching the pitchers. Shortly after his return to Philadelphia, in early April, he was admitted to Graduate Hospital, suffering from exhaustion. Forced to retire, Bender still insisted that his wife, Marie, go to Shibe Park and watch his pitchers whenever the team played in Philadelphia. Afterward she would report to the hospital to tell her husband "exactly what was going on."[28]

On the evening of Saturday, May 22, 1954, Bender, still hospitalized, suffered a heart attack and died. He had just turned seventy years old.[29] Five days later he was laid to rest at Ardsley Park Cemetery in Roslyn, Pennsylvania, just outside Philadelphia. Among those in attendance were former teammates Amos Strunk, Rube Oldring, and Frank Baker; Roy, Earle, and Connie Mack Jr.; and the 1954 Athletics team, the last to play in Philadelphia.[30]

Sadly, Bender was forced to suffer insensitive characterizations based on his Native American heritage even in death. The headline announcing his death in the Sporting News read, "Chief Bender Answers Call to Happy Hunting Grounds."[31]

Marie Bender traveled to Cooperstown alone that August. As she stepped to the platform behind the National Baseball Library to speak on behalf of her late husband, there was, according to one observer, "a collective throb of the heart."[32] She was brief in her remarks, offering humble thanks for the honor bestowed upon her late husband, the first Native American to be so honored. When presented with the bronze plaque that would grace the Hall, she brushed away the tears to gaze upon the following words:

CHARLES ALBERT BENDER
"CHIEF"
Philadelphia A.L. — 1903–1914
Philadelphia N.L. — 1916–1917
Chicago A.L. — 1925

Famous Chippewa Indian. Won over 200 games. Pitched for
Athletics in 1905–1910–1911–1913–1914 World Series. Defeated
New York Giants 3–0 for A's only victory in 1905. First pitcher
in World Series of 6 games (1911) to pitch 3 complete games.
Pitched no-hit game against Cleveland in 1910. Highest A.L.
percentages in 1910–1911–1914.[33]

"It was," as Marie Bender said later, "a sad but beautiful moment.
So beautiful that it made the sadness a thing of dignity and glory."[34]
Just like her husband's struggle to be respected by white society.

9

LEGACY

On a chilly, rainy October morning in 2003, a few dozen people gathered under a small tent adjacent to "Indian Field" on the U.S. Army barracks at Carlisle, Pennsylvania. They came to dedicate a blue and gold Pennsylvania state historical marker honoring Charles A. Bender, who once displayed his pitching brilliance on that same field during the era when it was part of the Indian Industrial School's campus.

No one from Bender's family was present. No one could be located. No one who played or coached with him attended the ceremony. They were all dead. Instead, the small gathering consisted of officials from the Pennsylvania Historical Museum Commission (PHMC), the Carlisle Barracks, the Cumberland County Historical Society (CCHS), the Philadelphia Athletics Historical Society (PAHS), and a few members of the local press.

After some brief remarks by Linda Witmer, director of the CCHS, John Bloom, a professor of American studies who taught at the University of Maryland and a scholar on the Carlisle Indian School, John Wesley of the PHMC, and I, representing the PAHS, dedicated the marker, which reads:

> CHARLES ALBERT "CHIEF" BENDER (1884–1954)
> One of Baseball's greatest pitchers. Bender played for the
> Philadelphia Athletics from 1903–14, helping them to win 5

pennants and 3 world championships. After winning 212 games over 16 seasons and becoming one of the first World Series stars, he was inducted into the Baseball Hall of Fame in 1954. His mother was one-half Chippewa and he attended Carlisle Indian Industrial School on this site from 1898–1901.

It was, as Marie Bender had said of her husband's Hall of Fame induction ceremony half a century earlier, "a sad but beautiful moment."

Some of us rejoiced in the ceremony because we had at least a historical understanding of Bender's struggle to be accepted by a hostile white society. Others were present simply to show their respect for his professional achievements. Regardless of the reasons for our attendance, we all realized that Carlisle was the most fitting place for such a marker.

"Chief Bender's pitching prowess blossomed here," said Bob Warrington, the member of the PAHS who nominated Bender for the marker. "This was where he came of age and where he was first noticed by professional baseball."[1]

Although Mandowescence lived on the campus for just four years, he left his heart there, along with his Chippewa culture. For better and worse, the Carlisle Indian Industrial School was his home. He understood that it was his choice to attend the school. It was his choice to become part of the white man's world. And it was his choice to pursue the white man's dream of achieving fame and material prosperity. Only after leaving Carlisle, however, did Bender come to understand the complexity of being an American Indian in a hostile white society. Thus he left behind a bittersweet legacy that is both a validation and an indictment of baseball as the national pastime.[2]

To be sure, the game, by allowing Native Americans to participate during the early twentieth century, made an effort to become more inclusive. The rhetoric of democracy applied not only to "hyphenated Americans," those who immigrated from Europe and their offspring, but to the peoples who inhabited the continent before it was taken over by the white race.[3] As a result, Major League Baseball could celebrate the game as a truly *national* pastime because it reflected the demographics of American society—with the exception of African Americans, that is, who were confined to their own Negro Leagues until 1947.

Fig. 38   On October 17, 2003, Charles A. Bender was honored with a Pennsylvania historical marker, erected near Indian Field at the Carlisle Army Barracks, formerly the Carlisle Indian Industrial School. Among those who gathered to dedicate the marker were *(left to right)* John Bloom, professor of history, Shippensburg University; Robert Warrington, Philadelphia Athletics Historical Society; Linda Witmer, director of the Cumberland County Historical Society; the commander of the Carlisle Army Barracks; John Wesley, director of the Pennsylvania Historical and Museum Commission; and William Kashatus, author. (Robert D. Warrington)

If not for Bender's example, however, the sportswriters and owners would have buried Native American hopes for the integration of baseball, much as they had eliminated black players from the game. Bender's remarkable playing ability and dignified behavior disproved their notions of the Indian's racial inferiority and opened the door to the majors for more than 120 Native Americans who played baseball during the first half of the twentieth century, seventy-two of them pitchers, like Bender.[4]

Some historians view baseball's integration of Native Americans as a "window of opportunity" in which Indians could influence American society on their own terms. Philip J. Deloria in *Indians in Unexpected Places* (2004), for example, argues that "sports allowed Native people to help shape a critical dialogue existing within American modernity." If whites worried about "corruption and effeminacy in the [emerging] industrial cities," Indian participation in baseball "offered solace based on masculinity, whiteness, and class." Indeed, Native Americans, "as both historical losers and pure masculine primitives, performed as both objects of white desire and colonized people taking advantage of what some saw as the only fair playing field in the history of white-Indian relations."[5] Deloria views Bender in particular as a representative of "racial gifts" (specifically, "physical power and mental equilibrium") that Indians brought to baseball for a "racist audience," who viewed him as "a spectacle of a lost time of natural physicality" and "nostalgia for community, spirituality, and nature."[6]

Similarly, Jeff Powers-Beck, in *The American Indian Integration of Baseball* (2004), views Native Americans like Bender as "integrators" who used baseball as "a tool of assimilation" as well as "means of cultural resistance." Like tribalism, baseball gave the Indian an opportunity to assert himself as an individual while also uniting with other members of a team. Native Americans brought their speed, visual acuity, and natural physicality to the game, challenging white players to compete on their terms. The discrimination and racism they experienced only made them stronger by making baseball an "important proving ground for American Indian courage." At the same time, their collective triumph over name-calling, race-baiting, and mob mockery "promised new opportunities for both Indian and non-Indian communities."[7]

Neither of these contemporary interpretations considers Bender's example a "tragic" one because of his ultimate success as a baseball player. But they miss the point. "Tragedy" stresses the vulnerability of human beings, whose suffering is brought on by a combination of factors, some that are caused by their own actions and others that are beyond their control. While the suffering is undeserved with regard to its harshness, the outcome is not always negative. In fact, there are occasions when the tragic hero's plight results in a satisfactory—even positive—outcome.[8]

Bender's tragedy is rooted in the process of Indian assimilation, which imposed Euro-American behavior and customs on Native American peoples, who reacted to that imposition by accepting some of those behaviors and customs and rejecting others. Born into a metis culture that adapted a traditional Anishinaabe emphasis on tribal integrity to a more market-oriented, individualistic value system, Bender chose to become the product of a materialistic white society based on the accumulation of land and capital that had been stolen from his own people. As a young Carlisle student, he believed that the only future he had rested in that society. His decision to join the white mainstream and compete—physically, socially, and financially—on its terms may very well have been a matter less of accommodation than of personal survival. Nevertheless, he made a conscious decision to distance himself from the White Earth Reservation and the lifestyle he had known there. To his credit, Bender did much more than "survive."

He was a mainstay of the Philadelphia Athletics' pitching staff for more than a decade and posted impressive World Series victories against the legendary New York Giants in 1905, 1911, and 1913. His 6–4 record and 2.44 earned run average in world championship competition is still among the very best in the history of the game. He also registered nine straight complete games in World Series competition, which is a record that still stands today. Accordingly, A's manager Connie Mack regarded his Chippewa hurler as his "greatest money pitcher," who was at his best when the stakes were the highest.[9] It was Mack's greatest compliment, considering that the A's also had such future Hall of Famers as Rube Waddell and Eddie Plank on the same pitching staff.

When Bender believed that Mack was taking advantage of him in salary negotiations, he jumped to the renegade Federal League for three times the amount of money. When the Federal League released him without honoring their contractual obligations, he took it to court, something he did not hesitate to do in the future when he felt cheated in a business deal. Bender then went on to enjoy more than a decade as a player-manager in the minor leagues. Having a steady—and profitable—income from his sporting goods stores, he no longer felt the pressure of his earlier years in the major leagues and played the game for the sheer love of it. Bender had not only achieved the "American Dream," he had mastered it. When he completed his major league career, Connie Mack's "money pitcher" had compiled a 212–127 record, 1,711 strikeouts, and a 2.46 ERA, statistics that earned him election to baseball's Hall of Fame a year before his death. As in all "tragedies," however, the success came at a price.

Bender, both consciously and unwittingly, became the product of two worlds, one white, the other Indian. While he was successful at accumulating the land and capital valued by the former, he could never escape the latter. Tragically, he defined himself more by his success at a white man's game than by his intrinsic value as a person of Native American extraction. He was bitter about his second-class treatment yet accepted his Indian identity stoically. While he responded with a tip of the cap to cheers for the "Chief," he signed autographs "Charley Bender." He joked with those who criticized his Native American background by calling them "foreigners in his land."[10] What sportswriters, teammates, and opponents viewed as "poise under pressure"—a quality they attributed to Bender's Native American background—was actually his inability, or unwillingness, to give expression to the demons inside him. "I was cool on the outside," he admitted years after his playing career had ended. "On the inside I burned up. My nerves reached such a pitch that I broke out in hives and spent hundreds of dollars on doctors."[11] That kind of pain, which was both psychological as well as physical, not only shortened his major league career, it no doubt contributed to the poor health he suffered later in life. Thus, if Bender did "lie down" during the 1914 World Series, it was no greater a sin than the race-baiting, mockery, sensationalist newspaper cartoons, and financial exploitation he endured throughout his career.

Just as tragic, Bender's experience was not far removed from that of the Native American people themselves. When the United States government took their land and put them on reservations, it stole their livelihood of hunting, fishing, and farming. The young were encouraged to attend off-reservation boarding schools as a means of annihilating native culture. In those schools they were told that a future in white society promised good employment, more money, and better urban homes. Instead, Indians found that they were exploited in poorly paying jobs and forced to live in the poverty-stricken sections of cities where cultural confusion and a constant sense of meaninglessness led to other problems, such as alcoholism. This was the federal government's plan for assimilation: strip the Indian of his culture, force him into the urban mainstream, where he would simply "disappear," and, in so doing, end all government obligation.[12]

Other racial and ethnic groups, with the exception of African Americans, were not forced to endure the same experience. For them, assimilation came voluntarily and, to a degree, on their terms. These "hyphenated Americans" reproduced the conditions of their native country. The existence, in many large cities, of Chinatowns and of Polish, Irish, Italian, and German enclaves reflects that fact. These groups established their own churches and fraternal organizations, where they continued to speak in their native language and celebrate their religious holidays. African Americans, for all the hardships they have suffered in white society, even founded schools and colleges that reflected their heritage.

Native Americans, by contrast, were forced to assimilate wholesale. Because they came from small tribes, they could not create urban neighborhoods where their customs and languages could be preserved. Instead, from the very beginning of the assimilation process in the off-reservation boarding schools, Indians from different tribes were forced to live together, losing their relatives, friends, and special sense of identity with a tribe that was bound by common practices and rituals.[13]

In the end, Charles A. Bender's story reflects the tragedy of Indian assimilation itself. By forcing Native Americans to accept white ways of thinking and living, the federal government and self-styled Indian reformers aimed to destroy the culture of a once proud people. *Nothing*—not reparations, financial profits from the gambling industry, or a bronze plaque at Cooperstown—can ever make up for that.

Perhaps we must find it in ourselves, both white and Native American, to respect each other for our humanity. That can happen only if we ask what it is we are destroying in ourselves and others in our constant pursuit for material success, and whether in that pursuit we have forgotten what it means to be human. Only then will we have learned something from Charles Bender and the tragedy of Indian assimilation.

APPENDIX

Charles Albert "Chief" Bender Major and Minor League Pitching Statistics

Year	Age	Team	League	G	IP	W	L	Pct.	H	R	ER	SO	BB	ERA
1903	19	Philadelphia	American	36	270	17	15	.531	233	116	92	127	67	3.07
1904	20	Philadelphia	American	29	205	10	11	.476	174	66	65	149	59	2.87
1905	21	Philadelphia	American	35	230	18	11	.621	199	105	72	142	83	2.83
1906	22	Philadelphia	American	36	240	15	10	.600	211	96	67	159	48	2.53
1907	23	Philadelphia	American	33	222	16	8	.667	183	72	50	112	31	2.05
1908	24	Philadelphia	American	18	139	8	9	.471	121	48	27	85	21	1.75
1909	25	Philadelphia	American	34	250	18	8	.692	196	68	46	161	45	1.66
1910	26	Philadelphia	American	30	250	23	5	**.821**	182	63	44	155	47	1.58
1911	27	Philadelphia	American	31	216	17	5	**.773**	198	66	52	114	58	2.16
1912	28	Philadelphia	American	27	171	13	8	.619	169	63	52	90	33	2.74
1913	29	Philadelphia	American	48	238	21	10	.667	208	78	58	135	59	2.19
1914	30	Philadelphia	American	28	179	17	3	**.850**	159	49	45	107	55	2.26
1915	31	Baltimore	Federal	26	179	4	16	.200	198	101	85	89	38	4.27
1916	32	Philadelphia	National	27	123	7	7	.500	137	71	51	43	34	3.73
1917	33	Philadelphia	National	20	113	8	2	.800	84	24	21	43	26	1.67
1918	34		(Voluntarily retired—worked in shipyards)											
1919	35	Richmond	Virginia	34	280	29	2	**.935**	209	53	—	**195**	22	—
1920	36	New Haven	Eastern	47	**324**	25	12	.676	256	104	70	252	71	1.94
1921	37	New Haven	Eastern	36	196	13	7	.650	168	70	42	131	59	1.93
1922	38	Reading	Int'l.	30	183	8	13	.381	172	76	49	88	33	2.42
1923	39	Baltimore	Int'l.	18	93	6	3	.667	109	65	52	44	30	5.03
1924	40	New Haven	Eastern	12	91	6	4	.600	94	38	31	55	18	3.07
1925	41	Chicago	American	1	1	0	0	.000	1	2	2	0	1	18.00
1927	43	Johnstown	Mid-Atl.	18	108	7	3	.700	74	18	16	39	13	1.33

MAJOR LEAGUE TOTALS—16 years 433 2,847 212 127 .650 2,455 987 829 1,711 667 2.46
MINOR LEAGUE TOTALS—7 years 195 1,275 94 44 .658 1,082 424 — 804 246 —

KEY: G = Games IP = Innings pitched W = Wins L = Losses Pct. = Winning percentage
H = Hits R = Runs ER = Earned Runs SO = Strikeouts
BB = Base on Balls ERA = Earned Run Average **Bold Statistics indicate league leader**

Bender's World Series Pitching Record

Year	Opponent	G	IP	W	L	Pct.	H	R	ER	SO	BB	ERA
1905	New York Giants	2	17	1	1	.500	9	2	2	13	6	1.06
1910	Chicago Cubs	2	18$^{2/3}$	1	1	.500	12	5	4	14	4	1.93
1911	New York Giants	3	26	2	1	.667	16	6	3	20	8	1.04
1913	New York Giants	2	18	2	0	1.000	19	9	8	9	1	4.00
1914	Boston Braves	1	5$^{1/3}$	0	1	.000	8	6	6	3	2	10.13
5	World Series	10	85	6	4	.600	64	28	23	59	21	2.44

NOTES

INTRODUCTION

1. Frederick G. Lieb, *Connie Mack: Grand Old Man of Baseball* (New York: G. P. Putnam's Sons, 1945), 98.

2. William F. Kirk, "Today Is the Day," *New York American*, October 9, 1905.

3. Jeffrey Powers-Beck, "'Chief': The American Indian Integration of Baseball, 1897–1945," *American Indian Quarterly* 25 (fall 2001): 508.

4. Ibid.

5. Charles A. Bender quoted in "Big Chief Bender, Mighty Pitcher, Leads Way to Victory for Athletics Over New York," *Philadelphia Inquirer*, October 11, 1905; for cartoon, see "The Big Chief at the Polo Grounds," ibid.

6. Connie Mack quoted in "Chief Bender Dies," *New York Times*, May 23, 1954.

7. Powers-Beck, "'Chief,'" 508–38. Powers-Beck identifies 133 athletes of Native American ancestry who played major league baseball between 1887 and 1945.

8. Vine Deloria Jr., *Custer Died for Your Sins: An Indian Manifesto* (New York: Macmillan, 1969). Deloria, of Dakota descent, offered a Native American perspective on race relations, Christianity, and federal bureaucracies in this groundbreaking work, which appeared on the *New York Times* best-seller list.

9. Dee Brown, *Bury My Heart at Wounded Knee: An Indian History of the American West* (London: Barrie & Jenkins, 1971). Other notable works on the subjugation of Native Americans during the nineteenth century include two books by Robert M. Utley, *Frontier Regulars: The United States Army and the Indian, 1866–1890* (New York: Macmillan, 1973) and *The Indian Frontier of the American West, 1846–1890* (Albuquerque: University of New Mexico Press, 1984); Robert A. Trennert Jr., *Alternative to Extinction: Federal Indian Policy and the Beginnings of the Reservation System* (Philadelphia: Temple University Press, 1975); Francis Paul Prucha, *American Indian Policy in Crisis: Christian Reformers and the Indian, 1865–1900* (Norman: University of Oklahoma Press, 1976); and Brian W. Dippie, *The Vanishing American: White Attitudes and U.S. Indian Policy* (Middletown: Wesleyan University Press, 1982).

10. See David Wallace Adams, *Education for Extinction: American Indians and the Boarding School Experience, 1875–1928* (Lawrence: University Press of Kansas, 1995); See also Tsianina Lomawaima, *They Called It Prairie Light: The Story of Chilocco Indian School* (Lincoln: University of Nebraska Press, 1994); Michael C. Coleman, *American Indian Children at School, 1850–1930* (Jackson: University Press of Mississippi, 1993); Genevieve Bell, "Telling Stories Out of School: Remembering the Carlisle Indian Industrial School, 1879–1918 (Ph.D. diss., Stanford University, 1998); and John Bloom, *To Show What an Indian Can Do: Sports at Native American Boarding Schools* (Minneapolis: University of Minnesota Press, 2000).

11. Harold Seymour, *Baseball: The People's Game* (New York: Oxford University Press, 1990), 379. Seymour's work deals exclusively with baseball. Others, including Native American writers who believe that whites have distorted the history of Indian sports, have written treatments that address a wide range of athletic activities among Indians, tracing them back to their tribal roots. Among the best works are Robert S. Culin, *Games of the North American Indians: Twenty-fourth Annual Report of the Bureau of American Ethnology* (Washington, D.C.: U.S. Government Printing Office, 1907); Joseph B. Oxendine, *American Indian Sports Heritage* (Lincoln: University of Nebraska Press, 1995); and Bloom, *To Show What an Indian Can Do.*

12. Ellen J. Staurowsky, "An Act of Honor or Exploitation? The Cleveland Indians' Use of the Louis Francis Sockalexis Story," *Sociology of Sport Journal* 15, no. 3 (1998): 299–316.

13. David L. Fleitz, *Louis Sockalexis: The First Cleveland Indian* (Jefferson, N.C.: McFarland, 2002); and Brian McDonald, *Indian Summer* (New York: Rodale, 2002).

14. Jeffrey Powers-Beck, *The American Indian Integration of Baseball* (Lincoln: University of Nebraska Press, 2004), 73. Powers-Beck's work is grounded in a large body of literature on critical race studies that argues that race is a cultural and social construct, not simply a biological fact. Among those who argue this point most effectively are David R. Roediger, *The Wages of Whiteness: Race and the Making of the American Working Class* (New York: Verso Books, 1991); and Michael Omi and Howard Winant, *Racial Formation in the United States: From the 1960s to the 1990s* (New York: Routledge, 1994).

15. Powers-Beck, *American Indian Integration of Baseball*, 31–50.

16. Ibid., 30. Philip J. Deloria, *Indians in Unexpected Places* (Lawrence: University Press of Kansas, 2004), makes a similar *structural* argument. He views Bender as an object of representation that explains how whites appeared to value Indians—as "balanced" and "stoic." At the same time, Deloria argues that Bender was able to navigate within the white mainstream, which was a system of meaning with both racist hostility and opportunities for affirmation. Unlike some other Native Americans, Bender did not give up on the system, and as a result he helped to change the structure of white society (120–35).

CHAPTER 1

1. Minavavana quoted in William W. Warren, *History of the Ojibway People* (1885; reprint, St. Paul: Minnesota Historical Society, 1984), 196–99.

2. George W. Knepper, "Breaching the Ohio Boundary: The Western Tribes in Retreat," in *The American Indian Experience*, ed. Philip Weeks (Wheeling, Ill.: Forum Press, 1988), 81–95.

3. Charles J. Kappler, ed., *Indian Affairs: Laws and Treaties* (Washington, D.C.: U.S. Government Printing Office, 1903), 3:4–5.

4. Ibid., 3:213–15, 258–60, 401–3, 421.

5. Gary Anderson and Alan Woolworth, eds., *Through Dakota Eyes: Narrative Accounts of the Minnesota Indian War of 1862* (St. Paul: Minnesota Historical Society, 1988), ix.

6. John L. O'Sullivan quoted in *Democratic Review* 15 (July 1845): 219; see also Julius Pratt, "John L. O'Sullivan and Manifest Destiny," *New York History* 14 (1933): 213.

7. See Reverend Josiah Strong, *Our Country* (New York, 1885), quoted in Frederick Merk, *Manifest Destiny and Mission in American History* (New York: Vintage Books, 1966), 240.

8. Carl Schurz, "Present Aspects of the Indian Problem," *North American Review* 133 (July 1881): 6–10; and Adams, *Education for Extinction*, 16–19.

9. *General Allotment Act* (Dawes Act), February 8, 1887, in *Documents of United States Indian Policy*, ed. Francis Paul Prucha (Lincoln: University of Nebraska Press, 2000), 170–73. For policy formation related to Indian assimilation, see Frederick Hoxie, *A Final Promise: The Campaign to Assimilate the Indians, 1880–1920* (Lincoln: University of Nebraska Press, 1984).

10. Henry Price quoted in *Annual Report of the Commissioner of Indian Affairs* (July 1888), 89, 262.

11. Lamar quoted in *Annual Report of the Secretary of the Interior* (1886), 4. See also *Annual Report of the Commissioner of Indian Affairs* (1881), 1–2.

12. Schurz "Present Aspects of the Indian Problem," 7.

13. Robert Tholkes, "Chief Bender—the Early Years," *Baseball Research Journal* (Cooperstown, N.Y.: Society for American Baseball Research, 1983), 9. According to Bender's birth certificate, his father's name was Alburtus, but the federal census gives it as William.

14. See "Annual Report of Philadelphia Educational Home" (1894), Charles A. Bender student file, record of graduates, Carlisle Indian Industrial School, file 1327, no. 5453, record group 75, National Archives and Records Administration, Washington, D.C.

15. See Frances Densmore, *Chippewa Customs* (1928; reprint, St. Paul: Minnesota Historical Society, 1979), 52–54; and M. Inez Hilger, *Chippewa Child Life and Its Cultural Background* (1951; reprint, St. Paul: Minnesota Historical Society, 1992), 35.

16. See Melissa L. Meyer, *The White Earth Tragedy: Ethnicity and Dispossession at a Minnesota Anishinaabe Reservation, 1889–1920* (Lincoln: University of Nebraska Press, 1994). White Earth was cobbled together from a variety of splinter bands of Anishinaabe from across Minnesota. Although traditional Anishinaabeg tended to see their differences in cultural rather than biological terms, metis tribal members tended to serve as intermediaries between the tribe and white society.

17. Ibid., 69–94.

18. Tholkes, "Chief Bender—Early Years," 9.

19. Gary W. Clendennen, "Minnesota's Greatest Baseball Player," *Minnesota Monthly* (August 1983): 16.

20. General Henry H. Sibley quoted in David Anderson, ed., *Before the Dome: Baseball in Minnesota When the Grass Was Real* (Minneapolis: Nodin Press, 1993), 21.

21. Ibid., 22–23.

22. Patty Loew, "Tinkers to Evers to Chief: Baseball from Indian Country," *Wisconsin Magazine of History* (spring 2004): 4–5; and Densmore, *Chippewa Customs*, 119.

23. Patty Loew, "The Lake Superior Chippewa and Their Newspapers in the Progressive Era" (Ph.D. diss., University of Wisconsin, Madison, 1998), 6.

24. Ibid., 7.

25. Powers-Beck, "'Chief,'" 521.

26. Tholkes, "Chief Bender—Early Years," 10.

27. Ibid.

28. Ibid.

29. Luther Standing Bear, *My People the Sioux* (Boston: Houghton Mifflin, 1928; reprint, Lincoln: University of Nebraska Press, 1975), 131.

30. Ibid.

31. Adams, *Education for Extinction*, 28–44.

32. Ibid., 21–24.

33. "Charter of the Educational Home, Philadelphia, PA," quoted in Tholkes, "Chief Bender—Early Years," 11.

34. Ibid.

35. Ibid.

36. See Meyer, *White Earth Tragedy*, 173–201; and D. S. Otis, *The Dawes Act and the Allotment of Indian Lands*, ed. Francis P. Prucha (Norman: University of Oklahoma Press, 1973); and Wilcomb E. Washburn, *The Assault on Indian Tribalism: The General Allotment Law (Dawes Act) of 1887* (Philadelphia: J. B. Lippincott, 1975). Between the passage of the Dawes Act and 1934, Native Americans lost 60 percent of the reservation land remaining in 1887 and 66 percent of the land allotted to them. In 1934 Congress passed the Tribal Reorganization Act, reversing the tenets of the Dawes Act by affirming the integrity of Indian cultural institutions and returning land to tribal ownership.

37. Meyer, *White Earth Tragedy*, 173–201.

38. Bender quoted in Tholkes, "Chief Bender—Early Years," 11.

CHAPTER 2

1. For an account of the arrival of students at the Carlisle Industrial School, see Barbara Landis, "A Virtual Glimpse of the Carlisle Industrial School," http://home.epix.net/%7Elandis/histry.html; and Standing Bear, *My People the Sioux*, 132–33. For design of the campus, see Jacqueline Fear-Segal, "Maps of Carlisle Industrial School" (Carlisle: Dickinson College, 2000).

2. Paul A. W. Wallace, *Indians in Pennsylvania* (Harrisburg: Pennsylvania Historical and Museum Commission, 1993), 3, 18–47; and C. A. Weslager, *The Delaware Indians* (New Brunswick: Rutgers University Press, 2000), 31–76.

3. Edwin B. Bronner, *William Penn's "Holy Experiment": The Founding of Pennsylvania, 1681–1701* (Westport, Conn.: Greenwood Press, 1978), 13, 57, 63–64.

4. See Steven G. Gimber, "Kinship and Covenants in the Wilderness: Indians, Quakers, and Conversion to Christianity, 1675–1800" (Ph.D. diss., American University, 2000). Gimber argues that in the late seventeenth and early eighteenth centuries, when the Lenni Lenape welcomed Quakers to their homeland, the similar religious beliefs of both groups served as the basis for their friendship. Quakers felt that their mystical belief in the presence of a divine light in each

person, as well as their own Christian example, would induce the Lenape to join their religious body. But the Lenape soon discovered that the Friends did not live up to their expectations for kinship. By the 1740s the Lenape were engaged in a concerted effort to preserve and recapture their own religious ideals. Quakers, many of whom had strayed from the principles of their faith by succumbing to material gain, also labored to restore the integrity of their faith. In the 1790s, Philadelphia Quakers, inspired by a humanitarian concern, tried to acculturate and convert Indians to their faith and teach them an agricultural way of life. Their efforts were fully supported by the federal government. But most Delaware did not participate, wanting to retain their own culture and determine which elements, if any, they would adopt.

5. Weslager, *Delaware Indians*, 188–91. Thomas and Richard Penn used an old, incomplete draft treaty from 1686 to press their scheme. The draft granted the proprietary additional Lenape lands north along the Delaware, "as far as a man could walk in a day and a half." Pretending that this was a valid treaty, the Penns persuaded four Delaware chiefs of their obligations to honor it. In 1737 the Penns hired three athletes—Solomon Jennings, Edward Marshall, and James Yates—to make the "walk" in record time. At 6:00 A.M. on the morning of September 19, these three "walkers" set out from Wrightstown Meeting House in Bucks County and made their way up through Plumstead, past "the head of the Perkiomen branch" to the Lehigh River, and continued into the Pocono Mountains. To aid them, underbrush was cut away and horses were provided to carry supplies and boats to ferry them across streams. As a result, this so-called "Walking Purchase" was stretched to cover sixty miles, twice the distance originally intended.

6. Ibid., 214–38. Once they lost their Pennsylvania lands in the late 1760s, the Delaware settled for years at a time along the Susquehanna River in central Pennsylvania, on the other side of the Allegheny Mountains in western Pennsylvania, and in Ohio. Disillusioned by the Revolutionary War, a band of Delaware broke from the main body and moved into Missouri, where they later took the name "Delaware Nation." During the nineteenth century, various bands of the Delaware Nation spent time in east Texas and Arkansas before settling in Anadarko in south central Oklahoma, where they continue to live today. The Delaware tribe, on the other hand, settled in Kansas on a two-million-acre parcel reserved for them by the federal government in the 1830s. In 1868 the U.S. government forced them to move to northeast Oklahoma, where they resettled on Cherokee Nation land. The Delaware tribe continues to live there today.

7. Richard H. Pratt, *Battlefield and Classroom: Four Decades with the American Indian, 1867–1904*, ed. Robert M. Utley (New Haven: Yale University Press, 1964), 10–11. The most noted of the twenty-five off-reservation boarding schools were Carlisle, Chilocco (Oklahoma), Chemawa (Oregon), and Haskell (Kansas).

8. Ibid., ix; Linda F. Witmer, *The Indian Industrial School: Carlisle, Pennsylvania, 1879–1918* (Carlisle: Cumberland County Historical Society, 1993), 1–2; James Wilson, *The Earth Shall Weep: A History of Native America* (New York: Grove Press, 1998), 289–329; and Elaine G. Eastman, *Pratt, the Red Man's Moses* (Norman: University of Oklahoma Press, 1935), which is considered the standard biography of Pratt.

9. Pratt, *Battlefield and Classroom*, 5.

10. Witmer, *Indian Industrial School*, 3–8.

11. Pratt, *Battlefield and Classroom*, 190.

12. Mary Lou Hultgren and Paulette Fairbanks Molin, *To Lead and to Serve: American Indian Education at Hampton Institute, 1878–1923* (Virginia Beach: Virginia Foundation for the Humanities and Public Policy, 1989), 17–22.

13. President Rutherford B. Hayes quoted ibid., 21.

14. Pratt, *Battlefield and Classroom*, 335.

15. Witmer, *Indian Industrial School*, 13–14.

16. Pratt, *Battlefield and Classroom*, 220.

17. Ibid., 222–23.

18. Witmer, *Indian Industrial School*, 24–29.

19. Standing Bear, *My People the Sioux*, 141.

20. Wilson, *Earth Shall Weep*, 315.

21. Merrill Gates, president of Mohonk Conference, quoted in Wilson, *Earth Shall Weep*, 315.

22. Witmer, *Indian Industrial School*, 29–33.

23. Pratt, *Battlefield and Classroom*, 311.

24. Adams, *Education for Extinction*, 157–62.

25. Pratt quoted in *The Indian Helper* (Carlisle student newspaper), March 18, 1898.

26. Powers-Beck, "'Chief,'" 521.

27. Charles A. Bender student file, record of graduates, Carlisle Indian Industrial School, file 1327, no. 5453, record group 75, National Archives and Records Administration, Washington, D.C.

28. See John Bender student file, ibid., folder 377; Mrs. Harris Sessions, "Charles and Elizabeth Bender," Bender player file, National Baseball Hall of Fame Museum and Library, Cooperstown, New York; and the *Carlisle Arrow*, April 9, 1915. Bender's other siblings, Anna, Emma, Elizabeth, Fred, and George, attended Hampton Institute in Virginia. See Paulette Molin to Genevieve Bell, August 5, 1996, Charles A. Bender file, Cumberland County Historical Society, Carlisle, Pennsylvania.

29. Powers-Beck, *American Indian Integration of Baseball*, 183.

30. Marianne Moore quoted in Robert Cantwell, "The Poet, the Bums, and the Legendary Red Men," *Sports Illustrated*, February 15, 1960, 76.

31. Bender, student file, Carlisle Indian Industrial School.

32. See Webster Grim, ed., *Bucks County, Pennsylvania, Directory* (Doylestown, Pa.: James D. Scott, 1898), 224, 228, 246, 247; see also *Federal Census, 1900* (Bucks County, Pennsylvania): vol. 47, dist. 18, p. 1, line 70; vol. 48, dist. 41, p. 2, line 56, and dist. 44, p. 4, line 48.

33. Bender quoted in Tholkes, "Bender—Early Years," 8–9. Carlisle had several Quaker connections. Alfred J. Standing, an English Quaker, recruited students and served as an assistant superintendent of the school between 1879 and 1899. Sisters Susan and Mary Anna Longstreth, Philadelphia Quakers, were prominent benefactors. In addition, Carlisle's outing system sent many students to Quaker families in southeastern Pennsylvania. See Witmer, *Indian Industrial School*, 39.

34. William C. Kashatus, "A King Crowns the World's Greatest Athlete," *Pennsylvania Heritage* (fall 1996): 34–35. Pratt had mixed feelings about fielding a football team. On the one hand, he understood and encouraged the importance of the sport for building school spirit and discipline. On the other hand, he feared the game's "accidental or intended violence." During the fall of 1890, when one of Carlisle's players returned from a game against Dickinson College with a broken leg, Pratt ended the football program. But the following year several students appealed to him to reinstate it, which he reluctantly agreed to do. See Pratt, *Battlefield and Classroom*, 46–47.

35. Powers-Beck, *American Indian Integration of Baseball*, 14, 33.

36. Bloom, *To Show What an Indian Can Do*, 37; and Philip Deloria, "'I Am of the Body': Thoughts on My Grandfather, Culture, and Sports," *South Atlantic Quarterly* 95, no. 2 (1996): 321.

37. Indian agent quoted in Bell, "Telling Stories Out of School," 146.

38. Powers-Beck, *American Indian Integration of Baseball*, 181–92. Carlisle also produced some ballplayers who enjoyed fine minor league careers, among them Bill Garlow, John Bender, William Newashe, Charles Guyon, and Joe Guyon.

39. *Carlisle Daily Herald*, April 15, 1901.

40. Ibid., May 2, 1901.

41. Powers-Beck, *American Indian Integration of Baseball*, 183.

42. *Carlisle Evening Sentinel*, April 21, 1902.

43. Bender, student file, Carlisle Indian Industrial School.

44. Powers-Beck, *American Indian Integration of Baseball*, 200.

45. "Carlisle Student Petition to Oato Bills," March 21, 1914, Linnen Report, Carlisle Indian School correspondence, 1914, record group 75, National Archives and Records Administration, Washington, D.C.

46. Powers-Beck, *American Indian Integration of Baseball*, 47–50. In fact, Bender returned to Carlisle after his first season with the Athletics to coach the baseball team in February and March before he had to report to spring training. See Carlisle Indian Industrial School newsletter, *Redman and Helper*, March 18, 1904.

47. Powers-Beck, *American Indian Integration of Baseball*, 183.

48. J. G. Taylor Spink, "A Long-Delayed Feather for the Chief," *Sporting News*, December 30, 1953.

49. Dillsburg Baseball Club to Mr. Chief Bender, September 22, 1942, National Baseball Hall of Fame Museum and Library, Cooperstown, New York.

50. Bender quoted in "Chief Bender Turns Back the Calendar—38 of 'Em," *Sporting News*, December 31, 1942.

51. Ibid., and Clendennen, "Minnesota's Greatest Baseball Player," 16.

CHAPTER 3

1. Lloyd M. Abernethy, "Progressivism, 1905–1919," in *Philadelphia: A 300-Year History*, ed. Russell F. Weigley (New York: W. W. Norton, 1982), 524–32.

2. Ibid., 537–48.

3. Lincoln Steffens, "Philadelphia: Corrupt and Contented," *McClure's Magazine* 21 (July 1903): 249.

4. Lieb, *Connie Mack,* 3–11.

5. Lee Allen, *The American League Story* (New York: Hill and Wang, 1965), 7.

6. John M. Rosenburg, *The Story of Baseball* (New York: Random House, 1970), 39–40.

7. David M. Jordan, *The Athletics of Philadelphia: Connie Mack's White Elephants, 1901–1954* (Jefferson, N.C.: McFarland, 1999), 15–16. Shibe purchased original investor Charles Somers's stock in the A's. Mack owned another 25 percent and two Philadelphia newspapermen, Frank Hough and Sam Jones, shared the remaining 25 percent.

8. Wilfred Sheed, "Manager: Mr. Mack and the Main Chance," in *The Ultimate Baseball Book,* ed. Daniel Okrent and Harris Lewine (Boston: Houghton Mifflin, 1981), 106.

9. Robert Warrington, "The Story of the 1902 American League Champion Athletics," *Along the Elephant Trail* (newsletter of the Philadelphia Athletics Historical Society) 6 (winter 2002): 4; and J. M. Murphy, "Napoleon Lajoie: Modern Baseball's First Superstar," *National Pastime* (spring 1988): 14–15. Mack continued to snare players from the Phillies just before the opening of the '02 season, when he lured right fielder and future Hall of Famer Elmer Flick, pitcher Bill Duggleby, and shortstop Monte Cross to his A's. Nor was Mack the only American League manager to raid the Phillies roster. The St. Louis Browns stole pitcher Red Donahue, who posted a 21–13 record in 1901, and Washington snared power-hitter Ed Delahanty, a future Hall of Famer, third baseman Harry Wolverton, and pitchers Jack Townsend and Al Orth, the latter a twenty-one-game winner in 1901.

10. Jordan, *Athletics of Philadelphia,* 19–20.

11. Warrington, "Story of the 1902 Champion Athletics," 4.

12. *Philadelphia Ball Club, Limited, v. Lajoie,* 202 Pa. 210, 217, 219, 221 (1902). Although Cross, Flick, and Duggleby weren't named in the litigation, the ruling also applied to them.

13. John McGraw quoted in Sheed, "Mr. Mack and the Main Chance," 108.

14. Jordan, *Athletics of Philadelphia,* 23–24; and Warrington, "Story of the 1902 Champion Athletics," 4. Fraser willingly returned to the National League.

15. Connie Mack quoted in *Philadelphia Public Ledger,* April 22, 1902.

16. Alan H. Levy, *Rube Waddell: The Zany, Brilliant Life of a Strikeout Artist* (Jefferson, N.C.: McFarland, 2000), 9–61.

17. Warrington, "Story of the 1902 Champion Athletics," 4–5.

18. Geoffrey C. Ward and Ken Burns, *Baseball: An Illustrated History* (New York: Knopf, 1994), 65–69; and G. Edward White, *Creating the National Pastime: Baseball Transforms Itself, 1903–1953* (Princeton: Princeton University Press, 1996), 60.

19. E. Suehsdorf, "Eddie Plank," in *The Ballplayers: Baseball's Ultimate Biographical Reference,* ed. Mike Shatzkin (New York: William Morrow, 1990), 873.

20. Connie Mack, quoted in Jack Kavanaugh, "Chief Bender," ibid., 68.

21. Bender quoted in J. G. Taylor Spink, "Albert Bender's Four Decades on the Mound," *Sporting News,* December 31, 1942.

22. Ibid.

23. Levy, *Rube Waddell*, 125; and Lieb, *Connie Mack*, 95.

24. Bender quoted in Spink, "Bender's Four Decades in the Mound."

25. Rick Wolff, ed., *The Baseball Encyclopedia*, 8th ed. (New York: Macmillan, 1990), 153–54.

26. Bender quoted in Spink, "Bender's Four Decades on the Mound."

27. "Athletics Win and Lose on Opening Day at Boston," *Philadelphia Inquirer*, April 21, 1903.

28. Bender quoted in Spink, "Bender's Four Decades on the Mound."

29. Rich Westcott, *Philadelphia's Old Ballparks* (Philadelphia: Temple University Press, 1996), 16.

30. "Bender's Benders Tie Up New York," *Philadelphia Inquirer*, April 28, 1903.

31. Louis Menand, *The Metaphysical Club: A Story of Ideas in America* (New York: Farrar, Straus and Giroux, 2001), 102–3.

32. Samuel G. Morton, *Crania Americana; or, A Comparative View of the Skulls of Various Aboriginal Nations of North and South America* (Philadelphia: J. Dobson, 1849), 5–7.

33. Menand, *Metaphysical Club*, 102–3. Morton was a mentor to such other self-styled anthropologists as Louis Agassiz, whose theories on race were enlisted by the Confederacy to prove the racial inferiority of African Americans during the Civil War.

34. "Daguerreotypes taken of former stars of the Diamond: Charles Albert (Chief) Bender," Bender file, National Baseball Hall of Fame Museum and Library, Cooperstown, New York.

35. Bender quoted in Spink, "Bender's Four Decades on the Mound."

36. Charles Dryden, "Big Chief Bender Loses Wampum Belt," *Philadelphia North American*, June 28, 1903.

37. Powers-Beck, *American Indian Integration of Baseball*, 74.

38. Charles Nelan, "Bender Hunting for His Wampum Belt in St. Louis," *Philadelphia North American*, June 28, 1903.

39. Wolff, *Baseball Encyclopedia*, 153.

40. Bender quoted in "Chief Bender Turns back Calendar—38 of 'Em," *Sporting News*, December 31, 1942.

41. "Pitcher Bender a Benedict," *Sporting Life*, October 15, 1904.

42. *Carlisle American Volunteer*, December 21, 1904.

43. Wolff, *Baseball Encyclopedia*, 157–58; and David Neft et al., *The Sports Encyclopedia: Baseball* (New York: Grossett and Dunlap, 1974), 32.

44. Neft et al., *Sports Encyclopedia*, 32.

45. "Big Chief Bender Tells His Most Successful Styles of Pitching the Ball," *Baseball Magazine* 7 (August 1911): 64.

46. Spink, "Bender's Four Decades on the Mound."

47. Levy, *Rube Waddell*, 179–80; and Robert Warrington, "The 1905 Athletics: American League Champions," *Along the Elephant Trail* 5 (fall 2001): 8.

48. Jordan, *Athletics of Philadelphia*, 33–34.

49. See "Big Chief Bender Put Two Games on Ice," *Philadelphia Inquirer*, October 6, 1905.

50. Charles Dryden, "Bender's Arm and Bat Win Two and Put Pennant Near," *Philadelphia North American*, October 6, 1905.

51. See "Grand Baseball Pennant Is Won by Athletics, the Defeat of Chicago Giving Them the Championship of the A.L.," *Philadelphia Inquirer*, October 7, 1905.

52. Wolff, *Baseball Encyclopedia*, 158.

53. See Albert G. Spaulding, *America's National Game* (New York, 1911), 189–90.

54. White, *Creating the National Pastime*, 86–89.

55. See Eliot Asinof, *Eight Men Out: The Black Sox Scandal and the 1919 World Series* (New York: Henry Holt, 1987), 207–8. The account of Waddell's game fixing was detailed in a 1920 newspaper interview by former Phillies president Horace Fogel.

56. Connie Mack quoted in Lieb, *Connie Mack*, 92–93.

57. Wolff, *Baseball Encyclopedia*, 2630; and Jordan, *Athletics of Philadelphia*, 35.

58. "Big Chief Bender, Mighty Pitcher, Leads Way to Victory for Athletics over New York," *Philadelphia Inquirer*, October 11, 1905.

59. Lieb, *Connie Mack*, 98–99.

60. "New York Wins Championship of World," *Philadelphia Inquirer*, October 15, 1905.

61. Charles Dryden, "New York Shut Out 3–0 by Athletics," *Philadelphia North American*, October 11, 1905.

62. "Big Chief Bender, Mighty Pitcher, Leads Way to Victory for Athletics over New York," *Philadelphia Inquirer*, October 11, 1905.

63. Charles Zuber, "Glory for Indian," *Sporting Life*, October 21, 1905.

64. Powers-Beck, *American Indian Integration of Baseball*, 73.

CHAPTER 4

1. Powers-Beck, *American Indian Integration of Baseball*, 22.

2. For biographical accounts of Sockalexis, see McDonald, *Indian Summer*; Fleitz, *Louis Sockalexis*; and Trina Wellman, *Louis Francis Sockalexis: The Life-Story of a Penobscot Indian* (Bangor, Me.: Department of Indian Affairs, 1975).

3. McDonald, *Indian Summer*, 240–41; David Nevard, "Wahooism in the U.S.A.," *Red Sox Journal* 11 (December 1995): 5; Powers-Beck, *American Indian Integration of Baseball*, 116, 175; and Staurowsky, "An Act of Honor or Exploitation?" Elmer Bates, a sportswriter for the *Sporting Life*, initially made the claim that Sockalexis's remarkable performance inspired Cleveland's fans to refer to the Spiders as the "Indians." See Elmer E. Bates, "Cleveland Chatter," *Sporting Life*, March 27, 1897, 3. Although team officials did not refer to Sockalexis when they adopted the Indian mascot in 1915, many writers claim that he was the inspiration for it.

4. John McGraw quoted in Nathan Aaseng, *American Indian Lives: Athletes* (New York: Facts on File, 1995), 2.

5. See "A Broken Idol," *Cleveland Daily Press*, July 31, 1897; "A Rumor of Family Troubles," *Cleveland Plain Dealer*, August 3, 1897; and "Does Wagner Want Him?" *Cleveland Plain Dealer*, August 6, 1897.

6. See "Drink Ruins a Great Player," *Nebraska State Journal*, June 11, 1908; and "Sockalexis, Fat and Lazy, Takes Ease in His Tribe," *Philadelphia North American*, August 4, 1912.

7. Powers-Beck, *American Indian Integration of Baseball*, 176.

8. Bender quoted in *Chicago Daily News*, October 19, 1910.

9. Lawrence Baldassaro and Richard A. Johnson, eds., *The American Game: Baseball and Ethnicity* (Carbondale: Southern Illinois University Press, 2002), 3–4.

10. It is interesting to note that African Americans were not the only racial group to be banned from professional baseball in the early twentieth century. In 1915 the Pacific Coast League turned away two Asian American players because of the objections of fans and other players. Similarly, dark-skinned Latinos were told to play in the Negro Leagues, though light-skinned Cubans and other Hispanics were invited to play in the white professional leagues. See Baldassaro and Johnson, *American Game*, 164, 177–78.

11. See Robert Peterson, *Only the Ball Was White* (Englewood Cliffs, N.J.: Prentice-Hall, 1970), 54. Comiskey quoted in Charles Alexander, *John McGraw* (New York: Penguin Books, 1988), 75–76.

12. Powers-Beck, *American Indian Integration of Baseball*, 72; and Kara Briggs and Dan Lewerenz, *Reading Red Report 2003: A Call for the News Media to Recognize Racism in Sports Team Nicknames and Mascots* (San Francisco: Native American Journalists' Association, 2003), 32. For nicknames as indicators of ethnicity, see Baldassaro and Johnson, *American Game*, 37–39, 41–48, 62–63, 122–25, 157–58.

13. Joseph Oxendine quoted in Powers-Beck, "'Chief,'" 510.

14. Powers-Beck, *American Indian Integration of Baseball*, 72. In later years Bender yielded to the public popularity of the nickname and signed autographs and even legal documents "Chief Bender."

15. Clendennen, "Minnesota's Greatest Baseball Player," 18.

16. Bender quoted in "Big Chief Bender, Mighty Pitcher," *Philadelphia Inquirer*, October 11, 1905.

17. "Big Chief Bender the Whole Show," ibid., May 6, 1906.

18. "Athletics Hammer Tannehill in 9th," ibid., May 9, 1906.

19. "Bender Pitches A's to victory, Fair Hiawatha Applauds Performance," *Philadelphia North American*, April 4, 1907.

20. "A Just Protest?" *Sporting Life*, April 6, 1907.

21. "Indian Pitcher Lays Aside Finance Story to Tell Experience," *St. Louis Post-Dispatch*, July 23, 1905.

22. Ibid.

23. "Chief's Mother-in-Law Says He's Just the Cheese," *Carlisle American Volunteer*, October 19, 1905.

24. Rube Oldring Jr., "Rube Oldring: The Pride of the Left Field Stands," *Along the Elephant Trail* 5 (winter 2001): 7.

25. Wolff, *Baseball Encyclopedia*, 1299–300.

26. Quotation from *Baseball Magazine* in Oldring Jr., "Rube Oldring," 7.

27. "Indian Pitcher Lays Aside Finance Story."

28. Rube Oldring Jr., interview by author, Bridgeton, New Jersey, December 21, 2004. See also Earl L. McCormick, "Dinner with the Chief," *South Jersey Magazine* (winter 1992): 49.

29. Jordan, *Athletics of Philadelphia*, 37.

30. Wolff, *Baseball Encyclopedia*, 160, 164.

31. Francis C. Richter, "Quaker Quips," *Sporting Life*, August 21, 1907.

32. Jordan, *Athletics of Philadelphia*, 38–40; and Westcott, *Philadelphia's Old Ballparks*, 23–24.

33. Mack quoted in "Bender Not Signed," *Carlisle Evening Sentinel*, February 25, 1909.

34. Jordan, *Athletics of Philadelphia*, 40–41. For player statistics, see Wolff, *Baseball Encyclopedia*, 173.

35. Mack, "The Stuff That Stars Are Made Of," *Saturday Evening Post*, April 27, 1912.

36. See Connie Mack, *My 66 Years in the Big Leagues* (Philadelphia: John C. Winston & Co., 1950), 196; and *Sporting News*, February 26, 1931. Mack's effort to protect Collins's amateur status was in vain. Interestingly, Columbia revoked Collins's eligibility not because of playing for the A's, which apparently was not discovered until years later, but for playing semipro ball at Plattsburg.

37. Jack Kavanagh, "Eddie Collins," in Shatzkin, *Ballplayers*, 209–10.

38. Mack, "Stuff That Stars Are Made Of."

39. Harvey Frommer, *Shoeless Joe and Ragtime Baseball* (Dallas: Taylor, 1992), 13; and David L. Fleitz, *Shoeless: The Life and Times of Joe Jackson* (Jefferson, N.C.: McFarland, 2001).

40. Robert Warrington, "Philly's Links to the Black Sox Scandal," *Along the Elephant Trail* 1 (spring 2001): 12.

41. Asinof, *Eight Men Out*, 56.

42. Douglas Wallop, *Baseball: An Informal History* (New York: Signet, 1969), 121.

43. Bruce Kuklick, *To Every Thing a Season: Shibe Park and Urban Philadelphia, 1909–1976* (Princeton: Princeton University Press, 1991), 39–41.

44. Emil Beck quoted in Westcott, *Philadelphia's Old Ballparks*, 16–17

45. Ibid., 18.

46. Ibid., 104.

47. Ibid., 105.

48. Ibid., 105–6; Kuklick, *To Every Thing a Season*, 53; and Lawrence S. Ritter, *Lost Ballparks: A Celebration of Baseball's Legendary Fields* (New York: Penguin Books, 1992), 178.

49. Westcott, *Philadelphia's Old Ballparks*, 108–10; and Kuklick, *To Every Thing a Season*, 29, 30.

50. Westcott, *Philadelphia's Old Ballparks*, 110.

51. William Weart, "Athletics Open Shibe Park with Sellout Crowd," *Evening Telegraph*, April 13, 1909; Horace Fogel, "Shibe Park, the Crowned Jewel of Baseball World," *Evening Bulletin*, April 13, 1909.

52. Jordan, *Athletics of Philadelphia*, 44–45.

53. Ibid., 45.

54. Wolff, *Baseball Encyclopedia*, 176.

55. Frommer, *Shoeless Joe*, 20; and Asinof, *Eight Men Out*, 56–57.

56. Jordan, *Athletics of Philadelphia*, 45; Lieb, *Connie Mack*, 127–28.

57. Jordan, *Athletics of Philadelphia*, 46.

58. Mack quoted in Wallop, *Baseball: An Informal History*, 144–45.

59. Wolff, *Baseball Encyclopedia*, 1673.

60. Billy Evans quoted in Aaseng, *American Indian Lives*, 5.

61. Wolff, *Baseball Encyclopedia*, 1673.

62. Connie Mack quoted in "Chief Bender Dies," *New York Times*, May 23, 1954.

63. Mack, "Stuff the Stars Are Made Of."

CHAPTER 5

1. Spink, "A Long-Delayed Feather for the Chief."

2. "Pitcher Bender a Benedict," *Sporting Life*, October 15, 1904.

3. Tholkes, "Chief Bender—Early Years," 8.

4. Charles A. Bender, "Record of Graduates and Returned Students, U.S. Indian School, Carlisle, Pennsylvania," Bender student records, file 1327, no. 5453, record group 75, National Archives and Records Administration, Washington, D.C.

5. According to one legend, the $100,000 Infield got its name when a sportswriter asked Mack if he would part with the four infielders if he was offered $100,000. Mack supposedly replied, "I'd turn it down. I wouldn't take $100,000 for my infielders." See Mac Davis, *Baseball's All-Time Greats*. (New York: Grosset and Dunlap), 26.

6. Lowell Reidenbaugh, *Baseball's 25 Greatest Teams* (St. Louis: Sporting News, 1988), 223.

7. Lieb, *Connie Mack*, 125.

8. Reidenbaugh, *Baseball's 25 Greatest Teams*, 219.

9. Mack quoted in Lieb, *Connie Mack*, 126.

10. Ibid.

11. Mack quoted in Lieb, *Connie Mack*, 129.

12. Rob Neyer and Eddie Epstein, *Baseball Dynasties* (New York: W. W. Norton, 2000), 46.

13. William B. Mead and Paul Dickson, *Baseball: The President's Game* (New York: Walker and Co., 1997), 24–25.

14. Reidenbaugh, *Baseball's 25 Greatest Teams*, 221.

15. "Bender Wins No-Hit Game by 4–0 Score," *Philadelphia Inquirer*, May 13, 1910.

16. Oldring quoted in Spink, "A Long-Delayed Feather for the Chief."

17. Ibid.

18. Bender quoted in Spink, "Albert Bender's Four Decades on the Mound."

19. Bender quoted in "Bender Wins No-Hit Game by 4–0 Score."

20. Wolff, *Baseball Encyclopedia*, 1673.

21. "Chief Bender, Hall of Fame Pitcher, Dies," *New York Herald Tribune*, May 24, 1954.

22. Ty Cobb quoted in Neyer and Epstein, *Baseball Dynasties*, 47.

23. Bender quoted in Billy Evans, "Pitchers' Greatest Requisite Control," *Baseball Magazine* 4 (December 1913): 62.

24. Ibid.

25. Ibid.

26. Bender quoted in Aaseng, *American Indian Lives*, 6.
27. Ibid.
28. Lieb, *Connie Mack*, 131.
29. Mack quoted ibid., 125.
30. Neyer and Epstein, *Baseball Dynasties*, 59–60.
31. Mack quoted in Lieb, *Connie Mack*, 132.
32. Reidenbaugh, *Baseball's 25 Greatest Teams*, 221.
33. Ibid. The October 1, 1910, appearance was Russell's first and last as a major leaguer.
34. Ibid., 223.
35. "Clippings Aid Bender to Win," *Chicago Record Herald*, May 3, 1914.
36. Jimmy Isaminger, "Bender Heroic," *Philadelphia Inquirer*, October 18, 1910.
37. Ibid.
38. "Bender Hurls A's Past Cubs," *Chicago Daily News*, October 19, 1910.
39. "Bender's Great Work," *Carlisle Evening Sentinel*, October 19, 1910.
40. Frederick Lieb, "1910 World Series—A Commentary," in *The 1910 Chicago Cubs World Series Program*, vol. 42 (reprint, Santa Clara, Calif.: RDO Publications, 1984).
41. Eddie Collins Jr., interview by author, Kennett Square, Pennsylvania, July 12, 1995.
42. Eddie Joost, interview by author, Santa Rosa, California, December 23, 2004.
43. Neyer and Epstein, *Baseball Dynasties*, 56.
44. Mack quoted in Lieb, *Connie Mack*, 146–47.
45. Neyer and Epstein, *Baseball Dynasties*, 62.
46. Ibid., 54. The introduction of the cork-centered baseball in 1911 is credited with the significant increase in run production between 1910 and 1911. There was a jump from 7.28 to 9.21 runs scored per game, or a 26.5 percent increase, in the American League. In the National League, the increase was more modest, from 8.06 to 8.84 runs per game, a 9.6 percent increase.
47. Frank Baker quoted in Reidenbaugh, *Baseball's 25 Greatest Teams*, 224.
48. Stuffy McInnis quoted ibid., 225.
49. See "Caught on the Fly," *Sporting Life*, October 7, 1911; and "John Bender Dies in Baseball Game," *Carlisle Evening Sentinel*, September 30, 1911.
50. Warren Goldstein, "Chief Bender," *Encyclopedia of North American Indians*, ed. Frederick E. Hoxie (Boston: Houghton Mifflin, 1992), 58.
51. "Chief Bender Turns Back Calendar—38 of 'Em," *Sporting News*, December 31, 1942.
52. Frederick Lieb, "1911 World Series—A Commentary," in *The Great World Series Program Collection*, vol. 20 (reprint, San Jose, Calif.: RDO Publications, 1981).
53. Jordan, *Athletics of Philadelphia*, 53.
54. Lieb, *Connie Mack*, 151.
55. Ibid.
56. Aaseng, *American Indian Lives*, 7–8.
57. Powers-Beck, *American Indian Integration of Baseball*, 76–86.
58. Richter quoted in Eric Enders, *100 Years of the World Series* (New York: Barnes and Noble Books, 2000), 30.

59. Christy Mathewson, *Pitching in a Pinch* (New York: Dodd, Mead, 1912), 58.

60. Enders, *100 Years of the World Series*, 30.

61. Lieb, *Connie Mack*, 155.

62. Ibid., 154.

63. "Chief Bender Signal Tipper," *Philadelphia Inquirer*, October 22, 1911.

64. Lieb, "1911 World Series—A Commentary."

65. Chief Meyers quoted in Lawrence S. Ritter, *The Glory of Their Times: The Story of the Early Days of Baseball Told by the Men Who Played It* (New York: Vintage Books, 1985), 180–81.

66. Cy Morgan quoted in L. E. Sanborn, "Chief Bender's Keen Eyes Athletics' Signal Detector," *Sporting Life*, April 6, 1912, 4.

67. Enders, *100 Years of the World Series*, 32.

68. Lieb, *Connie Mack*, 158–59.

69. James A. Isaminger, "World Series Echo," *Sporting Life*, March 9, 1917.

70. Jordan, *Athletics of Philadelphia*, 55.

71. Wolff, *Baseball Encyclopedia*, 1673.

72. "Chief Bender Turns Back Clock," *Sporting News*, December 31, 1942.

73. Kuklick, *To Every Thing a Season*, 41.

74. Mack, *My 66 Years in the Big Leagues*, 50.

75. Mack quoted in "The Fallen Stars of the 1912 Season," *Philadelphia Telegraph*, September 21, 1912.

76. Robert Warrington, "The 1913 World Champion Athletics," *Along the Elephant Trail* 7, no. 6 (2003): 5.

77. Jordan, *Athletics of Philadelphia*, 58–59.

78. Neyer and Epstein, *Baseball Dynasties*, 58. Coombs contracted typhoid fever at the A's spring-training camp. He appeared to recover early that season and rejoined the team briefly. Suffering a relapse, he returned home to Maine, where he was diagnosed with spinal typhoid, a condition that is generally fatal. Coombs spent months confined to the hospital. He eventually recovered and pitched a few games for the A's in 1914. Released by the club the following season, he signed with the Brooklyn Dodgers and won a total of forty-three games over the next four seasons before retiring in 1918.

79. Jordan, *Athletics of Philadelphia*, 60.

80. Harold Seymour, *Baseball: The Golden Age* (New York: Oxford University Press, 1971), 82.

81. "Giants Humbled by Athletics," *Odanah Star*, October 8, 1913.

82. See Bill Crawford, *All American: The Rise and Fall of Jim Thorpe* (New York: John Wiley and Sons, 2004). While Thorpe could run the bases well and play the outfield with above-average skill, he had great difficulty hitting. During five seasons in New York, he played in a total of just 117 games and hit a paltry .190. "I felt like a sitting hen, not a ballplayer," Thorpe complained. Never the star performer he was on the gridiron or track, the Olympic gold medalist played for several minor league teams, his last official game coming in 1928 when he was forty.

83. Chief Meyers quoted in *New York American*, May 25, 1913.

84. Ed A. Goewey quoted in *Leslie's Illustrated Weekly*, November 13, 1913.

85. Frederick Lieb, "1913 World Series: A Commentary," *The Great World Series Program Collection*, vol. 26 (reprint, San Jose, Calif.: Robert D. Opie, 1982).

86. Ibid.

87. Mack quoted in "Clean Living and Quick Thinking," *McClure's Magazine* 43 (May 1914): 61–62.

88. Grantland Rice, *The Tumult and the Shouting: My Life in Sport* (New York: A. S. Barnes, 1954), 227.

89. Lieb, "1913 World Series: A Commentary."

90. Wolff, *Baseball Encyclopedia*, 1673.

91. Bender quoted in "Indian Pitcher Lays Aside Finance Story to Tell Experience," *St. Louis Post-Dispatch*, July 23, 1905.

CHAPTER 6

1. Associated Press Biographical Service, "Biographical Sketch of Charles Bender" (May 15, 1942), National Baseball Hall of Fame Museum and Library, Cooperstown, New York; and Powers-Beck, *American Indian Integration of Baseball*, 53. Ty Cobb, Detroit's star outfielder, was earning $12,000 a year in 1914, and Pittsburgh shortstop Honus Wagner was earning $10,000. See Ward and Burns, *Baseball: An Illustrated History*, 122–23.

2. Mack quoted in "Bender Not Signed," *Carlisle Sentinel*, February 25, 1909.

3. Ibid.

4. Wolff, *Baseball Encyclopedia*, 1673.

5. White, *Creating the National Pastime*, 49.

6. "Bender Calls Braves 'Bush Leaguers,'" *Philadelphia North American*, October 12, 1914.

7. Gene Schoor, *The History of the World Series* (New York: William Morrow, 1990), 57–58; and Enders, *100 Years of the World Series*, 39.

8. "Athletics at 10 to 6 in Wall Street Betting," *Boston Globe*, October 9, 1914.

9. John I. Taylor, "Former Red Sox President Sees Walkover for Athletics," *Boston Globe*, October 8, 1914.

10. Frank Hough, "A's Favored on Past Performances," *Philadelphia Inquirer*, October 5, 1914.

11. Ty Cobb, "A Slowball Pitcher Best Against Athletics, Says Cobb," *Philadelphia Public Ledger*, October 8, 1914; and Cobb, "Boston Surprised National League; Will They Surprise the Athletics?" *Philadelphia Public Ledger*, October 9, 1914.

12. Johnny Evers and George Stallings quoted in George Young, "Stallings Thinks Braves Will Surprise Athletics," *Philadelphia Public Ledger*, October 8, 1914.

13. T. H. Murnane, "Mack Threatened by Braves Chief," *Boston Globe*, October 9, 1914.

14. "Stallings in Scrap; Calls Bluff by Fan," *Boston American*, October 9, 1914.

15. *Philadelphia Public Ledger*, October 2, 1914.

16. "Far Greatest Rush for World Series Tickets Ever Seen," *Philadelphia Public Ledger*, October 8, 1914.

17. "Baseball Scalpers Released by Judge," *Philadelphia North American*, October 9, 1914.

18. "Police Are Accused in Ticket Scandal," *Boston American*, October 9, 1914.

19. T. H. Murnane, "Mack Threatened by Braves Chief," *Boston Globe*, October 9, 1914.

20. "Story of the 1914 World's Series," *The Reach Official American League Baseball Guide* (New York: Reach Sporting Goods, 1915), 101.

21. Ibid.

22. O'Leary, "First Game in Series Won By Braves, 7–1," *Boston Globe*, October 9, 1914.

23. Ibid.

24. "Story of the 1914 World's Series," 101.

25. Ibid.

26. George M. Young, "Boston Easily Defeats Athletics by 7–1 Score," *Philadelphia Public Ledger*, October 10, 1914. See also "Bender Knocked Out of Game One, A's lose, 7–1," *Philadelphia Inquirer*, October 10, 1914.

27. Mack quoted in Lieb, *Connie Mack*, 177.

28. James C. Isaminger, "Bender Falls to Savage Onslaught of Stallings' Men," *Philadelphia North American*, October 10, 1914.

29. George Stallings quoted in "Braves Slamming of Bender Surprised George Stallings," *Boston Globe*, October 10, 1914.

30. "A's down 2–0 to Braves; Series Moved to Boston," *Philadelphia Inquirer*, October 11, 1914; T. H. Murnane, "Greatest of All World Series Games Is Won and Saved in the Ninth," *Boston Globe*, October 11, 1914.

31. "Story of the 1914 World's Series," 103.

32. James C. Isaminger, "Young Pitcher Will Be Mack Choice in Third Title Clash," *Philadelphia North American*, October 12, 1914; and Walter E. Hapgood, "Braves, Sensation of Baseball World, Out-Hit the A's," *Boston Herald*, October 12, 1914. One explanation for Bender's poor performance is that in all previous World Series games he pitched on overcast days, when it was more difficult to see and hit his fastball and nickel curve. But Game One of the 1914 Series was bright and sunny, taking away that advantage. After Bender lost the opening game, Ty Cobb, in a ghostwritten column, predicted that the Chief's defeat "practically eliminates him" from pitching in any more of the games, unless "it would be on a cloudy day." See Ty Cobb, "Athletics Not Only Outbatted, but Outguessed," *Philadelphia Public Ledger*, October 10, 1914.

33. "Boston Defeats Athletics for Third Time, 5–4," *Philadelphia Inquirer*, October 13, 1914.

34. Ty Cobb, "Spirit of Overconfidence Beat Athletics," *Philadelphia Public Ledger*, October 14, 1914.

35. Richard A. Johnson, *Boston Braves* (Charleston, S.C.: Arcadia, 2001), 30.

36. Cobb, "Spirit of Overconfidence Beat Athletics."

37. Rube Bressler quoted in Ritter, *Glory of Their Times*, 199–200.

38. Benjamin Shibe quoted in *Philadelphia Inquirer*, October 15, 1914.

39. See "Cupid Strikes Out 'Bullet Joe' Bush," *Philadelphia Inquirer*, October 11, 1914; "Hard Luck," ibid., October 15, 1914; and John Foster, "Why A's Lost the Series," *Spaulding Baseball Guide* (spring 1915): 3–6.

40. Connie Mack quoted in *Philadelphia Bulletin*, October 14, 1914; and *Philadelphia Inquirer*, October 15, 1914.

41. For suspicions of game fixing and the 1914 Word Series, see Sheed, "Mr. Mack and the Main Chance," 108; Kuklick, *To Every Thing a Season*, 49; Frederick Ivor-Campbell, "Team Histories," in *Total Baseball*, ed. John Thorn and Pete Palmer (New York: Warner Books, 1989), 80; Daniel E. Ginsburg, *The Fix Is In: A History of Gambling and Game-Fixing Scandals* (Jefferson, N.C.: McFarland, 1995), 83; Jordan, *Athletics of Philadelphia*, 69–70; and Warrington, "Philly's Links to the Black Sox Scandal," 1, 12–13. Warrington persuaded me to write this book by making an especially strong case for a "corrupted" World Series. Many of the arguments in this chapter were originally identified by him in a letter to me of October 15, 2003.

42. For statistics, see Thorn and Palmer, *Total Baseball*, 124, 767.

43. Mack, *My 66 Years in the Big Leagues*, 35–36.

44. Mack quoted in Lieb, *Connie Mack*, 173–83.

45. Spaulding, *America's National Game*, 189–90.

46. White, *Creating the National Pastime*, 86–88; and Ginsburg, *Fix Is In*, 52–99. The three incidents of alleged game fixing involved (1) John W. Taylor, a pitcher for the Chicago Cubs, who was accused of taking $500 to lose games in the city series against the White Sox in 1904; (2) John McGraw, manager of the New York Giants, who was accused of bribing players on the Boston Braves and Philadelphia Phillies to lose to his team in 1908; and (3) suspicious play on the part of the St. Louis Browns during the last regular-season games—a doubleheader against the Cleveland Indians—in 1910. The suspicious play resulted in Napoleon Lajoie of the Indians beating out Ty Cobb of the Detroit Tigers for the American League batting championship. The belief was that the St. Louis players hated Cobb so much that they purposely allowed Lajoie to win the title by getting eight hits in nine at-bats, six of which were bunt singles.

47. White, *Creating the National Pastime*, 88.

48. "Bender Goes to Baltimore," *Carlisle Evening Sentinel*, December 8, 1914; "Bender Joins Feds," *Philadelphia North American*, September 25, 1915; and Jordan, *Athletics of Philadelphia*, 70. Bender's Federal League contract was called a "square-deal" contract in which the player is guaranteed a salary and a position for the term of the pact with no ten-day clause to save the owner if he finds he made a bad bargain. A year later, in 1915, the owner of the Baltimore Terrapins, disgusted with Bender's poor 4–16 record, released the Indian hurler and refused to pay the $7,500 balance of the square deal. See "Bender Enters Suit," *Sporting Life*, October 2, 1915.

49. Mack, *My 66 Years in the Big Leagues*, 35–36.

50. James Isaminger, "Bender Released by Federal League," *Philadelphia North American*, September 25, 1915.

51. Ibid.

52. For World Series shares, see "Each Player's Share," *Philadelphia North American*, October 14, 1914.

53. Jordan, *Athletics of Philadelphia*, 70. After the 1914 Series ended, A's pitcher Bob Shawkey was quoted as saying that both Bender and Plank were "bothered a whole lot with rheumatism and will probably never pitch winning ball in the American League again."

54. Eddie Collins to Grantland Rice, quoted in Aaseng, *American Indian Lives*, 4–5.

55. Collins interview.

56. Mack, *My 66 Years in the Big Leagues*, 35–36; and Lieb, *Connie Mack*, 181–82.

57. Neyer and Epstein, *Baseball Dynasties*, 60–61; and Wallop, *Baseball: An Informal History*, 148–49.

58. Jordan, *Athletics of Philadelphia*, 69.

59. Mack, *My 66 Years in the Big Leagues*, 36.

60. Jordan, *Athletics of Philadelphia*, 75–77.

61. Bender quoted in *Philadelphia Inquirer*, December 6, 1914.

62. Bender quoted in Spink, "Bender's Four Decades on the Mound."

CHAPTER 7

1. "Mack Asks Waivers on Bender and Plank," *Philadelphia Public Ledger*, November 1, 1914.

2. "Chief Bender Turns Back Calendar—38 of 'Em," *Sporting News*, December 31, 1942.

3. "Big Shake Up for Mackmen," *Philadelphia Public Ledger*, November 2, 1914.

4. Jordan, *Athletics of Philadelphia*, 71.

5. Mark Millikin, "Home Run Baker—A Take of a Local Baseball Legend at His Peak," *Charlestown (Md.) Star Democrat*, April 12, 2000; and Rich Pagano, *The Delaware County Baseball League: The Early Years* (Aston, Pa.: Delco Baseball League, 2004), 8–9.

6. Mack, *My 66 Years in the Big Leagues*, 36.

7. Collins interview.

8. Jordan, *Athletics of Philadelphia*, 69.

9. William C. Kashatus, *Connie Mack's '29 Triumph: The Rise and Fall of the Philadelphia Athletics Dynasty.* (Jefferson, N.C.: McFarland, 1999), 159–70.

10. Neyer and Epstein, *Baseball Dynasties*, 49.

11. James C. Isaminger, "Chief Bender Released by Baltimore Feds," *Philadelphia North American*, September 25, 1915.

12. Harold Seymour, *Baseball: The Golden Age*, paperback ed. (New York: Oxford University Press, 1989), 199–212; and White, *Creating the National Pastime*, 65–66.

13. Seymour, *Baseball: The Golden Age*, 217–18; James H. Bready, *Baseball in Baltimore: The First 100 Years* (Baltimore: Johns Hopkins University Press, 1998), 125–30.

14. "Bender Goes to Baltimore," *Carlisle Evening Sentinel*, December 8, 1914; and Bready, *Baseball in Baltimore*, 126–28.

15. Seymour, *Baseball: The Golden Age*, 219.

16. Bender quoted in "Bender's Praise for the Federal League," *Philadelphia North American*, May 8, 1915.

17. Bender quoted in Spink, "Albert Bender's Four Decades on the Mound."

18. Bender quoted in "Men 40 Can Play Ball, Says Chief Bender," Associated Press article, December 10, 1923, Charles Albert Bender player file, National Baseball Hall of Fame Museum and Library, Cooperstown, New York.

19. Powers-Beck, *American Indian Integration of Baseball*, 75–76.

20. See "Chief Bender Hurt," *Carlisle Evening Sentinel*, November 16, 1914; "Chief Bender in Crash," *New York World Telegram*, November 29, 1917; and "Chief Bender Faces Big Suit," *New York World Telegram*, February 27, 1919.

21. Carroll W. Rasin, president, Baltimore Terrapins, to Charles A. Bender, August 30, 1915. Bender file, National Baseball Hall of Fame Museum and Library, Cooperstown, New York.

22. "Bender Enters Suit Against Federal League," *Sporting Life*, October 2, 1915.

23. Bender quoted in Grantland Rice, "Bender Not Quite Done," *Baseball Magazine* (September 1915): 8.

24. Rich Westcott and Frank Bilovsky, *The Phillies Encyclopedia*, 3d ed. (Philadelphia: Temple University Press, 2004), 33, 424.

25. Ibid., 34.

26. Bender quoted in Spink, "Bender's Four Decades on the Mound."

27. Pagano, *Delaware County Baseball League*, 10.

28. Paulette Molin to Genevieve Bell, August 5, 1996, Bender File, Cumberland County Historical Society, Carlisle, Pennsylvania; and Mrs. Harris Sessions, "Charles and Elizabeth Bender" (manuscript), National Baseball Hall of Fame Museum and Library, Cooperstown, New York.

29. "Indian Named Mother of the Year," Associated Press article, April 28, 1950, Bender player file, National Baseball Hall of Fame Museum and Library, Cooperstown, New York.

30. Ibid.

31. Bender quoted in Spink, "Bender's Four Decades on the Mound."

32. Frank V. Phelps, "Bender," in *Biographical Dictionary of American Sports*, ed. David L. Porter (New York: Greenwood Press, 1987), 33–34; and Clendennen, "Minnesota's Greatest Baseball Player," 16.

33. Phelps, "Bender," 33–34; Dan Daniel, "Daniel's Dope," *New York Telegram*, December 12, 1930; and "Pitches His Wigwam on Coogan's Bluff," *New York Times*, December 18, 1930.

34. Neil J. Sullivan, *The Minors: The Struggles and the Triumph of Baseball's Poor Relation from 1876 to the Present* (New York: St. Martin's Press, 1990), 67–230. Sullivan argues that from 1920 to 1945 the minor leagues flourished despite the major leagues' attempt to bully and subordinate them by capitalizing on their own big-city markets and consolidating their power in a gradually evolving governance hierarchy.

35. Bender quoted in Spink, "Bender's Four Decades on the Mound."

36. "Bender Will Pitch and Manage New Haven Team, While Meyers Will Catch," Associated Press article, February 20, 1920, Bender player file, National Baseball Hall of Fame Museum and Library, Cooperstown, New York.

37. "Daguerreotypes: Charles Albert (Chief) Bender," October 21, 1937, ibid.

38. Bender quoted in Spink, "Bender's Four Decades on the Mound."

39. Phelps, "Bender," 33–34; "Daguerreotype: Chief Bender"; and William Braucher, "Chief Bender Tries to Lift Erie Team," *New York Times*, May 16, 1932.

40. Edward C. Burbauer, "Chief Bender Is Fired and Re-hired by Erie within Span of Few Hours," *Philadelphia Bulletin*, August 4, 1932.

41. "Chief Bender Sues House of David," *Carlisle Evening Sentinel*, August 2, 1934; and "Chief Bender Sues Bewhiskered Nine," *New York World Telegram*, August 4, 1934.

42. Charles Bender, "Baseball Players as Shooters," essay, March 6, 1915, Bender player file, National Baseball Hall of Fame Museum and Library, Cooperstown, New York.

43. "Ballplayers Hit 'Em with a Gun," *American Shooter*, January 1, 1916, 33, 44.

44. Earl L. McCormick, "Dinner with the Chief," *South New Jersey Magazine* (winter 1992): 51–52.

45. See advertisement for "Chief Bender Sporting Goods Company," *Philadelphia Public Ledger*, May 9, 1915.

46. See *Grantee Index to Deeds, Cumberland County, Pennsylvania*, vol. 8D, 325; vol. 8Q, 329; vol. 9W, 258; vol. 12A, 37; vol. 12B, 200; vol. 12D, 187; vol. 12M, 108; and vol. 14G, 348, Cumberland County Historical Society, Carlisle, Pennsylvania.

47. Powers-Beck, *American Indian Integration of Baseball*, 48–49.

48. Ibid., 49.

49. Witmer, *Indian Industrial School*, 82, 88–89.

50. "Welcome Planned for Chief Bender," *Carlisle Evening Sentinel*, August 25, 1930.

51. Senator Leon Prince quoted in "Chief Bender, Indian School Student, Here After Thirty Years," ibid., August 28, 1930.

52. "Fans Declare Bender Game Season's Best," ibid., August 29, 1930.

53. Bender quoted in "Chief Bender, Indian School Student, Here After Thirty Years."

CHAPTER 8

1. Bender quoted in Spink, "Albert Bender's Four Decades on the Mound."

2. Kashatus, *Connie Mack's '29 Triumph*, 147–70.

3. Jordan, *Athletics of Philadelphia*, 135.

4. Lieb, *Connie Mack*, 268.

5. Ibid., 273–74.

6. Jordan, *Athletics of Philadelphia*, 151–63.

7. Harry Robert, "The Philadelphia Athletics," *Sport Magazine* (February 1951): 28.

8. Mack quoted in "Mack Retires from Athletics," *Philadelphia Bulletin*, October 18, 1950.

9. "Chief Bender to Coach for Macks," *Philadelphia Inquirer*, November 15, 1950.

10. Joost interview.

11. Wolff, *Baseball Encyclopedia*, 2196.

12. Mack, *My 66 Years in the Big Leagues*, 169.

13. Wolff, *Baseball Encyclopedia*, 2196.

14. Bobby Shantz, interview by author, Ambler, Pennsylvania, December 15, 2004.

15. Bobby Shantz to Chief Bender, September 4, 1952, quoted in "Prize Pupil Shantz Paid Glowing Tribute to Chief," *Sporting News*, December 30, 1953.

16. Lester McCrabb, interview by author, New Holland, Pennsylvania, December 20, 2004.

17. "Chief Bender, Hall of Fame Pitcher, Dies," *New York Herald Tribune*, May 24, 1954.

18. Oldring interview.

19. Joost interview.

20. Oldring interview.

21. Powers-Beck, *American Indian Integration of Baseball*, 68.

22. Bender quoted in "Chief Bender Answers Call to Happy Hunting Grounds," *Sporting News*, June 2, 1954.

23. Art Morrow, "Bender, Mack's Greatest Money Pitcher, Gets Some of It in Gifts," *New York Times*, September 5, 1952.

24. Bender quoted in Spink, "A Long-Delayed Feather for the Chief."

25. National Baseball Hall of Fame Museum and Library, *National Baseball Hall of Fame and Museum* (Cooperstown, N.Y.: National Baseball Hall of Fame and Museum, 1975), 37; and Robert Warrington, "Charles Albert 'Chief' Bender: A Biographical Profile," *Native American Casino Magazine* (November 2003), available from the Philadelphia Athletics Historical Society, Bender player file. Others elected with Bender in 1953 were Dizzy Dean, Al Simmons, Ed Barrow, Harry Wright, Bobby Wallace, and umpires Tom Connolly and Bill Klem. Unfortunately, there are those baseball historians who believe that Bender was a "marginal Hall of Famer, given that he won only 210 games in his career and he won 20 or more games in only two seasons." They also argue that "by the standards of his era, Bender simply wasn't very durable and he was washed up at the age of thirty-one." See Neyer and Epstein, *Baseball Dynasties*, 50.

26. Sid C. Keener to Charles A. Bender, April 28, 1954, Bender player file, National Baseball Hall of Fame Museum and Library, Cooperstown, New York.

27. Joost interview.

28. "Chief Bender Answers Call to Happy Hunting Grounds."

29. "Chief Bender, Hall of Fame Pitcher, Dies."

30. "Chief Bender Burial," *Philadelphia Inquirer*, May 28, 1954. After the 1954 season the Athletics left Philadelphia for Kansas City, eventually relocating in Oakland, California.

31. "Chief Bender Answers Call to Happy Hunting Grounds."

32. Sid. C. Keener to Mrs. Bender, August 19, 1954, Bender player file, National Baseball Hall of Fame Museum and Library, Cooperstown, New York.

33. Baseball Hall of Fame Museum and Library, *National Baseball Hall of Fame and Museum*, 37.

34. Mrs. Chief Bender to Mr. Keener, Aug. 17, 1954, Bender player file, National Baseball Hall of Fame Museum and Library, Cooperstown, New York.

CHAPTER 9

1. Bob Warrington quoted in Dan Miller, "Pitcher Comes Home, Indian School Athlete Gets Major-League Honor," *Harrisburg (Pa.) Sunday Patriot News*, October 19, 2003.

2. See Edward J. Rielly, "The American Indian in America's National Pastime," paper delivered at the sixteenth annual Cooperstown Symposium on Baseball and American Culture, June 4, 2004, National Baseball Hall of Fame Museum and Library, Cooperstown, New York. Rielly argues that baseball at the turn of the century presented many opportunities as well as difficulties in the assimilation of Native Americans. As a result, the game can be considered "both an indictment and reason for being called the national pastime."

3. Lawrence Baldassaro and Richard A. Johnson, eds., *The American Game: Baseball and Ethnicity* (Carbondale: Southern Illinois University Press, 2002). This collection of nine essays examines the various ethnic and racial groups that entered major league baseball in the twentieth century. The specific groups examined are African Americans, Anglo-Americans, Asian Americans, German Americans, Irish Americans, Italian Americans, Jewish Americans, Latin Americans, and Slavic Americans.

4. Powers-Beck, *American Indian Integration of Baseball*, 177–80. Powers-Beck provides a complete list of both American Indian major league players and major league players of American Indian ancestry who played between 1897 and 1945.

5. Deloria, *Indians in Unexpected Places*, 13. Deloria argues that this "window of opportunity" closed in 1934 with the Indian Reorganization Act, which gave Native Americans "a small measure of political autonomy, which they continued to build on throughout the twentieth century" (237).

6. Ibid., 120–22. Baseball's obsession with the Indian manifested itself in the adoption of caricatures like "Chief Wahoo," the mascot of the Cleveland Indians, and "Chief Knock-a-homo," the mascot of the Atlanta Braves. These mascots perpetuate stereotypes that damage the dignity and self-respect of Native Americans. See Powers-Beck, *American Indian Integration of Baseball*, 169–76; Nevard, "Wahooism in the U.S.A.," 1–4; and Briggs and Lewerenz, *Reading Red Report*, 2003.

7. Powers-Beck, *American Indian Integration of Baseball*, 176.

8. For a definition of "tragedy," see F. R. Adrados, *Festival, Comedy, and Tragedy* (London: Brill Academic Publishers, 1975); Peter D. Arnott, *An Introduction to the Greek Theatre* (Bloomington: Indiana University Press, 1959); and D. Masters Bain, *Servants and Others in Greek Tragedy* (Chapel Hill: University of North Carolina Press, 1981).

9. Connie Mack quoted in "Chief Bender Dies," *New York Times*, May 23, 1954.

10. Aaseng, *American Indian Lives*, 3.

11. Bender quoted in "Men 40 Can Play Ball," *New York Times*, December 10, 1923.

12. See Barbara Helen Hill, "Home: Urban and Reservation," in *Genocide of the Mind: New Native American Writing*, ed. MariJo Moore (New York: Thunder's Mouth Press, 2003), 22.

13. See Vine Deloria Jr., "Foreword," in Moore, *Genocide of the Mind*, xii–xiii.

SELECTED BIBLIOGRAPHY

Adams, David Wallace. *Education for Extinction: American Indians and the Boarding School Experience, 1875–1928*. Lawrence: University Press of Kansas, 1995.

Bloom, John. *To Show What an Indian Can Do: Sports at Native American Boarding Schools*. Minneapolis: University of Minnesota Press, 2000.

Cantwell, Robert. "The Poet, the Bums, and the Legendary Red Men." *Sports Illustrated*, February 15, 1960, 74–84.

Clendennen, Gary W. "Minnesota's Greatest Baseball Player." *Minnesota Monthly Magazine* (August 1983): 15–18, 25.

Deloria, Philip J. *Indians in Unexpected Places*. Lawrence: University Press of Kansas, 2004.

Ginsburg, Daniel E. *The Fix Is In: A History of Baseball Gambling and Game Fixing Scandals*. Jefferson, N.C.: McFarland, 1995.

Jordan, David M. *The Athletics of Philadelphia: Connie Mack's White Elephants, 1901–1954*. Jefferson, N.C.: McFarland, 1999.

Kashatus, William C. *Connie Mack's '29 Triumph: The Rise and Fall of the Philadelphia Athletics Dynasty*. Jefferson, N.C.: McFarland, 1999.

Kuklick, Bruce. *To Every Thing a Season: Shibe Park and Urban Philadelphia, 1909–1976*. Princeton: Princeton University Press, 1991.

Lieb, Frederick G. *Connie Mack: Grand Old Man of Baseball*. New York: G. P. Putnam's Sons, 1945.

Loew, Patty. "Tinkers to Evers to Chief: Baseball from Indian Country." *Wisconsin Magazine of History* (spring 2004): 1–3.

Mack, Connie. *My 66 Years in the Big Leagues*. Philadelphia: John C. Winston, 1950.

McDonald, Brian. *Indian Summer*. New York: Rodale, 2003.

National Archives and Records Administration. "Charles A. Bender, Student File." Record of Graduates, Carlisle Indian Industrial School. File 1327, no. 5453, record group 75. National Archives and Records Administration, Washington D.C.

Neyer, Rob, and Eddie Epstein. *Baseball Dynasties*. New York: W. W. Norton, 2000.

Oxendine, Joseph B. *American Indian Sports Heritage*. Lincoln: University of Nebraska Press, 1995.

Powers-Beck, Jeff. *The American Indian Integration of Baseball*. Lincoln: University of Nebraska Press, 2004.

Pratt, Richard H. *Battlefield and Classroom: Four Decades with the American Indians, 1867–1904*, ed. Robert M. Utley. New Haven: Yale University Press, 1964.

Ritter, Lawrence S. *The Glory of Their Times: The Story of the Early Days of Baseball Told by the Men Who Played It*. New York: Vintage Books, 1985.

Spink, J. G. Taylor. "Albert Bender's Four Decades on the Mound." *Sporting News*, December 31, 1942.

———. "A Long-Delayed Feather for the Chief." *Sporting News*, December 30, 1953.

Staurowsky, Ellen J. "An Act of Honor or Exploitation? The Cleveland Indians' Use of the Louis Francis Sockalexis Story." *Sociology of Sport Journal* 15, no. 3 (1998): 299–316.

Warren, William W. *History of the Ojibway People*. 1885; reprint, St. Paul: Minnesota Historical Society, 1984.

Warrington, Robert D. "Charles Albert 'Chief' Bender: A Biographical Profile." *Native American Casino Magazine* (November 2003): 32–34.

Weigley, Russell F., ed. *Philadelphia: A 300-Year History*. New York: W. W. Norton, 1982.

Westcott, Rich. *Philadelphia's Old Ballparks*. Philadelphia: Temple University Press, 1996.

Wilson, James. *The Earth Shall Weep: A History of Native America*. New York: Grove Press, 1998.

White, G. Edward. *Creating the National Pastime: Baseball Transforms Itself, 1903–1953*. Princeton: Princeton University Press, 1996.

Witmer, Linda F. *The Indian Industrial School: Carlisle, Pennsylvania, 1879–1918*. Carlisle: Cumberland County Historical Society, 1993.

Wolff, Rick, ed. *The Baseball Encyclopedia*. 8th ed. New York: Macmillan, 1990.

INDEX

Page numbers in *italics* indicate
illustrations

Agassiz, Louis, 42, 173 n. 33
Albright College, 26
Alexander, Grover, 134
Allen, Elvin, 24
Ames, Leon "Red," 48, 96
American Association, 35
American League, 32–34, 46, 66, 89,
   132, 146, 148
Anishinaabe. *See* Chippewa
Arapaho Indians, 17
Ardsley Park Cemetery (Roslyn, Pa.),
   152
Arellanes, Frank, 73
Armstrong, Samuel C., 18

Baker, Frank "Home Run," 66, 68,
   74, 75, 80, 81, 83, 90, 92, 94,
   96, 99–101, 105, 107, 115, 119,
   130, 140, 152
Baker, William, 134
Balenti, Mike, 26
Baltimore Orioles, 35, 58, 131, 132
Baltimore Terrapins (Federal League),
   xv, 112, 123, 131–34, 182 n. 48
Barry, Jack, 66, 68, 74, 80, 81, 94, 116,
   117
Baseball Magazine, 62
Battle of Little Bighorn (1876), 19
Beck, Emil, 69–70
Beck, Joseph E., 24
Becker, David Beals, 96
Bender, Alburtus (father), 3–5, 9
Bender, Charles A. "Chief," ix–xv,
   7–28, 40–46, 45, 51–53, 57–63,
   74, 76, 77–79, 83–88, 86,

102–8, 111–28, 116, 131–34, 135,
   137, 138–53, 147, 151, 155–62
   at Carlisle, 11–28
   cartoons of, 43–44, 51–53
   description of, 23–24, 40, 57, 59
   discrimination against, ix, 40–41,
      133
   and education, 7–28
   Hall of Fame induction, 152–53,
      186 n. 25
   hobbies, 140
   legacy, 155–62
   marriage, 45–46, 60–61, 79
   minor league career, 136–40
   "money pitcher" nickname, 77
   no-hitter, 83–85
   salary, 102, 111, 123–24, 125–26, 129,
      131, 182 n. 48
   statistics, 43–44, 51, 63, 74, 77, 109,
      111–12, 124, 134, 153, 155–56, 163
   tragedy of, 159–60
   youth, xi, xvi, 5–28
   and World Series, (1905) ix–x,
      50–53, 59, (1910) 89–92, (1911)
      96–97, 100–102, (1913) 104–5,
      107–8, (1914) xii–xv, 111–28, 150,
      181 n. 32
Bender, Elizabeth, 136
Bender, John (brother), 24, 27, 94–95
Bender, Marie Clement (wife), 45–46,
   60–61, 79, 142, 152–53, 156
Bender, Mary Razor (mother), 5, 10
Bernhard, Bill, 33–34, 35
Blackfoot Indians, 136
Black Sox Scandal (1919), 88, 123, 125,
   125–26, 131
Bloom, John, vii, 155, 157,
Bonner, Frank, 34

191

House of David Baseball Club, 140
Hough, Frank, 103, 113
Huff, Emma Bender, 136
Hurst, Tim, 73
Husting, Bert, 34

Iroquois Indians, 16
Isaminger, Jimmy, 90, 118

Jackson, Joseph "Shoeless Joe," xiii,
    62, 68–69, 74, 80, 88–89
James, Bill, 113, 118–19, 121
Jennings, Hughie, 73, 129–30
Johnson, Bancroft "Ban," 32, 97
Johnson, George H., 26
Johnson, Walter, 83, 89, 132
Jones, Sam, 103
Joost, Eddie, ix, 146, 148, 152

Keener, Sid, 150
Kerzog, Buck, 96
Kilby, Ralph, 139
Killian, Ed, 63–64
Kiowa Indians, 17, 19
Krause, Harry, 74, 75, 81–82, 87, 94

Lajoie, Napoleon "Nap," 33–34, 47
Lamar, Lucius Q., 3–5
Landis, Judge Kenesaw Mountain, 132
Lapp, Jack, 66, 102, 104
Lawrence, Kans., x
Lenni Lenape Indians. *See* Delaware
    Indians
Leroy, Louis, 25–26
Leslie's Illustrated Weekly, 105
Lincoln Institution (Philadelphia), 7
Livingston, Paddy, 74
Loew, Patricia, vii
Lord, Bristol "Bris," 51, 84, 88–89, 94,
    104

Mack, Connie, ix–xi, xiv, 31, 31–40,
    52–53, 60, 62, 65–70, 76,

80–83, 92–95, 102–3, 111–12,
    124–28, 127, 129–31, 145–46, 148,
    159–60
  breaking up championship
    dynasty, 129–31
  elected to Hall of Fame, 146
  playing career, 31–32
  relationship with Bender, 60,
    65–66, 77, 95, 102, 109, 111–12,
    124, 145, 159–60
  retirement, 146
  roster raiding, 32–34, 123, 172 n. 9
Mack, Connie, Jr., 146, 152
Mack, Earle, 146, 152
Mack, Roy, 146, 152
Mandowescence (Charles Bender's
    Indian name), xi, 1, 5, 7–8,
    9–12, 28, 156
Manifest Destiny, 2
Maranville, Walter "Rabbit," 113, 115
Mathewson, Christopher "Christy,"
    ix, 48, 50, 51, 96, 97, 99–101,
    104, 107–8, 140
Marquard, Richard William "Rube,"
    96, 99, 104–5
McConnell, Ambrose "Amby," 73
McClean, Larry, 108
McCrabb, Lester, vii, 149
McDonald, Brian, xii
McFarland, Eddie, 42–43
McGillicuddy, Cornelius. *See*
    Connie Mack
McGillicuddy, Tom, 82
McGinnity, Joseph "Iron Man," ix,
    48, 51
McGowen, Frank, 139
McGraw, John, ix, xiii, 34, 46, 50,
    56–57, 58, 95–100, 104
McInnis, John "Stuffy," 80, 81, 92, 94,
    96, 117
McIntire, Harry, 91
McScudden, Gerald, 24
Menomini Indians, 1

ABOUT THE AUTHOR

William C. Kashatus, a professional historian and educator, holds a Ph.D. in history from the University of Pennsylvania. A regular contributor to the *Philadelphia Daily News*, he is also the author of several baseball books. He lives in Chester County, Pennsylvania.

ALSO BY *William C. Kashatus*

September Swoon: Richie Allen, the '64 Phillies, and Racial Integration

Lou Gehrig: A Biography

The Philadelphia Athletics: Images of Sports

Diamonds in the Coalfields: Remarkable Baseball Players from Northeast Pennsylvania

Mike Schmidt: Philadelphia's Hall of Fame Third Baseman

Was It as Good for You? Tug McGraw and Fans Recall the 1980 World Series (with Tug McGraw)

Connie Mack's '29 Triumph: The Rise and Fall of the Philadelphia Athletics Dynasty

One-Armed Wonder: Pete Gray, Wartime Baseball, and the American Dream